Lake Onta

× Fort
Niaga

se of Peace
Elevation

Elevation

r Plan

Niagara Falls

The Great Island

LAKE ERIE

THUNDERGATE: The Forts of Niagara

THE AMERICAN FORTS SERIES
as planned by Stewart H. Holbrook

GUNS AT THE FORKS
(Forts Duquesne and Pitt)
by Walter O'Meara

LOUISBOURG: KEY TO A CONTINENT
by Fairfax Downey

SUTTER'S FORT: GATEWAY TO THE GOLD FIELDS
by Oscar Lewis

THREE FLAGS AT THE STRAITS: THE FORTS OF MACKINAC
by Walter Havighurst

FORT LARAMIE AND THE SIOUX INDIANS
by Remi Nadeau

FORTS OF THE UPPER MISSOURI
by Robert G. Athearn

THUNDERGATE: THE FORTS OF NIAGARA
by Robert West Howard

★ ★ ★

Other Subjects in Preparation

VINCENNES: PORTAL TO THE WEST
by August Derleth

FORT MIMS
by P. D. East

SAGEBRUSH SOLDIERS: THE STORY OF FORT CHURCHILL
by Ferol Egan

FORT LEAVENWORTH
by George Walton

Books by Robert West Howard

THE HORSE IN AMERICA
THE GREAT IRON TRAIL
TWO BILLION ACRE FARM
THE RACE WEST
THIS IS THE WEST (editor and contributor)
THIS IS THE SOUTH (editor and contributor)
HOOFBEATS OF DESTINY (editor and contributor)
RODEO: LAST FRONTIER OF THE OLD WEST
(editor and contributor)
THE BENCHMARK (editor and contributor)
EDUCATIONAL PLANNING BY NEIGHBORHOODS (with Paul Essert)

Young Adult and Juvenile Titles

THE REAL BOOK OF FARMS (juvenile)
THE FIRST BOOK OF FARMS (juvenile)
THE FIRST BOOK OF NIAGARA FALLS (juvenile)
THE WAGONMEN (young adult)
THE BOATMEN (young adult)
THE SOUTH PASS STORY (young adult)
ELI WHITNEY (juvenile)
THE FLAG OF THE DREADFUL BEAR (juvenile)
THE WONDERFUL WORLD OF BOOKS (contributor)

THUNDERGATE

The Forts of Niagara

Robert West Howard

Prentice-Hall, Inc., Englewood Cliffs, N. J.

To the memory of my parents

The Rev. Charles James Howard
of Herkimer, N. Y.

Clara Jane West
of Rotterdam Junction, N. Y.

Thundergate: The Forts of Niagara
by Robert West Howard

Library of Congress Catalog Card Number: 68-16321

Printed in the United States of America • *T*

PRENTICE-HALL INTERNATIONAL, INC., *London*
PRENTICE-HALL OF AUSTRALIA, PTY. LTD., *Sydney*
PRENTICE-HALL OF CANADA, LTD., *Toronto*
PRENTICE-HALL OF INDIA PRIVATE LTD., *New Delhi*
PRENTICE-HALL OF JAPAN, INC., *Tokyo*

ACKNOWLEDGMENTS

Credit for details "beyond dull fact" in this manuscript belongs to those Case ... Swart ... West ... Howard ancestors who followed William Johnson up the Mohawk's plow-way. The yarn-spins in Grandpa Jim's East Herkimer barn, Uncle Herb's Ilion parlor, Grandma West's Syracuse kitchen, and Uncle Frank's Niskayuna den were my initial stimulants for trying to learn what happened during the 1678–1866 struggles between the St. Lawrence and Mohawk peoples.

I was born at Addison, New York, on the Butler-Brant trail, grew up in the Hudson plow-way and Catskills, and worked (??) on Susquehanna valley, Mohawk valley and Onondaga "salt lake" newspapers. There I absorbed folklore and enjoyed the friendship and advice of Dr. Alexander C. Flick, New York's great State Historian. Dr. Bertrand M. Wainger, Harry "Butch" Malone, the late Leslie Ernenwein and other staffers of Upstate's Federal Writers Project became my fact and folklore sources, too, during the 1935–37 fun of researching and writing *New York: A Guide to the Empire State*.

Contemporary thanks are due the late Stewart H. Holbrook; John Gudmundsen, now an editor with Yale University Press; Paul M. Angle, former director of the Chicago Historical Society; Drs. Robert McCaul and Mark Krug of the University of Chicago; Dr. Frederick Rath of the New York State Historical Society, and the distinguished author-librarian, Richard M. Dillon of Sutro Library, San Francisco. Pierre Brunet and W. I. Smith of the

670444

Public Archives of Canada at Ottawa sustained that magnificent institution's reputation for courtesy and thoroughness. Dr. William Fenton, Dr. Hugh Flick and Miss Juliet Wolohan of the New York State Department of Education provided numerous research materials. The interviews and wanders with Mr. and Mrs. S. Grove McClellan, Donald E. Loker and Hubert E. Torrence were of critical value. Despite projects in Canada, France and the Netherlands, U. S. Steel's naval architect and Great Lakes shipping authority, Bernard E. Ericson, answered all of my questions about Niagara's ships, and provided several of his drawings for use in *Thundergate*.

But two people deserve co-author bylines for their multitude of contributions: My wife, Elizabeth Zimmermann Howard, and my agent, Malcolm Reiss of Paul R. Reynolds & Son.

Robert West Howard
Rochester, New York

CONTENTS

SECTION FIVE: THE FIGHT FOR THE LAKES

SECTION SIX: ALL THE PAST WE LEAVE BEHIND

AGAIN IN NOVEMBER

A Preface

Kitchen fluorescent lights began to pulse like lovesick lightning bugs. Electric stove burners dimmed from cherry to weak orangeade to slag. A stumble through the twilight revealed that floor lamps, furnace, dehumidifier, television, clocks, switch box and street lights were all dead lumps. It was November 9, 1965. A defective relay at a Niagara power plant had paralyzed the 80,000-square-mile area between the St. Lawrence and the Hudson as thoroughly as the deadly struggles for this Great Lakes Throatway had done between 1679 and 1866.

Again in November!!!!

November 1626: The first European to explore the thirty mile tumble of the Niagara River crossed the portage trail.

November 1679: The first French fort at the Niagara's Lake Ontario mouth was burned and abandoned after Seneca-British plotting.

November 11, 1778: The massacre of Cherry Valley's women and children by the Butler Rangers and Indians out of Niagara terrorized the new United States of America.

November 1779: The "Great Starving Time" of five thousand Indians and Loyalist refugees began at Fort Niagara. It was directly responsible for the creation of the Royal Province of Upper Canada thirteen years later.

November 1792: The decision to ban "human slavery" in Upper Canada, made by the province's first Parliament at Newark,

xi

enabled the flight of more than seventy-five thousand refugee slaves to this "Land of Promise" between 1795 and 1863. So the Underground Railroad, the Fugitive Slave Act, *Uncle Tom's Cabin* and many of our majestic "spirituals" entered American folklore.

November 19, 1795: The Jay Treaty surrendered Fort Niagara and the east shore of the Niagara gorge to the United States, and hence "New West" migrations veered from the Pittsburgh-Ohio Valley route to the easier, more logical Great Lakes route.

October-November 1812: The states' rights refusal of New York and New England militia to cross the Niagara to "foreign soil" perpetuated the War of 1812 through the savage burnings of York, Newark, Black Rock, Buffalo and Washington and the major battles of Lake Erie, Chippewa and Lundy's Lane.

November 1830: The migration of members of the Church of Jesus Christ of the Latter-day Saints over the Niagara ridge began the American saga of the Mormon Trail and Deseret.

November 1866: Fear of American aggression, focused by the Fenians' raid across the Niagara during the summer of 1866, persuaded the Canadian provinces to petition Great Britain for unification as the Dominion of Canada.

Of course, none of the news reports that squealed out of transistor radios during the 1965 Big Blackout chose to recall this 340-year sequel of fear-out-of-Niagara. Yet, for any imaginative listener the rumors of "Communist sabotage?"... "Mysterious power ray?"... "UFO sighted near the Niagara gorge?" were mere technologic adaptations of the terror gossip that had swept the same St. Lawrence-Hudson plow-ways after other Niagara crises in 1679 . . . 1756 . . . 1759 . . . 1778 . . . 1779 . . . 1783 . . . 1793 . . . 1812 . . . 1813 . . . 1830 . . . 1837 . . . 1864 . . . 1866.

The Big Blackout echoed past turmoil and underlined the importance of the Niagara gorge and her grim brood of forts as a great place of crisis in American and Canadian civilization.

The first Fort Niagara was built in 1679, twenty years before the Virginians chose Middle Plantation as their colony's capital and renamed it Williamsburg. The massive chateau-fort built on the same promontory at the mouth of the Niagara River in 1725 and 1726 is the oldest surviving post-Indian structure between Montreal and the southern Rockies.

The Anglo-American epic of conquering the West began at, and with, Fort Niagara. La Salle selected its site and built the first sailing ship for the Upper Lakes on a Cayuga Creek shore behind the Falls. After him came Lahontan . . . the Joncaires . . . Bienville . . . Sir William Johnson . . . Robert Rogers . . . Pontiac . . . Joseph Brant . . . Moses Cleaveland . . . James Fenimore Cooper . . . Jedediah Smith . . . De Witt Clinton . . . Winfield Scott . . . Zebulon Pike . . . Henry Leavenworth . . . Wells and Fargo . . . the railroaders . . . Walt Whitman . . . Horace Greeley . . . Grover Cleveland . . . Alexander Graham Bell.

As a heritage place, Niagara and her forts tower beside Plymouth Rock, St. Augustine, Santa Fe, Faneuil Hall, Quebec's Citadel, and the lovely St. Lawrence-Saguenay junction at Tadoussac.

Niagara's destiny was determined by the glaciers that plowed two channels to the sea.

SECTION ONE

THE DESTINY MAKERS

And stepping westward seemed to be
A kind of heavenly destiny.

William Wordsworth,
STEPPING WESTWARD

ONE

THE ICE PLOW

Glaciers gouged the channel for the Niagara River through the dolomite-on-shale ridge that became the east dike of the upper Great Lakes. Between 20,000 and 2000 B.C., the glacier's melt-off created Niagara Falls, its gorge, and the massive ruts of the St. Lawrence and Mohawk–Hudson valleys. Thus a "great deluge" plowed out the geopolitical potentials for Thundergate's twelve forts, score of battles and centuries of terror.

Hundreds of millions of years ago, glaciers began to form on the northern third of the Earth. "Siberian winter established itself," the great naturalist Louis Agassiz deduced, "over a world previously covered with a rich vegetation and peopled with large mammalia. . . . Death enveloped all nature in a shroud, and the cold, having reached its highest degree, gave to this mass of ice, at the maximum of tension, the greatest possible hardness."

At climax, this shroud towered more than ten thousand feet above sea level. At Niagara's site it was as high as Pike's Peak.

The ages of melt-off between the four glacial eras shaped and reshaped the topography of future Canada and the northeastern United States. The melt-off of the fourth and most recent glacial age, the Wisconsin, began about 40,000 B.C. Its avalanches and floods plowed out the basins of the Great Lakes, then bulldozed the Finger Lakes among rock folds of the Allegheny foothills.

By 10,000 B.C., the Wisconsin's icewall had retreated north of the modern shorelines of Lakes Erie and Ontario, but it still covered much of Canada's rock shield. Thus the runoff forced a series of channels southeast through the lowest pass in the mountains. Between 10,000 and 5000 B.C., these torrents established a channel from the eastern rim of Lake Erie across central New York and down the Mohawk and Hudson valleys to the ocean.

As the melt-off continued, the torrent veered to a new channel running northeast that created both the St. Lawrence valley and Lake Champlain. When the Britons built Stonehenge and the Aryans of the Caspian steppes were learning how to tame and ride horses, most of New York was a lake with the triangular island of the Adirondack Mountains at its northeast.

By the time the Aryan horsemen created the centaur myth through their invasions of Greece and the hunters of Ur had discovered that they could harvest gold by sluicing creek mud over sheep pelts, New York and lower Canada were assuming contemporary topography. The Great Lakes runoff fixed on the St. Lawrence channel. A marshy ridge west of the site of Rome, New York, became the only barrier between the Mohawk and the St. Lawrence flow-ways.

A shield of Silurian dolomite two hundred miles west of Rome's site had held firm against the glaciers and floods except at a half-mile area where it overlaid layers of shale. Between 10,000 and 3000 B.C., this weak spot became the sole discharge route of the four Upper Lakes—Erie, Huron, Superior and Michigan.

The thirty-mile channel thus plowed due south to north dropped 327 feet from the level of Lake Erie to the level of Lake Ontario. More than half of this drop occurred at the crest of the dolomite-shale ridge. An average of 200,000 to 500,000 cubic feet of water per second thundered down a 167-foot precipice. The gargantuan force tore the rock crest away at an average rate of five feet a year. Thus the third largest waterfall on Earth moved southwest at a rate of five hundred feet each century, creating a great gorge and whirlpool rapids in its wake.

The Throatway was ready.

⌒⌒∘⌒⌒

TWO

THE TRUE PEOPLE

Bronze-hued refugees from Asia discovered the thundering Throatway of the lakes and the marshy prairies to the east before 5000 B.C. Upstate New York was still a lake. Ice dams between the sites of Montreal and Quebec veered the flow-off south across the Lake Champlain bowl to the upper Hudson.

The black muck and Podzolic brown earth of the lake shore, swelling every mile or two into a conical drumlin hill, nourished nut trees, grapevines, berry bushes and man-high grasses, providing food for numerous mammoths, mastodons, bison, deer, bobcats and black bear. The creeks and forested bays invited beaver and muskrat colonies which, of course, lured the murderous mink. Sturgeon and salmon, some as large as sharks, rainbowed the St. Lawrence rapids each spring in the race to spawning grounds up Ontario's creeks and in shadowed inlets of the lower Throatway.

This environmental wealth invited permanent settlement. The transition from nomad to farmer began the same awkward genesis that was underway in Eurasia. It was crippled, however, by the absence of horses, donkeys, cattle, or swine. Dogs were the largest semi-domestic animals.

The canoe was invented sometime between 4000 and 2000 B.C. With it, the bronzemen became water travelers and pioneered regional trade. Tools fashioned from Michigan copper, arrowheads chipped from Wyoming obsidian, Rocky Mountain grizzlybear teeth doweled into warclubs, ornaments glittering with chips

of Florida and Mississippi pearl-shell—all these testify to the
extent of Upstate New York's trade by canoe before A.D. 1000.
This trade established the Throatway as a place of crisis. It became the only barrier to canoe travel for more than a thousand
miles.

The earliest fort ruin so far discovered on the Throatway portage was built by the Moundbuilders of the Ohio–Indiana valleys
near the site of Lewiston. The human skeletons found beside it
were buried about A.D. 160. They had been cremated, either by
Moundbuilder priests or by the conquerors of the fort.

Perhaps the legend of the virgin in a canoe sent over the falls
each spring as sacrifice to Hawenio, the Majestic Voice, symbolized the battles for control of the portage that occurred
between A.D. 160 and 1600. During this millennium, the Great
Lakes receded to almost contemporary shorelines. Scores of palisaded villages overlooked crop fields of maize, pole beans,
pumpkins, squash and herbs. Orchards of fruit trees and ropy
jungles of berry bushes and grapevines deckled the forest edge.
Three portage trudges barred the canoe journey from Lake Ontario to the hunting and fishing grounds of the Long Island–
New Jersey shore. Northeast from the foot of Ontario only one
furious rapid delayed the 600-mile paddle down the St. Lawrence
to the sea. The sturgeon and salmon swarmed upriver during the
Fish-running Moon of mid-March in such quantities that two
men armed with clubs could fill a canoe with the silvery creatures
in ten minutes.

Mongol ponies were racing the terrors of Genghis Khan's Golden
Horde across Russia into Poland and Hungary when a new sequence of invaders came through the Throatway. One tribal alliance, whose members called themselves the Hurons, conquered
the Ontario–St. Lawrence paddleway. Some of the refugees from
the conquest fled south through the Adirondacks toward the
Mohawk–Hudson junction. About the same time, tribes with
similar folkways, wild pride, and lithe tall bodies conquered the
western end of the Genesee–Mohawk plow-way.

Until 1500, or perhaps 1550, the communal bark-and-pole
villages that these invaders developed between the Genesee

River's south-north valley and the site of Schenectady displayed the aborigines' traditional insularism. The villagers feuded over hunting grounds, plundered one another's crops, and kidnapped the women they fancied. When the tribe nearest the Mohawk-Hudson junction—whose braves called themselves the Kaniengehaga, People of the Place of the Flint—fought with the Hudson valley's Mahicans for farm and hunting rights, no warriors from the western villages offered to help them. Similarly, when the villagers in the Genesee valley—the Nundahwagegah, or People of the Hill—renewed the struggle for control of the Throatway portage, the eastern villagers stayed away.

Yet the five regional tribes evolving along the plow-way had common beliefs and folkways. All of them practiced a matriarchal form of government under which civic administrators, the sachems, were nominated by a women's council. All worshipped supreme deities identified as Sky Holder and Hawenio, the Majestic Voice. They believed in an eternal life for the soul and the brotherhood of all animate and inanimate matter. They were deathly afraid of witchcraft, animal and human. The brave man was a stoic and could resist pain without a murmur or eye flick. Like most aboriginal groups, they believed that human flesh imparted certain virtues to the consumer. Moreover, it had a very delicate flavor. But the fingers were invariably bitter and should be discarded.

Human ego-drive seems always to have motivated the habit of choosing one individual as the genius and semideity for each ethnic or social revolution. Thus the sagas of Beowulf, the Argonauts, Robin Hood, the Cid, Jimmu and Hsia evolved. It was logical for a folk hero to grow from the "mysterious invader" gossip that unified these plow-way villages into the Five Nations Confederacy about 1550.

The two founders of the Confederacy, according to oral traditions first recorded in writing about 1750, were Degeniwidah, a philosopher and ideaman, and Haionawatha, an orator and politician.

But French, English, Portuguese and Spanish fishing fleets were on the Newfoundland and Georges Banks by 1500. The beaches of the lower St. Lawrence became their favored sites for repairing ships, refilling water kegs, and sundrying their choicest cod and halibut splits.

Then the Juan Ponce de Leon and Pánfilo de Narváez expeditions invaded Florida between 1513 and 1522.

Jacques Cartier's ships explored the St. Lawrence in 1534 and, the next year, anchored off the site of Montreal long enough for Cartier to portage around the rapids and guess that the river was a Northwest Passage to China. Naturally, he named the rapids La Chine.

In 1539, Hernando de Soto's army began a four-year plundering from Florida across the Mississippi to the Kansas-Oklahoma prairie. The Coronado Expedition's search for "the Golden Cities" ravaged northeastward through Arizona, New Mexico, Oklahoma, Colorado and Kansas during the same years.

The pedlar was the most important news source in every primitive society. No pedlar of Florida bird feathers, Great Smoky Mountain mica, or Gulf of St. Lawrence wampum shell could, between 1500 and 1550, avoid the gossip about the pale-faced men, the massive beasts they rode, the shiny metal coats they wore, or the death-dealing firesticks they carried. Tidbits of half truth and quarter truth babbled as excitedly from village to village as rumors about little green men from Mars and mushroom-shaped space ships gushed from front pages and newscasts during the 1960's. Any Indian could have deduced "paleface invasion" out of these sequential 1500–1550 reports from Florida . . . from the Mississippi valley . . . from the lower St. Lawrence. Then he would ponder methods of adequate defense for his environment and his kin.

The Mohawk plow-way union that developed between 1550 and 1600, with or without Degeniwidah and Haionawatha, was based on a Grand Council of forty-nine sachems representing the five tribal groups (the Kaniengehaga, Tiionenyote, Ononytageh, Kweniogwen and Nundawahgageh). This Council met at the principal village of the central group, the Onondagas. Its edicts were by majority rule. The sachem delegates of each tribe had to reach agreement before casting the tribe's single ballot. If there was a tie, the Onondagas could cast the deciding ballot.

The fears of "paleface invasion" were realized during the summer of 1609. The Kaniengehaga, still without assistance from the other tribes, had continued their vendettas against the Hurons and the Mahicans. That July 30, a Kaniengehaga hunting-and-plunder party battled with Samuel de Champlain, a French guard and sixty Huron warriors near Crown Point on Lake Champlain. Champlain and his white companion fired their guns and killed two Kaniengehagas.

Six years later, during the summer of 1615, Champlain and a few soldiers accompanied a Huron raid across Lake Ontario and up the Salmon River toward the Confederacy's capital on Onondaga Hill. Champlain sent Etienne Brulé west over the Throatway portage to rouse Huron allies along Lake Erie for a campaign that would plunder through the Five Nations' villages. Brulé failed. Champlain was wounded during the siege of an Onondaga village near Lake Oneida. The invaders limped back to the St. Lawrence.

Champlain's obvious alliance with the Hurons insured friendly Five Nations overtures toward the Dutch who founded the Fort Nassau trading post, near the site of Albany, in 1614, and toward Arent van Curler, the humane founder of Schenectady. (Van Curler made such a profound impression on the sachems that every New York governor throughout the seventeenth and eighteenth centuries was formally addressed as "Corlaer" by Five Nations orators.) With Dutch friendship came the first trades for iron utensils, iron hatchets and guns.

Three ominous truths must have become obvious to the sachems and tribal grandmothers between 1615 and 1640: First, both the French and the Dutch had decided that the most desirable products of the region were the pelts of fur-bearing animals, preferably beaver. Second, the white men's eagerness for pelts was so avid that the animals in the Mohawk and St. Lawrence plow-ways would soon be killed off. Then the fur plunder must move west beyond the Throatway. And third, the Five Nations could monopolize the fur supplies to the Dutch and perhaps to the French by terrorizing the Hurons and their allies away from the Throatway and the Ontario-St. Lawrence route.

Equally puzzling, but of less immediacy, was the feud between the French and the Dutch about God and His gentle Son. The Dutch, it seemed, were possessed of a kind of witchcraft called "Heresy," according to the black-robed French priests. But the Dutch called the French, "Papists," and considered them guilty of a kind of witchcraft. It was just as politic for a Dutchman to kill a Papist or for a Frenchman to kill a Heretic as it was for a Five Nations warrior to kill a Huron!

Efforts to make treaty agreements with both the Hurons and the French during the 1620's and 1630's indicate that the decision to terrorize was reached with reluctance. From these sachem deliberations came a policy that would be handed down as "The Constitution of the Five Nations." It ruled that:

> when the Confederate Council of the Five Nations has for its object the establishment of the Great Peace among the people of an outside nation, and that nation refuses to accept the Great Peace, then by such refusal they bring a declaration of war upon themselves from the Five Nations. Then shall the Five Nations seek to establish the Great Peace by a conquest of the rebellious nation. . . . War must continue until the contest is won by the Five Nations.

During this period, too, the Grand Council and tribal orators began to promote the term, "Ongweh Oweh," as a collective name for all the people of the Confederacy. It was excellent jingoism that meant "the True People" and could even mean "the Only Real People."

Ruthless destruction of the Huron communities began during the early 1640's. By 1660, the Five Nations controlled the upper St. Lawrence valley, the Ontario basin, the Niagara portage, and the Lake Erie shores, and sent raiders as far south as Georgia.

Coincidentally, fear-inspiring torture methods were perfected. One Mohawk ritual, witnessed by Father Le Jeune, a Jesuit mis-

sionary, during 1635 or 1636, made such a harrowing impact that
he described it in detail in his annual report:

Towards eight o'clock in the evening, eleven fires were lighted
along the cabin, about one brass distant from each other. The
people gathered immediately, the old men taking places above,
upon a sort of platform, which extends, on both sides, the entire
length of the cabin. The young men were below, but were so
crowded that they were almost piled upon one another, so that
there was hardly a passage along the fires. Cries of joy resounded
on all sides; each provided himself, one with a firebrand, another
with a piece of bark, to burn the victim. Before he was brought
in, the Captain Aenons encouraged all to do their duty, representing to them the importance of this act, which was viewed, he
said, by the Sun and by the God of war. He ordered that at first
they should burn only his legs, so that he might hold out until
daybreak; also for that night they were not to go and amuse
themselves in the woods. He had hardly finished when the victim entered. I leave you to imagine the terror that seized him at
the sight of these preparations. The cries redoubled at his arrival; he is made to sit down upon a mat, his hands are bound,
then he rises and makes a tour of the cabin, singing and dancing;
no one burns him this time, but also this is the limit of his rest—
one can hardly tell what he will endure up to the time when they
cut off his head. He had no sooner returned to his place than the
war Captain took his robe and said, "Oteiondi"—speaking of a
Captain—"will despoil him of the robe which I hold"; and added,
"The Atachonchronons will cut off his head, which will be given
to Ondessone, with one arm and the liver to make a feast."
...After this each one armed himself with a brand, or a piece
of burning bark, and he began to walk, or rather to run, around
the fires; each one struggled to burn him as he passed. Meanwhile, he shrieked like a lost soul; the whole crowd imitated his
cries, or rather smothered them with horrible shouts. One must
be there, to see a living picture of Hell.

The whole cabin appeared as if on fire; and, athwart the flames
and dense smoke that issued therefrom, these barbarians—crowd-
ing one upon the other, howling at the top of their voices, with
firebrands in their hands, their eyes flashing with rage and fury

—seemed like so many demons who would give no respite to this poor wretch. They often stopped him at the other end of the cabin, some of them taking his hands and breaking the bones thereof by sheer force; others pierced his ears with sticks which they left in them; others bound his wrists with cords which they tied roughly, pulling at each end of the cord with all their might. Did he make the round and pause for a little breath, he was made to repose upon hot ashes and burning coals. . . .

Behold in part how passed the night. . . . As soon as day began to dawn, they lighted fires outside the village, to display there the excess of their cruelty to the sight of the Sun. The victim was lead thither. . . . Two of them took hold of him and made him mount a scaffold 6 or 7 feet high; three or four of these barbarians followed him. They tied him to a tree which passed across it, but in such a way he was free to turn around. There they began to burn him more cruelly than ever, leaving no part of his body to which fire was not applied at intervals. When one of these butchers began to burn him and to crowd him closely, in trying to escape him, he fell into the hands of another who gave him no better reception. From time to time they were supplied with new brands, which they thrust, all aflame, down his throat, even forcing them into his fundament. They burned his eyes; they applied red-hot hatchets to his shoulders; they hung some around his neck, which they turned now upon his back, now upon his breast, according to the position he took in order to avoid the weight of this burden. If he attempted to sit or crouch down, someone thrust a brand from under the scaffolding which soon caused him to arise. . . . They so harassed him upon all sides that they finally put him out of breath; they poured water into his mouth to strengthen his heart, and the Captains called out to him that he should take a little breath. But he remained still, his mouth open, and almost motionless. Therefore, fearing that he would die otherwise than by the knife, one cut off a foot, another a hand, and almost at the same time a third severed the head from the shoulders, throwing it into the crowd, where someone caught it to carry it to the Captain Ondessone, for whom it had been reserved, in order to make a feast therewith. As for the trunk, it remained at Arontaen, where a feast was made of it the same day. . . . On the way (home) we encountered a Savage who was carrying upon a skewer one of his half-roasted hands.

Occasionally women captives and children were sacrificed as offerings to the war god, Aireskoi. But decisions on the prisoners to be tortured, as well as allocation of the villages where spectacles and feasts were to be held, were made by tribal councils of grandsires, chiefs and medicine men. Families who adopted a prisoner, or prisoners, to "replace" a dead relative had the right to request a torture-and-feast if a prisoner should prove unsatisfactory.

"The Platform Torture appears to have been based upon human sacrifice to the Sun or War God, Aireskoi," Nathaniel Knowles deduced in his classic study, "The Torture of Captives by the Indians of Eastern North America":

> The penetration of torture into Algonkian cultures was seemingly not deep and was recognized as being of [Five Nations] origin. Perhaps due to an upsurge of war, the importance and numerical amount of human sacrifice increased, thereby leading to a spread of terror which was utilized and emphasized to obtain submission of their enemies.

The ritual of "running the gauntlet" as part of the formal ceremony of adoption in a Five Nations family was a sadistic contemporary of the Platform Torture. Any male captive worthy of adoption, the mores edicted, must test his hardihood by dodging, twisting, clawing his way down the village street toward his new family's home. Along the route crouched rows of neighbors-to-be, armed with war clubs, lances and snow-snake sticks. The captive who fell or displayed fear before reaching the threshold of his new home was either slain at once or dragged off to the prisoners' pen to be fattened for a Platform Torture.

One chief, Knowles reported, "was reputed to have adopted and subsequently burned forty prisoners because none of them proved worthy to succeed his dead brother. Another chief reputedly had eighty victims tortured to honor the shade of his brother."

The Five Nations' ferocities caused the Hurons to give the Confederacy the collective hate-name, *Iroquois*, meaning "the vipers who strike without warning." The crucifixion of Jesuit missionaries and French traders persuaded the French to adopt this name in their journals and official correspondence.

The Dutch and their British successors used the formality of *The Five Nations* in their documents and at council orations. But they did substitute the Mahican hate-name, *Maqua,* or *Mohawk,* meaning "the human flesh eaters," as their name for both the Kaniengehaga and the river whose "Eastern Gate" they guarded. Similarly, the tribesmen of the Genesee were renamed the *Sinnaker* or, as governmental clerks soon began to simplify it, the *Seneca.* The nation that had wrested control of the Finger Lakes and Upper Susquehanna valley took the name of *Cayuga.* The nation owning the portage trail between Lake Oneida and the Mohawk headwaters as well as the central Mohawk valley became known as the *Oneida.*

As guardians of the Confederacy's "Western Gate," the Senecas controlled the portage trail around the great falls. Being pragmatic realists, they named the falls and its thirty-mile channel *Oughniagara,* meaning "the throat." Their vigilance forced the French and their red allies to use the deadly Ottawa River–Georgian Bay route to the Michigan and Wisconsin fur lands.

Thus the Five Nations, never able to send more than twenty-five hundred warriors into battle, became the masters of both glacial plow-way approaches to Thundergate. Their reign of terror would shape American civilization for 150 years. The first Frenchman who lived long enough to outwit them was Robert Cavelier, Sieur de la Salle.

SECTION TWO

NEW FRANCE

*Monsieur de la Salle was the only man who entered
into that great Trade by building a little Ship, which
was made on the Lake Errie near the Place where I have
supposed the English will build a good Fort. The Sieur
de la Salle had indeed removed an obstacle which others
of the French had attempted to do in vain; that is to say
the Iroquois had granted him the Liberty to transport
his goods from the French towns to the Lake of Errie
with the like freedom to return to the said towns by the
same way with all the Skinns above mentioned for which
he traded upon the Lakes by means of his great Bark.
The said Sieur de la Salle had built a Fort for that purpose with Pyles pitcht into the ground at Niagara where
he had made a Magazin. . . . The Skinns which I have
given an account of would bring very great Profit to the
English for those of Muscovy (the Sables only excepted)
do not come near them in beauty.*

—Baron de Lahontan in a secret report to the ministers of Queen Anne, about 1710

∾ↄᕒ∾

A ROAD TO MEXICO

Plague and cognac were far more effective weapons than guns in the New France struggle against the Five Nations. By 1660, the redmen had become such hapless alcoholics that a source for cognac, like the Dutch schnapps and British gin, was a critical force in political decisions. During 1663, a plague of measles and influenza killed more than a thousand in the Mohawk-Genesee villages. The desire-for-cognac and the weakening-by-plague influenced the sachems toward a peace treaty with New France.

By 1667, Albany's court records reveal, Jesuit missionaries were returning to Schenectady to rent horses for the journey to the "lande of the Maquaes." The missions they established were a pioneer step toward the creation of a French fort at Niagara.

Robert Cavelier, better known later as Robert Cavelier de La Salle, landed at Montreal during the late summer of 1666. At 23 he had scorned his family's prosperous wholesaling business in Rouen and had rebelled against the rigor of teaching at a Jesuit school. His elder brother was an abbé at the Hospice of St. Sulpice, one of the two stone buildings amid the shabby sprawl of cabins, warehouses and windmills that made up the settlement of Mont Real.

The Hospice claimed ownership of both shores of the La Chine Rapids, a three-hour walk west of town. The forests along its bluffs were virgin hardwoods. The soil was rich loam. Construction of a cart-road to Montreal would be simple, except that the rapids were a favorite place for the Onondagas, Cayugas and Senecas during the Fish-running Moon.

However, young La Salle took the dare. By 1667, he had a village platted near the rapids, had persuaded a few families to settle, and had further amazed the Sulpicians by inviting a band of Seneca hunters to spend the winter at his trading post.

Perhaps it was the smattering of Seneca dialect that he picked up that winter. Perhaps it was the eternal roar of the rapids out of the West. Either or both caused the development of the village to become as boring to Cavelier as the Jesuit classrooms and the Rouen warehouses.

During the spring of 1669, the young Seigneur of La Chine canoed to Quebec and obtained permission to explore west up the St. Lawrence. He sold the La Chine development back to the Sulpicians for a thousand dollars, which he used to buy and outfit four canoes.

On August 10, La Salle and two Sulpician missionaries landed on Irondequoit Bay within the present city limits of Rochester. Some of his Seneca guests of the previous winter were with him. They guided him to the Senecas' principal village "on a hill in the midst of a clearing nearly two leagues in circumference."

A Jesuit missionary, Fremin, was in the village, but there is no mention in available records that he made any effort to help La Salle or the Sulpicians. However a Dutch "bush runner" from Schenectady was trading there. He offered to help La Salle obtain the sachems' permission to explore west through Seneca territory, but the sachems refused.

La Salle and the Sulpicians returned to Irondequoit Bay and then—on advice of his winter guests—headed northwest across the lake to a landing in the vicinity of Hamilton, Ontario. Here, on September 25 or 26, they met Louis Joliet, who was returning to Quebec after a search across Michigan, Wisconsin and eastern Minnesota for the source of the Indians' copper.

Joliet showed La Salle and the Sulpicians his new maps of the upper Great Lakes. He, too, had heard that two great rivers rolled south and west of the Great Lakes to Mexico and, perhaps, the Pacific. He advised a route west across the ridge to the valley of the Grand River and thence down it to Lake Erie. Too much danger of Seneca torture made the Niagara portage inadvisable.

The Sulpicians took Joliet's advice. Their journeys during 1669 and 1670 gave Europe a first description of Lake Erie. But Cavelier was intent on discovering one of the great rivers that flowed to Mexico. No record exists of his journeys during the next two years, but legend insists that he returned alone to the Seneca castle at Boughton Hill and persuaded the sachems to provide him with a guide and safe conduct through the Alleghenies to the headwaters of the Ohio. During the spring and summer of 1670, he allegedly explored down the valley as far as the falls at the site of Louisville, Kentucky. Then, most students of his life believe, he crossed Indiana to the foot of Lake Michigan, and followed it north past Mackinac to the Georgian Bay-Ottawa portage back to Montreal. (Louis Joliet's published maps of the Great Lakes and the Upper Mississippi valley credited La Salle with the first French exploration of the Ohio valley.)

The prairie, forest and navigable waterways west of Niagara excited the dream of a New France that would dwarf France herself. Its colonization would limit the British to a precarious foothold on the Atlantic coastal plain between the St. Lawrence valley and Spanish Florida. The first step essential to development of such a New France must be control of Lake Ontario and the Niagara portage.

Louis de Buade, Count of Palluau and Frontenac, had spent the remnants of his family's fortune on bribes and entertainment to secure Louis XIV's seal on his appointment as Governor of New France. Now he was learning that feuds among the Catholic orders, traders and town officials were as perilous to the colony's future as the arrogance of the Five Nations. He believed that an aggressive program of colonization was the best hope of ending the squabbles and corruption. Consequently, he welcomed La Salle's dream of discovering and fortifying the road to Mexico.

A river called Cataraqui by the Indians entered Lake Ontario from the north opposite the beginning of the St. Lawrence. A trading post-fort located there could attract some of the Five

Nations' fur trade, and it would be the most defensible supply base between the La Chine Rapids portage and the Niagara portage.

Frontenac sent La Salle to the Seneca capital on Boughton Hill to invite the sachems to a conference at Cataraqui during August 1673. The sachems accepted, and took him to a meeting of the Grand Council on Onondaga Hill.

More than two hundred Five Nations sachems and warriors met with Frontenac at Cataraqui. They considered his speech about peace and the desirability of a trading post convenient to the Onondaga, Cayuga and Seneca castles (villages). Finally when Frontenac told them that he wished to make Robert Cavelier de la Salle commandant and head-trader of the post, they approved.

The Fort Frontenac that Captain La Salle developed on the Cataraqui-Ontario shore was an impressive outpost for New France. Its timber barracks, mill, bakery and smithy were enclosed on the land side by cut-stone walls and on the lake shore by spike-tipped log walls. Nine cannon guarded it. Although the military garrison totaled only twelve soldiers and two officers, the masons, laborers, farmers and *coureurs de bois* employed there could provide a fighting force of more than a hundred against raids by the New England Puritans or the New York Anglo-Dutch.

Four *"barques pontées,"* each grossing ten to fifteen tons, were built on the beach. They are believed to have been rigged with two masts carrying large lug-sails and a stay-sail or two. They were used as trading vessels and patrol boats and as supply carriers between the fort and the head of La Chine Rapids.

By 1676, the Frontenac community included a Seneca-Onondaga longhouse, a dozen tenant farms, and a chapel served by two Recollet friars, Luc Buisset and Louis Hennepin.

About this time, pride of achievement encouraged the thirty-three-year-old captain to use an inherited title. Robert Cavelier, Seigneur of Frontenac, became Cavelier, Sieur de la Salle, or simply Cavelier La Salle. (Americans have a passion for abbreviation, so he entered our history books as "La Salle.")

Now each year the *barques pontées* relayed more than a million dollars worth of beaver, mink, elk, bear, bison, deer and otter pelts down the St. Lawrence. Most of the bundles came through trades with the Seneca, Cayuga and Onondaga. Thus the fort and La Salle angered the Mohawks, Oneidas and Hudson valley traders as well as the Montreal merchants who were dependent on the Ottawa-Georgian Bay trade. Governor Edmund Andros of New York wrote angry protests to Governor Frontenac, claiming that, because of a treaty signed with Arent van Curler, the Five Nations were British wards and thus Fort Frontenac was violating a British protectorate. Plots to raid the fort and hatchet La Salle were whispered in the Mohawk castles. The Montrealers favored poison or some method that would publicly disgrace the young upstart and persuade the Sulpicians or Jesuits to bring charges against him.

In 1677, La Salle turned his command over to an aide and sailed to France. Letters from Frontenac won him an audience with Louis II de Bourbon, Prince de Condé. The prince consented to become La Salle's patron in presenting a petition to Louis XIV for approval of the next steps in the New France dream: a fort at Niagara; construction of sailing ships on the Upper Lakes; exploration down the Mississippi for a route to Mexico.

A route to Mexico that would be safe from British and Dutch raiders and Caribbean pirates was of timely interest to Louis XIV. Spain's great empire was in crisis. Her Philip II was a frail and seemingly sterile ruler. His death without heirs would mean a struggle for the succession between Louis's House of Bourbon, Austria's House of Hapsburg, and the rulers of Bavaria. Control of an inland route from New France to New Spain's gold and silver mines might help to secure the succession for the Bourbons, but it was not a promising enough investment for royal funds. La Salle would have to finance it himself.

The Royal Patent that Louis issued to La Salle on May 12, 1678, gave permission to explore the "country through which, to all appearance, a way may be found to Mexico." But Jesuit influences were strong at Versailles, so the permit forbade any trading in pelts, save those of the *cíbolo* (bison).

Prince de Condé recommended another protégé, Henry de

Tonti, as vice-commander of the expedition. Eight years before, Tonti's right hand had been blown off. Surgeons replaced it with a Toledo steel and leather creation, and "Iron Hand" Tonti was a Neapolitan who felt it perfectly proper to crack jawbones in maintaining troop discipline.

That September gossip about the Patent in Montreal caused at least two efforts to poison La Salle. One dinner host served "my own special salad," spiked with hemlock. Another mixed so much arsenic in the wine that it clouded. A scheme to prove La Salle a home wrecker and roué and to initiate a court case that would delay the expedition was foiled when La Salle happened to see the husband of his landlady hide behind a door down the hall moments before the landlady, her breasts bobbing out of a skimpy chemise, tiptoed into his bedroom with a flask of cognac.

The first ship of the expedition left Montreal early in October. La Motte de Lussière commanded its sixteen men. Father Louis Hennepin volunteered to go with them. La Motte was to obtain the Senecas' approval to build a base camp at the north end of Niagara portage and a shipyard camp behind the falls.

Arguments with merchants about supplies and repeated sabotage attempts delayed La Salle and Tonti until mid-December. Ice rimed the St. Lawrence and Ontario shores. The Five Nations' code of propriety, as well as the urge to visit his Seneca friends, caused La Salle to order a course to Irondequoit Bay.

A few of his friends at the Boughton Hill castle were lolling between hunts. They were glad to see him, but prospects were not good. Two Jesuits lived at the castle now. The sachems listened to them. Only the week before, they had told the sachems that La Salle was a "mad man." So La Motte's request to build the base camp and shipyard at Niagara had been turned down.

La Salle asked for an opportunity to defend himself against the Jesuit charges. After speeches that lasted most of a night, the sachems agreed he was not "a witch or mad" and promised friendship toward the fort and shipyard. A feast and the ritualistic torture of an Indian prisoner kept La Salle and Tonti at

Boughton Hill for several days. This and ice floes delayed their arrival at the Niagara River until January 3, 1679.

Father Hennepin had built a bark-and-pole chapel at the foot of the gorge, seven miles from the Niagara's mouth. He set up his portable shrine there in time to hold the Christ Mass. But the others were so frightened by the Seneca sachems' edict to La Motte that they left most of the stores on the boat.

La Salle reported the Senecas' reconsideration. Work began on a barracks and warehouse. That midnight, La Salle woke Tonti, whispered that he was too excited to sleep, and asked him to cross the portage trail that night so they could fix the shipyard site during the morning of January 4.

The ancient trail was easy to follow, but the first mile was so steep that they had to crawl hand over hand from bush to tree limb to boulder. They saw sunrise glory the falls. Two miles south, a creek emptied into the Upper Niagara. A small island just beyond offered ideal shelter for an anchorage. There was enough firm ground along the creek mouth for a shipyard, blacksmith shop and barracks. La Salle and Tonti were back at the base camp by late afternoon.

A storm wailed down the gorge that night. The pilot of the barque that had brought La Salle and Tonti uplake had moored the vessel carelessly. The moorings slipped. The vessel careened against the shore, lunged back toward deep water and sank.

The gale was prelude for a blizzard out of the northwest. Ice and snow formed a six-inch sheath along the river. La Motte's barque could not return to Frontenac before spring.

The expedition's forty men were organized into three squads. The master carpenter, the blacksmith and a few helpers crossed the portage to select and cut trees for the ship and upper camp. Twenty men, shivering through fifteen-minute relays, salvaged the anchor, chains, forge and bar iron from the wrecked barque. The third team finished the barracks and warehouse huts at the foot of the portage.

With these emergency tasks under way, La Salle and Tonti explored the shores of the Niagara toward its mouth. Rock bluffs jutted from a narrow beach at the eastern edge of the estuary. They were twenty-five to fifty feet high and almost as effective a rampart as the cliffs guarding Quebec. And, as in Quebec's Plain of Abraham, an almost level prairie dappled with hardwood trees and shoulder-high stands of bushes and dead grass extended south to the green and black gorge. La Salle and Tonti paced back and forth along the bluff's edge for hours while they argued gun placements, sentry posts, and the best location for a boat landing.

On January 14 and 15, La Salle and Tonti returned to the spot with the master carpenter and a dozen sawyers. During the next week, a log blockhouse was adzed and doweled. La Salle named it Fort Condé, and assigned a dozen men to man it. No military engineer would ever complain about La Salle's choice of Fort Niagara's site! ! !

FOUR

∿ঔ৯∿

THE CHARRED CROSS

The few tatters of fact about the *Griffon* have made this
first sailing ship on the Upper Lakes a subject of legend, treasure
hunts and pedantic essays.

Father Hennepin twice described, in his volumes of memoirs,
the construction of the vessel at the mouth of Cayuga Creek and
its size and rig. In 1682, he alleged that the *Griffon* was "a vessel
of only about 45 tons and which we might call an ambulant fort."
But by 1696, he had exaggerated the ship to a craft "of 60 tons"
with a keel, a deck under which the crew "hang'd their ham-
mocks," topmasts and a "beakhead adorned with a Flying Griffin,
and an Eagle above it." This elaborate vessel, the Father then
averred, "carry'd five small Guns, two whereof were Brass, and
three Harquebuze a-crock" plus "the same ornaments as Men of
War use to have."

The weather pattern of the Niagara between December and
April casts doubt on the 1696 description. Niagara is the North
Atlantic seaboard's weather funnel, spewing Rocky Mountain
blizzards and Arctic Circle "highs" down its plow-ways. Niagara's
winters, the surliness of the *Griffon*'s builders, La Salle's debts
and the difficulties of transportation all suggest that the size and
rig of the *Griffon* remain as much of a mystery as her 1680
disappearance.

Much of the equipment intended for the *Griffon*'s construction
was lost when the second barque was wrecked. All the metal,
rope, canvas and stores had to be packed across the portage in
temperatures that ranged from 40 to −15 degrees.

But, between January 22 and mid-March, La Salle's men built the ship. La Salle drove the first bolt of the hull on January 26, and the next day, accompanied only by a Seneca guide, he snow-shoed east up the Ontario's north shore to Frontenac. Tonti took command. He knew little about shipbuilding, and the crew, forced into half-rations by the Senecas' refusal to supply corn and meat, threatened to desert.

A Seneca woman, who seems to have become strumpet-in-resi-dence at the Cayuga Creek camp, told that her kinsmen were plotting to burn the *Griffon* in its crib and assassinate everyone in camp. Tonti doubled the guard, but two Seneca hunters at-tacked the blacksmith one afternoon. The smith bellowed for help and threw red-hot bolts at them.

One crewman did desert, after confiding to bunkmates that he would snowshoe to Schenectady and "become a Yorker." A few days later, the Seneca woman bragged that he had been captured and was being fattened at Boughton Hill for "the spring feast."

An hour after launching the ship, the crew abandoned the bark huts and moved on board. Thereafter, the hunters and fishermen took along a half-dozen guards. Trips across the portage were similarly cautious. As trillium and ladyslipper loveliness gave way to green jungle and rattlesnakes became as fearsome along the portage as the dread of a Seneca ambush, perhaps Moyse Hillaret, the surly master carpenter, did become bored enough to hobby out carvings of a griffon and an eagle. After all, the griffon was the beast rampant on Governor Frontenac's family coat of arms, and the eagle was a favorite symbol of Prince Condé and the Bourbons.

At last, a message gave Tonti the reason for La Salle's delay. A second message warned Tonti to maintain a twenty-four-hour watch on the ship.

La Salle's creditors in Montreal and Quebec had been threat-ened by the pro-Jesuit traders of the Ottawa River route and had demanded immediate payment of their bills. La Salle could not raise the money. The creditors went to court and asked that all of La Salle's properties at Fort Frontenac be seized.

The second message reported that Governor Andros of New

York had learned about the expedition and the construction of the *Griffon* and was plotting some method for removing this "danger to all ye indian trade and all ye King's plantations upon this continent."

The foreclosure proceedings frightened La Salle to a disastrous decision. In June, he ordered Tonti to take the *Griffon* up the Great Lakes to Green Bay (Wisconsin) and start trading for furs.

The decision to use the *Griffon* for fur trading was a gross violation of the Royal Patent as well as of the promise "not to trade furs" he had given the Seneca sachems.

Tonti-the-soldier did not have enough knowledge of seamanship to carry out the order—and the crew must have decided not to coach him. The current in the fourteen miles of the Upper Niagara was too swift, and the prevailing wind was out of the west. After several attempts that almost hurtled the ship into the Upper Rapids and over the falls, Tonti ordered an anchorage between Grand Island and Navy Island. He relayed word to Fort Frontenac that the *Griffon* was helplessly trapped.

La Salle arrived in early August. Having grown up in Rouen on a shore of the Seine, he was familiar with the ancient sailor practice of "cordelling" a ship upstream through rapids. He ordered a rope attached to the mainmast and prow, then sent a hauling gang ashore with its other end. Thus on August 7, using a technique that several of the crew must have known, the *Griffon* was easily "walked" up to Lake Erie.

The *Griffon* reached Green Bay in early September and by September 18 had a cargo of beaver, mink, otter and lynx pelts. La Salle, who planned to continue his exploration to the west, instructed the pilot to race the thousand miles to Niagara and then use the guards at Fort Condé to help with the portage to Lake Ontario. The furs were worth $150,000. They would bring him enough credit in Montreal to pay off his debts, soothe the Senecas with gifts of cognac, and bribe Prince Condé and others to overlook the "no fur trading" clause in the Royal Patent.

But the *Griffon* vanished. The popular belief is that she foundered with all hands during a storm on September 19 or 20. However, it is equally possible that the pilot delivered the ship and cargo to New York agents or *coureurs de bois* in the employ of La Salle's enemies. At an inlet of Lake Huron or the Strait of Detroit, it would have been a simple matter to plunder and sink the ship and then canoe the fortune in furs off to Montreal or Albany.

The possibility of the *Griffon's* destruction by New Yorker piracy is strengthened by the few known details of Fort Condé's surrender that winter.

La Salle had left two details of militia on the Niagara. One squad guarded a small store of ship supplies cached at the Cayuga Creek mouth. The second squad, commanded by a Sergeant Le Fleur, manned Fort Condé atop the bluff at the Niagara's mouth.

During November, either British agents from Albany persuaded the Senecas to attack Fort Condé or the garrison panicked, burned the fort and fled. Sergeant Le Fleur reached Albany some time that winter and became the messenger for another exchange of angry letters between Governor Andros and Governor Frontenac. Le Fleur eventually returned to New York, enlisted as a militiaman, and served in the garrisons of several Hudson valley forts.

The squad above the falls escaped harm. La Salle accepted the certainty that the *Griffon* was lost when he returned there in the late spring of 1680.

In mid-July of that year, Moyse Hillaret led fifteen deserters ashore at Cayuga Creek, won over the guards, plundered the cache of supplies and fled east toward New York. Hillaret had finally organized a rebellion against "Iron Hand" Tonti at Fort Crèvecoeur on the Illinois River; then he plotted the race down the Lakes to refuge with the New Yorkers. The stories the deserters seem to have told at Boughton Hill and Onondaga, as payment for safe conduct to Albany, convinced the Five Nations that La Salle and the tribes along the Lake Michigan shore were creating a fur-trade monopoly that would ruin their trades with Montreal and Albany.

During September more than a thousand Seneca, Onondaga and Cayuga warriors portaged to Lake Erie. Through October they ravaged villages and crop fields in the valley of the Illinois

River; planted tree-limb stakes in the ruins capped with the charred skulls of Illini warriors, women and children, and plundered their way home through the villages of Illini confederates in Indiana and Ohio.

No record indicates visits by La Salle or any of his associates to Boughton Hill or Onondaga after 1679 or any other effort at reconciliation. If La Salle did use the Niagara as a portage place in 1682 and 1683, he crossed furtively and made no effort to re-establish Fort Condé or the Cayuga Creek supply base.

In 1682, Le Febvre de La Barré, a gouty arch-conservative, replaced Count Frontenac as Governor of New France. Flattery and the offer of a silent partnership in fur-trade ventures of the Ottawa River-Georgian Bay route added La Barré to La Salle's enemies. He dismissed La Salle as commandant of Fort Frontenac.

French barques and canoes that ventured into Irondequoit Bay or Niagara for trade were plundered and their crews led off to the fattening pens. In the spring of 1684, a flotilla of Seneca canoes beached at Fort Frontenac. The warriors wheedled entrance by offering to trade. Once inside, they hurled their fur bales at the clerks, chased the guard into the barracks and held an all-night brawl. The next morning they kicked away the empty cognac and wine kegs, picked up their bales of fur and paddled home.

That same spring, *coureurs de bois* hurried up the Ottawa-Georgian Bay route with orders to the commandants of the Upper Lakes posts to organize an expedition for "revenge against the Iroquois." In June, more than seven hundred warriors and frontiersmen started for Niagara. Meanwhile, La Barré had assembled eleven hundred soldiers, militiamen and trappers at Montreal. His plan initiated a technique that would become routine at Thundergate: a pincers attack from east and west.

But La Barré's guides were stupid or bribed. They led his eleven hundred into a swamp at the southeast end of Ontario. Hundreds contracted malaria or, more probably, yellow fever. La Barré invited the Five Nations' sachems to a meeting. They came. In response to La Barré's scolding, however, their spokesman,

La Grande Gueule, said: "We may go where we please, and carry with us whom we please and buy and sell what we please. If your allies be your slaves, use them as such."

La Barré ordered a retreat back to Fort Frontenac, then sent a barque to Niagara to "request" the seven hundred from the Upper Lakes, who were fuming there, to "return peacefully to your homes." The fiasco brought La Barré's dismissal and the appointment of Jacques René de Brisay, the Marquis of Denonville, as governor.

Denonville's orders from Versailles were to "crush the Iroquois." He resorted to La Barré's pincers tactic, and again orders went over the Ottawa route to organize a western wing of the attack. "Iron Hand" Tonti commanded the 180 *coureurs de bois* and 300 Indians who paddled south from Mackinac during May 1687. En route they captured two flotillas of New York traders and seized their "tradegoods worth 10,000 beaver skins."

Denonville assembled two thousand Frenchmen and six hundred Indians at Fort Frontenac during June, then invited Seneca and Onondaga sachems across the lake for a parley. The sachems were seized as they entered the fort, chained and shipped to France, first as exhibits of Denonville's "victory," then to be sold as farm slaves.

More than two hundred *bateaux* and three hundred canoes carried the invasion up Lake Ontario between July 8 and 10 to join with Tonti's 480 men at La Salle's old landing place on Irondequoit Bay. After the men constructed "a fort for the protection of the boats and canoes," they began the march toward Boughton Hill.

Baron de Lahontan served with both the La Barré and the Denonville expeditions. His *Voyages to North America* is the best source for details. The only provisions issued to the troops before the march to Boughton Hill began, Lahontan reported, were

> ten biscuits a man, which each one carried for himself. We had but seven leagues to march in a great wood of tall trees, upon a smooth even ground. The *coureurs de bois*, with a party of sav-

ages, led the van and the rest of the savages brought up the rear, our regular troops and our militia being posted in the middle.

The first day the army marched four leagues, and the advanc'd guards made no discovery. The second day our advanced parties marched up to the very fields of the village without perceiving anything, tho' they passed within pistol shot of five hundred (Senecas) who lay flat upon the ground, and suffered them to pass and re-pass without molestation.

Upon their intelligence, we marched up with equal precipitation and confusion, being buoyd up with the apprehension that the Iroquois had fled, and that at least their women, children and superannuated persons would fall into our hands.

When we arrived at the bottom of the hill upon which the ambuscade was placed, at the distance of a quarter of a league from the village, they began to raise their wonted cry, which was followed by the firing of some muskets. Had you but seen, sir, what disorder our troops and militia were in amidst the thick trees, you would have joined with me in thinking that several thousands of Europeans are no more than a sufficient number to make head against five hundred barbarians. Our battalions were divided into straggling parties who fell into the right and left, without knowing where they went.

Instead of firing upon the Iroquois, we fired upon one another. Twas to no purpose to call in the soldiers of such and such a battalion, for we could not see 30 paces off: In fine, we were so disordered that the enemy were going to close in upon us with their clubs in their hands, when the savages of our side having rallied, repuls'd the enemy, and pursu'd 'em to their villages with so much fury that they brought off the heads of eighty, and wounded a great many. In this action we lost ten savages and a hundred French.

The Seneca ambush at the Victor swamp was the only battle of the campaign. When it failed, the Seneca, Onondaga and Cayuga war chiefs ordered all castles within a week's march of Irondequoit Bay to be burned. "We found nothing but ashes," Lahontan recalled. "We spent five or six days cutting down the Indian Corn with our swords. In all the villages we found plenty of horses, black cattle, fowl and hogs." This livestock is, of course, important evidence of the activity and agricultural pioneering by Dutch, British, and perhaps Swedish traders in the Five Nations territory.

"The forests through which we marched were replenished with oak, wall-nut and wild chesnut trees. . . . Having done the like exploits, we return'd to the lakeside."

Denonville's strategy disgusted the Hurons and Ottawas who had come down the Lakes with Tonti. Lahontan reported:

> Most of 'em return'd to their own country, remonstrating that "The French came out to fetch a walk, rather than wage war . . . their ardour, like a flash of fire, was extinguished as soon as kindled. Twas a fruitless adventure to draw together so many warriors from all parts, to burn some hutts of bark, that the enemy could rebuild in four days. The Senecas did not matter the spoiling of their corn . . . the other Iroquois nations were able to supply 'em." And in fine (the Indian allies concluded) since they had joined the French twice together to no purpose, they would never trust'm for the future, in spite of all the remonstrances they could make.

But Denonville did decide to rebuild Fort Condé. Lahontan continued:

> Two days after, we imbarqued for Niagara, which lay 30 leagues off, and arrived there in four days. As soon as the troops had debarqued, we imployd'em in making a fort of pales, with four bastions which was finished in three days.

The Chevalier de Troyes and 120 men were assigned to guard the portage. Provisions and ammunition "for eight months" were delivered from the *bateaux* to the greenwood warehouse.

The Governor stated in his report to Versailles:

> It is an indispensable necessity to establish and maintain a post of 200 men at Niagara where married farmers ought, in my opinion, be placed to make clearances and to people that place, in view of becoming with barks masters of Lake Erie. . . . Were the British once established there, they must be driven off, or we must bid adieu to the entire trade of the country.

The flotilla of *bateaux* and canoes may still have been visible on the horizon when De Troyes learned from his commissary officer that the winter would bring as much terror from starvation as from the Senecas. Most of the flour left for them was mouldy. The casks of biscuits and salt meat were awriggle with maggots. The wine had been fouled by seawater.

No boats had been left for the garrison's use. The Senecas established siege lines. The first hunting party sent out from the fort lost two men and returned without so much as a rabbit.

Scurvy and pneumonia killed De Troyes and eighty of the garrison before spring. Then in March, Father Jean de Lamberville and three soldiers succeeded in slipping through the Seneca lines. They hiked down Lake Ontario's north shore to Fort Frontenac.

A relief expedition came up the lake during April and fought into the fort. Father Jean Millet, a Jesuit, supervised the construction of an oak-log cross, eighteen feet tall, at the center of the muddy square where de Troyes and the eighty were buried. On its crossarm he traced the inscription:

Regnat, Vincit, Imperat Christus
(Christ rules, conquers, commands)

The new garrison tried to adapt to the Seneca sentinels just beyond musket range . . . the sudden death for hunting parties . . . the midnight arc of firebrands hurtling over the stockade. But in August, Denonville sent orders to abandon both Niagara and Frontenac.

The Senecas burned the shell of the second fort at the Niagara's mouth. The charred stump of Father Milet's cross became the only symbol of New France at Thundergate. Military might had failed. Now it was up to The White Indians.

FIVE

ᘓᕤᘔ

THE WHITE INDIANS

"Canagorah lyes on the top of a great hill, and in that, as well as in bignesse, much like Oondago, contayning 150 houses," Wentworth Greenhalgh jotted into his journal for 17 June, 1677.

> Here ye Indyans were very desirous to see us ride our horses, wch wee did; they made great feasts and dancing, and invited us yt when all ye maides were together, both wee and our Indyans might choose such as lyked us to ly with.

Greenhalgh's frankness about the extent of the Five Nations' hospitality to visitors provides an important clue to the success of the Dutch-Anglos and the initial failure of the French in winning both peace and the bulk of the fur trade. Thundergate did not become a French property until New France officials learned that a willingness to "choose such as lyked us to ly with" and become a White Indian * was the quickest and safest route to the Indian trade.

"Chastity appears to be of some repute among them," Nicholas van Wassenaer wrote about the Indian women in 1632. "They are unwilling to cohabit through fear of their husbands. But those who are single evince only too friendly a disposition." It was a resourceful move for early Dutch pedlars to go through a tribe's

---

* The term "White Indian" is more appropriate for the Dutch bushrunners, Louis Joncaire, et al., than "squaw man." The phrase "squaw man" seems to have originated in Ohio about 1820, then moved west. It could mean "a white man with an Indian wife" or "an Indian who did women's work."

marriage ritual, including the gauntlet run, and become adopted sons. These first White Indians became the middlemen for the distribution of rum, guns, ammunition, knives, blankets and other white-man-goods out of Albany, and the eastward flow—via canoe and pack ponies—of the pelts, ginseng root, corn and other commodities that the Five Nations produced through squaw farming or bullied out of Indian tribes on the Upper Lakes.

These "bushrunners," as Hudson valley merchants nicknamed them, soon discovered that the chastity of Indian wives vanished after a swig of "schnaps." The redman had no more resistance to gin, applejack, rum and other 100 to 160 proof liquors than he could develop against measles, chicken pox, mumps, diphtheria, yellow fever and other of the white man's diseases. He was a helpless alcoholic.

Under the influences of alcohol, Indian women relaxed to promiscuity. Their warrior husbands believed that sexual relations weakened men. During a war or a hunting season, Five Nations' men disdained love-making. (Consequently, women captured in Five Nations' raids were never raped.) Thus alcohol became an evil weapon of the white man, and the half-breed soon became commonplace.

The system of White Indian traders, alcoholism, half-breeds and abject dependence on white-man-goods became British policy after the conquest of New Netherland in 1664 and its reorganization as His British Majesty's Colony of New York. Largely because of White Indian influences, the lure of rum or applejack, and dependence on the new iron-and-gunpowder economy, military expeditions against the Five Nations were never a matter for pondering by the Royal Governors of New York.

The great Congregational divine Jonathan Edwards wrote:

> The principal articles of commerce between them, and their amicable invaders were musquets and gunpowder, for which the bow and arrow were relinquished, and spirituous liquors, which introduced madness at their feasts and inflamed domestic enmity and strife among them. Thus doubly armed for social and for self-destruction, the aborigines have been dwindling towards extinction.

Hence the interpreter used by the Senecas for their 1669 council with La Salle was "a surly Dutchman," and during the next two years La Salle met Scotch-Irish and Dutch traders out of New York and Virginia in the Ohio valley and on the Indiana prairie. Greenhalgh's trading journey up the Mohawk valley and across the Cayuga and Seneca plains nine years later is noteworthy only because he was the first New Yorker to keep a diary of such a journey and was enough of a student to jot down intimate details about everyday life at the longhouses.

The decision of the New York governors to perpetuate the Dutch technique of White Indian agents is validated in records from 1670 to 1700. Thus, during his Albany conference of mid-September 1696, "to renew the covenant chain with the five canton nations of Indians," Governor Benjamin Fletcher approved the payment of "£100 cash for messengers and intelligence of the Enemyes motion pd. by Mr. Dellius, Mr. Barker. Majr. Schuyler and Majr. Wessells." In prelude to his October 1 council with the sachems, the Governor's aides gave the following gifts to them from "the Kings Most Excellent Majesty" and "the government of New Yorke":

> 24 blew coats
> 24 laced hats
> 24 pr shoes with buckles
> 24 shirts
> 22 dozen hose
> 30 gun barrills and locks
> 30 grasse kettles
> 1 barrill powder
> 400 weight of lead
> 1000 flints
> 1 grose of tobacco pipes, wood and tinn
> 2 grose of knives
> 6 pound of vermilion
> 1 piece of duffils
> 2 cask of Swan shott
> 7 barrills powder
> 14 large kettles

7 pieces of white hamills for shirts
100 hatchetts
54½ lbs. tobacco in roll
2 grose pipes
Wampum £3.9
28 gallons rumm

The White Indian policy abetted by the pageantry of a week-long drunk, the conferences with the Governor and his staff, and the presentation of a pack-train of goods "Made in Great Britain" yielded vast dividends. A similar conference between Acting Governor Nanfan and the sachems in July 1701 culminated in the sachems' decision to deed the Confederacy's hunting grounds north of Lakes Ontario and Erie to "the Great King of England." This act, the ministers of George I decided, made the Five Nations formal wards of Great Britain and assured a corridor west through Niagara for New York traders. About this time, too, New York instituted the practice of assigning blacksmiths to the principal Five Nations castles to repair guns and iron tools, "physik" the horses and cattle and otherwise promote dependence on a "Made in Great Britain" economy.

There is reason to believe that pack ponies were first used on the Niagara portage about 1700 and that a village of Seneca porters developed at or near the site of Lewiston. Women and children carried the bundles up the steep bluff of the first mile. This climb was so difficult that they called it *Duh-jih-heh-oh,* or "the crawl on all fours." At the gorge top, men and ponies waited for the carry along the precipice edge and through the fearsome rockpile above Devil's Hole to a *bateau*-landing on Cayuga Creek.

Some *coureurs de bois* and French missionaries used the route. During the spring of 1702, Madame de la Motte-Cadillac and her infant son crossed the portage en route to the colony of Detroit which her husband had founded the year before. Madame Alphonse de Tonti, a sister-in-law of "Iron Hand," accompanied her. They were escorted by *coureurs de bois* and a squad of soldiers. The Senecas made no effort to stop them. Their only excitements were the crawl up Duh-jih-heh-oh, the caution against stepping on rattlesnakes in the Devil's Hole area and the wild glory of the falls and whirlpool rapids.

Louis Joncaire may have been responsible for their safety at Niagara. By 1704 he was a successful White Indian. Louis Thomas de Joncaire, Sieur de Chabert, was born in Provence, near Arles, in 1670 and came to Quebec as a soldier during 1687. He was captured with a dozen others about the time of the Denonville expedition. All thirteen were taken to the Boughton Hill castle and put in the prisoners' compound for fattening. The other twelve died on the torture platform.

But as Joncaire was being led into the longhouse, he broke his bonds, knocked out both his guards, rushed a war chief and knocked him down with a haymaker that broke the chief's nose. The grunts of admiration by the Senecas indicated that Joncaire deserved an opportunity to win adoption by running the gauntlet. He made it, and became a White Indian.

During the next decade, Joncaire's audacity in battle and on the hunt won him a respect that no Frenchman had attained since La Salle. He followed the Dutch bushrunner pattern of interpreter, trader, active agent for the governors of New France, and disburser of the gifts and silver medals "from your great Father across the Sea." He was elected a sachem of the Senecas and had at least one Seneca family. Also, on March 1, 1706, he married Magdelene le Guay at Montreal and spent enough time with her during the next seventeen years to father six daughters and four sons.

With elaborate casualness, Joncaire began to talk up the advantages of a trading post at Niagara. The suggestion appealed to a few of the sachems, "if it is operated by you."

The trading post had been plotted for more than a decade at Montreal, Quebec and Versailles. All of Joncaire's services to his Seneca "brothers," his lavish gifts each summer to the sachems and the high values of "Made in France" trade goods he offered for furs were supervised by the governors of New France, with the expenses underwritten by Louis XIV's treasurer. Joncaire's services were deemed so valuable that he was appointed a captain of the Marine Corps of New France.

On May 19, 1721, Baron de Longueuil, the lieutenant-governor of Montreal, arrived at the site of Lewiston to dedicate Joncaire's stockaded cabin and warehouse as the *Magazin Royal.* The three sailboats in his flotilla carried a guard of twenty soldiers plus valets and cooks. Two *maître* canoes, each paddled by eight men, were loaded with trade goods. Two days later, more canoes arrived, carrying trade goods and supplies for the posts at Detroit and Mackinac.

During the council meeting with Seneca sachems that preceded the dedication speech and flag raising, Baron de Longueuil protested that *Magazin Royal* was "not a fort" and that the soldiers he had brought down Lake Ontario "will not be stationed here." The sachems, who had detailed reports on every step of the construction, nodded. A week later, the Baron and his guards were at Onondaga Hill; he gave similar assurances there.

Governor William Burnet of New York received a report of both meetings and a description of *Magazin Royal.* Consequently, messengers were sent up the Mohawk with invitations for the Indians to attend a Council of Friendship at Albany. The September sessions were preceded by a distribution of linen shirts, red coats, stockings, scissors, mirrors, guns and ammunition, "twelve dozen jewsharps, six and a half barrels of tobacco and a hogshead of rum." When Burnet posed questions of French operations at Niagara, the Indian assurances of "friendship for the English" were vehement, and wampum belts were presented to pledge that "as soon as any French come to the Five Nations, we shall tell them to pull down that trading house and not come either to settle or trade among us any more." (It is possible that Joncaire was one of the blanketed figures who gave this pledge and then spent the rest of the night dancing and drinking the barrels of ale provided by "His Greate Majesty, George II." It would have appealed to his vanity.)

A few weeks after the sachems' pack trains carried their gifts over the sandhills toward Schenectady, Captain Peter Schuyler, Jr., escorted seven young Germans west. The three thousand Protestant refugees from the German Palatine, shipped to the Hudson valley a decade before, had been a severe burden to New York's government. Queen Anne's ministers had believed that turpentine, resin and tar for the Royal Navy could be obtained from the Hudson valley's forests; but the hemlocks crowning the Highlands and Catskills could not produce shipstores. The refugees' shantytown hovels that would a century later bestow the place names of *Rhinecliff, Rhinebeck* and *Newburgh* along the central Hudson shores became New York's greatest shame. Hundreds froze to death or died from malnutrition, malaria and yellow fever. One group managed a midwinter march through the Catskills and settled the Schoharie valley. In 1721, the rest were threatening to revolt and march on Albany.

Palatine settlements along Lake Ontario, Governor Burnet decided, would ease two crises. William Penn was successfully using German immigrants to pioneer the Susquehanna frontier of his Penn's Sylvania. A migration of Palatines from the Hudson valley to Irondequoit Bay would not only give New York a port and trading post to compete with *Magazin Royal,* but would end the expense and threats at the mid-Hudson shantytowns.

The Mohawks provided guides across the Oneida hills and down the rocky valley of the Oswego River to the Ontario shore. The Senecas had a delegation of welcome waiting when the canoes landed at Irondequoit. They offered to provide meat and corn throughout the winter in exchange for "a little rum and some tobacco."

The winter's blizzards and subzero weather frightened the seven young Germans as much as the proximity of the Senecas, the Jesuit missionaries and the French soldiers across the lake at Fort Frontenac. They gave a bitter report about "the wild west." As a result, the Palatine elders refused Governor Burnet's offer to establish them on Irondequoit Bay. A few weeks later, they accepted his new offer of homesteads at the east end of the Mohawk valley, between Schenectady and the Mohawks' castle at Canajoharie. Thus the "Mohawk Dutch" came into existence and the villages of *Palatine Bridge, Herkimer, Frankfort, Sprakers,* and *Stone Arabia* were founded before 1730.

But this solution of the Palatine crisis did not establish a New York trading center on Lake Ontario. The presence of *Magazin*

Royal at Niagara and Joncaire's obvious influence with the Senecas, Cayugas and Onondagas threatened to veer much of the fur trade from the west down the St. Lawrence and, coincidentally, make the Five Nations economic—and eventually political—subjects of New France.

During the summer of 1724, a flotilla of flatboats poled up the Mohawk to the head of navigation near the site of Rome. Then pack ponies took the cannon, gunpowder, trade goods and tools off toward Lake Ontario. That fall, the New Yorkers built a fort and trading post on a bluff overlooking the mouth of the Oswego River.

Thus, just 115 years after Samuel de Champlain and Henry Hudson began the struggle for control of the glacial plow-ways to Thundergate, New York obtained its first port on the Great Lakes. It was fifty miles southeast across Ontario from Fort Frontenac. Its harbor, too, had anchorage space for scores of sailing craft and canoes and ample beach space for docks and shipyards. Only three portages interrupted the 200-mile water route between Oswego and Schenectady. Consequently, Burnet and his advisors planned that boats out of Oswego would announce "better prices at Albany" to the spring and summer flotillas of canoes heading toward Frontenac or Montreal. France and Great Britain were at peace. The Five Nations sachems had failed to close Joncaire's *Magazin Royal*. Now there could be competitive bidding.

Thousands of packs of pelts went down the Mohawk from Oswego during 1725 and 1726. Gossip at Montreal and Quebec about this trade expanded to stories that "a fleet of warships is building at Oswego," and "an army is gathering there to besiege Frontenac and Niagara."

Baron Longueuil and his platoon of guards canoed from Montreal to Irondequoit Bay again during the summer of 1725. Joncaire was waiting. He had arranged meetings with the Senecas, Cayugas and Onondagas. "Our bark house at Niagara is old and beginning to decay," Longueuil told the sachems after the formal exchanges of wampum belts and gifts. "The roof is so leaky that we cannot keep our goods dry there any more. Now we wish to build a larger, finer House of Peace to replace it. And, in order to keep it supplied with good things for you and your children, we also wish to build larger ships to carry goods between Niagara and New France."

The debate lasted for weeks. The Oneidas and Mohawks sent delegates to Onondaga to protest. But, again, Joncaire's influence prevailed. Formal approval of a stone House of Peace and operation of larger barques between Frontenac and Niagara was delivered to Longueuil in Montreal during the late fall of 1725.

The ships were already under construction at Fort Frontenac. Plans of the fieldstone chateau to be built on the site of Fort Condé had been approved by Louis XV's engineers. Gaspard Chaussegros de Léry, the engineer who had recently built a massive fortress at Quebec and a city wall at Montreal, was already selecting the oak beams and granite blocks that would permit his House of Peace to use its casemented third story as the gundeck for cannon.

Although the construction costs of the two sailing ships launched at Fort Frontenac during the early spring of 1726 were paid by Louis XV's treasurer, no detailed description of the vessels has survived. Bernard E. Ericson, an authority on the naval history of the Great Lakes, believes that the vessels were two-masters of 50 to 60 tons, similar in lines to a schooner. They must have been substantially larger than the craft built by La Salle. Engineer De Léry decided that granite in the vicinity of Fort Frontenac was better building material than the black-green gneiss of the Niagara gorge. Consequently, the vessels were to ferry deck cargoes of granite blocks as well as the seasoned oak beams and joists, cannon, ammunition, ironwork, tools and supplies.

De Léry reported to Quebec:

> I arrived June 6 (1726) with a detachment of troops. I remarked in beginning this house that if I built it, like those in Canada, liable to fire, should war come and the savages invest it, as was the case formerly with Mons. Denonville's fort, if it caught fire the garrison and all the munitions would be wholly lost, and the control of the country as well. It was this which determined me to make a house proof against these accidents.

Instead of wooden partitions I have built bearing-walls, and paved all the floors with flat stones.... I have traced around a fort of four bastions; and in order that they may defend themselves in this house, I have made all the garret windows machicolated, the loft being paved with flat stones on a floor full of good oak joists upon which cannon may be placed above this structure.

Though large, this would have been entirely finished in September had not some French voyageurs coming from the Miamis and Illinois, in passing this post, spread the fever here so that nearly all the soldiers and workmen have had it. This has interfered with the construction so that it has not been completed in the time that I had expected. There remains about a fourth of it to do next year. This will not prevent the garrison or traders from lodging there this winter.

The batteries of cannon for the garret were shipped uplake during the spring of 1727, heavily wrapped in canvas. Then, between midnight and dawn, the bundles were unloaded and carried up to the chateau. The haul up the two flights of oak stairs and the attic installations were carried out as furtively. Captain Charles Le Moyne, son of Baron de Longueuil, was assigned as first commandant, with a garrison of a hundred men.

The news soon reached Albany. Governor Burnet requested a council with the Five Nations on September 7. Between the afternoon of the seventh and the evening of the ninth, the series of speeches pondered the fact that the Treaty of Utrecht between France and Great Britain in 1724 had conceded the Five Nations to be "subjects of Great Britain." Governor Burnet had prepared a treaty for the sachems. It assigned the property rights of a 60-mile strip of Lake Ontario's south shore, including the Niagara peninsula, to "our Great King," and pledged warrior support "against the French" to the garrison at Fort Oswego. The sachems made their marks on the treaty.

Thus the House of Peace became a fuse to explode the French and Indian War.

SIX

⌒⟋ᗡᕲ⟍⌒

THE BEAUTIFUL RIVER

"Where are the redman's lands?" a refugee Delaware warrior asked the Virginia trader, Christopher Gist, in 1752. "The French claim everything on the north shore of the Ohio. The British claim everything on the south side." The cogency so impressed Gist that he jotted it in his journal. Louis Joncaire's pioneering down the creek valleys southwest of Niagara initiated the 1739 to 1753 expeditions that claimed "The Beautiful River" for New France and thus caused the French and Indian War.

As the panther-proud procession of Christopher Gist . . . Daniel Boone . . . Davy Crockett . . . Mike Fink . . . Jedediah Smith . . . Jim Bridger would emphasize, the wilderness of the American West offered soul balms of beauty, solitude and resources that surpassed its physical hardships. Thirty years among the Senecas had conditioned Louis Joncaire to the same conviction. Once the House of Peace was built and the garrison installed, it became "another fort with too many damn people."

Moreover, Joncaire was 56 years old in 1726. His oldest Montreal son, Philippe Thomas, was a lithe 19 and had worked with him on trade journeys and spy missions since he was 12. Now Philippe too was an adopted Seneca and of course a father. The second Montreal boy, Daniel or "Little Chabert," was 10 and already demanding "a place in the boat and my own hatchet." Both of them would soon be ready to step into the old man's moccasins as New France's ambassadors to the Five Nations. Old age develops the greatest fear of all in a man! One more frontier?

La Salle's explorations of *La Belle Rivière* were all but forgotten. The hunger for fur pelts had drawn New France up the Lakes, then west across the prairie to the Mississippi. Now traders from Virginia and Pennsylvania were discovering the trails through the mountains. They called *La Belle Rivière* the Ohio and claimed that it must be British because of those royal charters that had granted their colonies land "to the South Sea."

The Five Nations claimed *La Belle Rivière,* too, by right of their 1650–1680 conquests. The families who migrated there from Onondaga, Cayuga and Seneca castles were still subject to Onondaga Hill decisions. The Delaware and Shawnee who were forced west into the valley and the great forest beyond also acknowledged the Five Nations as overlords.

Joncaire knew the portage places from Lake Erie's south shore to the creeks that would carry a canoe down to the Allegheny. He returned to them during the summer of 1727, and that autumn at Montreal reported that another five hundred Shawnee refugees from North Carolina had settled along the *Rivière du Boeuf* (Bull Creek), a fourteen-mile portage south of Lake Erie.

The advance of New France missions and trading posts down the Allegheny to the Ohio's headwaters and on to the Kentucky and Ohio prairie clearings between 1728 and 1738 are the clearest record of Joncaire's last great achievement. He explored, intrigued, guided and slipped back into shadow. His favorite summer home was at Venango, on the site of Franklin, Pennsylvania, where the paddleway from Rivière du Boeuf merged with the Allegheny.

Jesuit missionaries preached to Delaware, Shawnee and Seneca camps at the Ohio's Forks (Pittsburgh) in 1728. During 1732 the first New France trading post on the Allegheny was built near the site of Warren, Pennsylvania. From it, Toussaint le Cavelier peddled cognac, Provence lace, Marseille silks and Paris kettles each summer southwest as far as the falls of the Ohio. Receptions for delegations of Delaware, Shawnee and other *Belle Rivière* tribes became July and August routines at Montreal.

By 1731, young Philippe Joncaire was on the Ohio too. He was considered valuable enough to New France to be appointed a

Lieutenant. By 1736, "Little Chabert" displayed exceptional profi-
ciency for a 19-year-old. He wrote in his memoirs:

> In 1736 I was ordered to go among the Iroquois, to the Fort of
> Niagara, there to await the chiefs from the nations of the Sault S.
> Louis and from the Lake of the Two Mountains and to escort
> them to the Missisagues, in order to make a good peace between
> these allies of France. The negotiation succeeded; I returned to
> the fort, from which I twice repaired to the Five Nations, in or-
> der to keep them always peacably disposed.
>
> The tribes on the Ohio were suspected of being prevailed upon
> by the English to stir up the neighboring nations against the
> French. The suspicion was well founded. I was sent there in com-
> pany with chiefs of the Five Nations. I broke up the conspiracy,
> and remained all summer [1737] in that country, from which I
> came back to winter, partly at the Fort, partly among the Five
> Nations.
>
> In the spring of 1738 I was again charged with visiting differ-
> ent villages, in order to keep informed on what happened, and to
> assemble the councils, of which I sent a report to the Governor.
> As a general thing, when I was not on some military expedition,
> my ordinary employment, summer and winter, was to travel over
> this vast continent; in summer by canoe; in winter on snowshoes
> across the ice and snow; to cultivate friendship, check impru-
> dence, dispel plots and break off treaties of these people with the
> enemy. . . . These perpetual negotiations offer dangers as manifold
> and more formidable than those of battle, for they are concealed
> under the false appearance of peace and friendship. When the
> Indians break with anyone, they have no other way of showing
> it than by the tomahawk and gun; if one comes among them un-
> der these circumstances, a deputy is no more than an enemy in
> their eyes.

The pioneering of Louis Joncaire and his sons enabled the first
New France expedition down the Ohio to assemble at Niagara
during July 1739. Word had come from New Orleans that Governor Bienville of Louisiana (the Mississippi valley) was organizing a campaign against the Chickasaws in the Tennessee
Mountains. The administrators at Quebec decided to send an
army south to carry out a pincers operation against the Chickasaw

villages on Tennessee's Wolf River and at the bluffs near the site of Memphis. Charles Le Moyne, Baron de Longueuil, son of Joncaire's old friend and spokesman, commanded the expedition.

Louis Joncaire was 69 years old that summer. He did not, as his custom had been for the previous dozen springtimes, follow the crocus and pussywillow unfoldings west along the Erie shore and down the pine-dark creek to his beloved Venango. He waited impatiently at *Magazin Royal* for his hour of triumph. The Longueuil invasion route down the Allegheny to its swirling union with the Monongahela and the 600-mile float on through the snags, flumes and mossy canyons of *La Belle Rivière* were a product of Joncaire's intrigue with the Five Nations and their Delaware and Shawnee wards. The crowning glory of Louis Joncaire's life would be to personally lead the Longueuil army across the Lake Chautauqua portage to Venango, then—standing on the hemlock-fragrant bank of the Allegheny—wave it on to Ohio conquest.

But the glory-day never came. Joncaire died on June 29. Perhaps Longueuil had already arrived from Montreal, and the old man's death was aftermath of a feast and far too much cognac. Perhaps, as sometimes happened there, tempers flared during a drinking-time, Joncaire accepted a challenge to a duel and was killed.

The records are suspiciously silent about "cause of death" and equally mysterious about Joncaire's burial place. His remains may be in the Old French Cemetery south of the Fort. It is more probable that the corpse was turned over to the Senecas and carried, with all the formality due a sachem, south across the Genesee to Boughton Hill.

Chabert Joncaire took his father's place as pathfinder for the expedition. It totaled twenty-four militiamen, forty-five *voyageurs*, a drummer, 319 Indians, plus Longueuil, his staff, and Chabert, who recalled:

> We had 18 days of marching and provisions for only six days. Moreover, we were charged to observe and not to fight. We could not even fire a musket. When our provisions were consumed, we lived on acorns roasted in hot ashes.

The flotilla reached the site of Memphis without any major battles and met the flotilla that Governor Bienville had sent north from New Orleans. They built a fort and marched against the Chickasaw villages on Wolf River. Chabert reported:

> I served as interpreter. An understanding was reached. I led the chiefs of the Chickasaws to the Fort to ratify the treaty; after which the governor sent me back to Niagara whence I had to go all winter long (1740–41) from village to village, with as much of risk as of fatigue, to hold or regain several nations which the English had drawn to their side.

Through 1758, the exploits of Philippe and Chabert Joncaire in winning New France allies merged into Albany legends about a superman known only as "Jean Couer." The sons almost fulfilled Louis Joncaire's life goal and won all of the Five Nations for New France. But a wild Irishman named William Johnson settled in the Mohawk valley during the fall of 1738. He became the greatest White Indian of them all.

SECTION THREE

A DARING KIND OF WAR

An offensive, daring kind of war will awe the Indians and ruin the French. Block-houses and a trembling defensive encourage the meanest scoundrels to attack us.

—Brigadier General James Wolfe
   to General Jeffrey Amherst, 1758

SEVEN

A MAN OF MEATH

In 1738 New York was ruled by a fourth-generation aristocracy. The Van Rensselaers, De Lanceys, Livingstons, Schuylers and a few other Anglo-Dutch patroons had grown wealthy by means of the usual frontier-plunder pattern of rum, tenant farming, and exorbitant prices for trade goods. Now a new form of income was opening. The high taxes in New France and the superiority of the cotton and woolen goods produced by England's mills persuaded the development of a smuggling monopoly between Montreal and the Hudson valley.

The smuggling, the piety of new wealth and the strategy of settling the Palatine refugees up the Schoharie and Mohawk valleys as frontier protection against "Indiane troubles"—all these militated against perpetuation of the pioneer technique of White Indian diplomacy.

Consequently, the advisability of secret alliances with the Joncaires and other agents of New France was in debate at tribal council meetings of the Mohawk and Oneida castles. The Albany-Montreal smuggling had lowered the exchange rate on pelts. The Jesuit missionaries had converted hundreds of their red kinsmen, then had led them off to shack towns on the St. Lawrence to enjoy "the blessed peace of the Christian life" and be protected "from the sins of lust and drunkenness." By 1738, there were as many Mohawks at the Jesuit colony of Caughnawaga, near the La Chine, as there were at the Canajoharie castle. And—Hawenio forgive them! ! !—they were all becoming enthusiastic Frenchmen.

The Senecas, the largest and strongest nation of the Confederacy, were completely spellbound by the Joncaires and that great stone house at Niagara. The Cayugas and Onondagas, despite two-faced talk to Albany, were being strict neutrals in the New France-New York rivalry. What to do? Rum-and-ruin with the New Yorkers? Piety and the coughing-death at Caughnawaga? A pox on all white men! ! !

Survey crews working near Fort Hunter that summer symbolized another gnawing fear to the Indians because of the method by which that land had become the property of Captain Peter Warren, R.N. (Royal Navy).

When the Palatines were persuaded to settle in the Mohawk valley, Fort Hunter was built to defend them. Captain Walter Butler was transferred from Connecticut to the command of Fort Hunter. He was Irish, proud of his descent from the Dukes of Ormonde, and determined to wrest a fitting inheritance for his five-year-old son, John. Thus, after an afternoon's conference with Governor William Cosby at Albany, Captain Butler sent wampum belts to the sachems of Teantontalago, just across the Mohawk-Schoharie junction, and invited them to "a feast of brotherhood" at the Fort.

The feast became a merry three-day brawl. Captain Butler brought out the parchment document that Governor Cosby had read and approved the week before. Promises of large gifts of rum caused several of the sachems to squiggle their clan symbols along the bottom of the document. Thus Captain Butler became the owner of 86,000 acres of land at the Mohawk-Schoharie junction.

Governor Cosby's kickback was a 14,000-acre parcel. When he discovered that a similar rum feast had secured the same plot for the Corporation of Albany just a few weeks before, he had the Corporation's deed burned.

Cosby's appointee as Chief Justice of New York was James De Lancey, head of a wealthy patroon family. Captain Peter Warren had married De Lancey's sister, Susannah, and used De Lancey's advice on investments in Manhattan real estate. (One piece of farmland which he bought became New York City's Greenwich Village!)

When Governor Cosby died in 1735, Justice De Lancey told Warren about the 14,000-acre plot of good wilderness land up the Mohawk, with a sale price of twenty-five cents an acre. Captain Warren bought it and designated it "Warrensburg." Then he sent a letter to his sister, Ann.

Warren, too, was a scrawny red-haired Irishman. An ancestor had served the Plantagenets well enough to win the grant of a manor in the Boyne River valley of County Meath, near Dublin. But Peter Warren's father lost it in 1690 by siding with James II at the Battle of the Boyne. Family friends sponsored Peter's education and a career in the Navy. His luck held. He was captain of a frigate at 26. Prize money for the French and Spanish ships that his frigate captured in the West Indies and off the mouth of the St. Lawrence financed his real estate gambles.

However, his sister, Ann, had married a County Meath miller named Christopher Johnson. The Johnsons lived on a 200-acre farm owned by the Earl of Fingel. Their oldest son, William, was "a great lout of 23, too wild in his ways for the likes of here."

Captain Warren offered to bring William Johnson to New York and try him out as overseer of the Warrensburg property. The youth must also recruit Meath families who wished to make good in the Mohawk valley by developing their own 200-acre farms— after, of course, they had worked off the costs of passage and the price of the land!

William Johnson and ten families of Meath farmers landed at Boston during the spring of 1738, took schooner passage to New York and were brusquely inspected by Captain and Mrs. Warren. William Johnson towered above his uncle. He had jet black hair, as unruly as an Irish Hobby's mane. His wide-set eyes and firm chin and the hawk ferocity of his nose all announced the same tenacious pride that had made Grandfather Warren fight for the Stuarts' "lost cause" and enabled Christopher Johnson to provide for nine people from a tenant farm and grist mill.

Captain Warren's instructions to William filled a week. He ex-

plained the Mohawk's weather pattern, the brutish redskins, the
ignorant Palatines and the admirable aristocrats of Albany and
Schenectady. He had already shipped a splendid assortment of
supplies up river for the trading post that William would manage.
Obviously, the frontier would relish colored inks, linen writing
papers, bolts of tweed, loaf sugar, cinnamon, pepper and similar
niceties. Mrs. Warren gave William a letter of introduction to her
old friends, the Van Rensselaers at Albany.

Mr. Van Rensselaer just happened to have a half dozen "splendid" horses that he was willing to sell William. Three of them
demonstrated they were half dead from the "staggers" before they
reached Schenectady. Two others died of distemper. Thus began a 36-year feud between William Johnson and the Albany
aristocrats.

Most of Uncle Peter's advice, Johnson soon learned, had been
as naïve as his faith in patroon hospitality. The display of linen
papers, colored inks, tweed and spices on the split-log shelves of
the trading post evoked mutters of *"Mein Gott!"* from the Palatines and grunts from the Indians. Johnson closed the cabin,
bateaued the goods to Schenectady and exchanged most of them
for the bush knives, hatchets, snuff boxes, red and blue blankets,
guns, lead and hoes that, Captain Butler finally told him, composed the "usual Indian truck" essential to pelt trading. In
October, when the Palatines rafted and pack ponied their wheat,
potatoes, turnips and maize down to exchange for winter supplies,
he was ready for them.

One of the most valuable facets of William Johnson's genius
was his ability to "listen people out." The Palatines and the Mohawks soon sensed this. The Warrensburg cabin became a favored gossip spot. Its schnapps was neither watered down nor
furied with pepper-bin dust, either. Johnson stood every third
drink. Smoked herring is as Irish as peat-fragrant whiskey, and
there was a crockful of it on the counter for the nibbling. Somehow, too, this good listener learned the Schenectadians' trick of
mashing two-year-old cheddar in a little rum or brandy with a
sprinkle of caraway seeds. Daubed on a split shipbiscuit, this was
attar of paradise!

The gossip droned. Johnson listened. The lusts, intrigues and self-reliance of the frontier excited him. Perhaps there were stories about the exploits of "that old devil Jean Couer" and the pervading fear of raids out of Niagara and Caughnawaga like the one that had burned Schenectady fifty years before. All of it led Johnson to the conviction that his sole hope of success was friendship with—and understanding of—the Indians and the Palatines. He began to ask the meanings of Mohawk phrases, then evinced such a persnickety pedantry for the subtleties of pronunciation that he was introduced to Tiyonaga, a Mohawk sachem who took pride in his British nickname of "King Hendrick."

King Hendrick was one of the four Mohawks who had been taken to London in 1710 for an audience with Queen Anne. A hatchet scar creased a purple welt across his left cheek. His nose was pierced for the jewels that Mohawk warriors fancied. Bundled in a greasy trade blanket with a faded tricornered hat pulled down over his eyes, Hendrick gloried in playing the role of hapless aborigine. He drawled French and Whitehall English as easily as he gutturaled Mohawk, Seneca or Huron.

Johnson's eagerness appealed to Hendrick. Within a few months, the young giant from Meath was Hendrick's protégé and was being guided south and west on trades, hunts and initiation to castle concepts of hospitality.

Catherine Weisenbergh clerked the trading post during these absences. No description of her exists. Her birth, parentage and death records are yet to be deduced. The Johnson legend asserts that she was a busty Palatine daughter. She became Johnson's housekeeper during 1739. Her first-born was baptized Ann—for Johnson's mother—at Fort Hunter's Mohawk chapel on June 8, 1740, and was recorded as "a childe of Catherine Wysenbergh." Her son, John, was similarly recorded on February 7, 1742. The next baby that lived long enough for baptism was recorded as "Mary Wysenbergh" on October 14, 1744.

The children grew up as Ann, John and Mary Johnson. William Johnson brought in a governess for the girls and sent John to school in New York City. Only the Butlers and a few missionaries muttered about Catherine's continuing role as housekeeper and the nudity of her wedding-ring finger.

But the mutters were held to bedtime gossip—after the children were asleep. William Johnson was becoming too important. Catherine brought in the Palatines' trade. King Hendrick's sponsorship and Johnson's abandon to Mohawk mores made him the most popular trader on the Mohawk. During 1742, he became Warraghiyagey, "a man who undertakes great things," as well as a blood-brother Mohawk.

Johnson's mistresses throughout the Five Nations and the domination of the Mohawk, Molly Brant, over his household during his last decades have become legend. Some allege that he "sired more than 700 half-breeds" and scores of Mohawk Dutch. So much for the penalty of being a lusty Irishman, who, through the White Indian technique, won a knighthood, 100,000 acres of land and more wealth than the Van Rensselaers and Schuylers combined. There are records of only three Indian sons.

The most revealing folktale about Johnson's genius for listening and playing the waiting game was in print in 1841. "Hendrick was at the house of William Johnson when Johnson received several rich suits of clothes," alleged John W. Barber and Henry Howe. "Soon after, Hendrick came to Johnson and said, 'I dream.'

" 'Well,' Johnson asked. 'What did you dream?'

" 'I dream you gave me one of those suits of clothes.'

"This hint could not be mistaken or well avoided, and accordingly Hendrick received a suit.

"Sometime afterward, Johnson meeting Hendrick said, 'I dreamed last night.'

" 'Did you? What did you dream?'

" 'I dreamed you gave me a tract of land,' which he went on to describe.

"Hendrick at first paused at the enormity of the demand, but at length said, 'You may have the land. But we don't dream any more. You dream too hard for me.'

"The tract of land thus obtained is stated to have been 12-miles square, in the present County of Herkimer. The title to it was confirmed by the King. It was called 'The Royal Grant.' " (It still

is, and some of its residents along State Route 28 north of Herkimer believe the dream story is true!)

Europe's War of the Austrian Succession became King George's
War in America during 1744. By that time, William Johnson
claimed thousands of acres along the north side of the Mohawk
and was building a mansion there. Uncle Peter threatened and
fumed until victories in the Caribbean, his part in the capture of
Louisburg, and a victory over a French fleet off Cape Finisterre
won him a knighthood, fortune, a London mansion and a seat in
Parliament.

Philippe and Chabert Joncaire opened the war campaign in
the West by spreading rumors among the Seneca, Cayuga and
Onondaga that "the English are organizing a great army to burn
your castles and steal your land." The rage which this roused
erupted against the English packtrains and *bateaux* supplying
Oswego. Petitions to His Honour the Lieutenant Governor of
New York protested:

> the many hazzards and Difficulties we are subject to in our pas-
> sage thither from the ill treatment we meet with from the Indians
> in passing the castles. They board our Battoes with Axes knives
> &c and by force take what Rum they think proper keeping . . . and
> on our arrival at the great carrying place, the Oneida Indians
> force our goods from us at pleasure to carry over, and not content
> to making us pay a most exorbitant price for each Freight but rob
> us of our Rum, Stores and other Goods with a great deal of in-
> vective threatening language, and are generally so Numerous
> that we are Obliged to submit to those impositions or run the risk
> of being Murdered and Robbed of everything we have.

That November, four hundred French and two hundred Indians burned Saratoga and plundered down the Hudson valley
to the outskirts of Albany. When the waterway opened in the
spring of 1746, no boatmen would accept the contract to carry
supplies and trade goods to Oswego. Johnson volunteered. His
status as an adopted Mohawk and a friend of the Palatines secured the crews. The Mohawks, Oneidas and Onondagas guar-
anteed safe passage and no rum plunders at the portages.

That spring, too, Governor George Clinton learned that "certain persons will undertake upon proper encouragement to bring Jean Couer, a French priest, to Albany who is settled among the Sinnecas. And they are of opinion his removal from the Indians will be very great service to the British interest."

The kidnap effort failed. But during July the Governor's Council resolved, "That of the new levies now in this province . . . 6 or 700, together with 200 Indians, be employed against the French fort at Ongiara, at the same time as an attempt against Crown Point."

Governor Clinton requested Johnson to carry war belts to the castles. Johnson induced delegations from each Nation to be in Albany by early August. He led the Mohawks down Rose Hill to the city gates on August 8, his naked chest and arms daubed with war paint, his hair shaved to the single center ridge of the war-lock.

The conference dawdled for weeks. An epidemic of smallpox killed several sachems. Delegates from Massachusetts and Pennsylvania finally arrived. They repeated Governor Clinton's promise that "his Majesty will send many soldiers to drive out the French." Bounties for French scalps were argued and fixed: Ten pounds for males, but no payment for women or girls. If an adult male was brought in alive, he rated a £20 reward.

Finally, after a series of conferences with the sachems and his Council, Governor Clinton appointed Johnson to be New York's "Colonel of the Six Nations" * and empowered him to organize raids against New France, especially Niagara.

* During 1722, refugee Tuscaroras from Georgia had appealed for Five Nations' protection and land. They became wards of the Oneidas, but were never permitted to send delegates to the Grand Council meetings at Onondaga. However, Albany bureaucrats deemed it politic to use the term, "Six Nations," when dealing with the Confederacy.

⌒᷍ᴐᴄ᷍⌒

THE PINCERS

"The army of soldiers" didn't materialize. Schooners out of Gloucester, Marblehead and Boston influenced Massachusetts' politics. Control of the cod and halibut fisheries off Newfoundland was more expedient than a campaign to ease New York's threats; so William Pepperell's soldiers and Uncle Peter Warren's ships went off to besiege and plunder Louisburg.

Virginia, despite the fact that several of her Ohio valley traders were in Fort Niagara's dungeon, was too preoccupied by plans for chartering the Ohio Company and the Loyal Company that would colonize 1,300,000 acres of land beyond the Blue Ridge. Pennsylvania was similarly scheming; moreover, neither her Quakers nor her Mennonites approved of soldiers or warfare.

Thus King George's War demonstrated how the forty-five thousand whites of New France could consistently hoodwink and terrorize the one million whites living in the thirteen British colonies from Maine to Georgia. Fisheries, gimcrack peddles, and huge profits from slaveships and rum established the New England aristocracy. Tobacco in Virginia . . . rice and indigo in South Carolina and Georgia . . . the diversified-agriculture and sharp-trade skills of the Pennsylvanians—these interests nourished dictatorial cliques in each colony. Too intent on local problems and profits, the colonists refused to build the north-south highways or even wagons and coaches necessary for the beginning of intercolony unity. These factors, plus jealousies about the Royal land grants "to the South Sea"—based, of course, on the ignorance of seventeenth-century cartographers—and the religious schisms among New England Puritans; Maryland-Georgia Catholics; Pennsylvania Quakers and Mennonites; and New York Episcopalians, Lutherans and Presbyterians all helped New France to divide and bully.

William Johnson did harangue a hundred Mohawks and a few Oneidas into raids across the Adirondacks. They brought back a few scalps and prisoners. Johnson had learned showmanship. He took the prisoners, the scalps and a band of painted warriors into Albany, then down to New York City and paraded them through the streets with an honor escort of militia. The display was gaudy, but failed to impress the Senecas, Cayugas and Onondagas, or even a majority of New York's Assembly. Only one company of militia was sent west to reinforce Fort Oswego during the three years of the war.

The Onondagas and Cayugas held to impassive neutrality; the Senecas interrupted trade with the Joncaires and with Fort Niagara only long enough to send assurances of "our great love for the King" to Albany. By 1748, when the Treaty of Aix-la-Chapelle ended the war—and returned Louisburg and Cape Breton to New France—the Mohawks and Oneidas were whispering again about the advisability of a secret pact with the French.

Through it all, Fort Niagara's garrison never exceeded a hundred soldiers. In 1744, the garrison varied from thirty to sixty-four soldiers with six officers. During 1745, William Johnson's war dances and harangues caused another company, plus sixty "Nipissing and Algonquin" warriors to be sent down from Frontenac. But from 1746 to 1748, the principal concern was about a cave-in of the bluff near the House of Peace, the weather rot of the stockades and the price increases in trade goods caused by Peter Warren's blockade off the Gaspé Peninsula.

In the summer of 1749, Governor Beauharnais agreed that it would be sound strategy to build another fort at the mouth of the Humber River, forty miles across Ontario from Niagara. The Mississauga Indians had a village there called Toronto. Some western Indians were bringing pelts to Oswego via the Humber.

An officer, fifteen soldiers, and a few *habitant* workmen were sent over to do the job.

The Marquis de Beauharnais, one of the bar-sinister sons of Louis XIV, had been Governor General of New France since 1726. The British indolence about the West during King George's War, and the Virginia-Pennsylvania plans for colonizing *La Belle Rivière*, encouraged him to a daring project.

During June 1749, a flotilla of 23 *maître* canoes swirled in to the Fort Niagara landing. Captain Pierre Joseph de Céloron de Blainville commanded the 20 soldiers, 180 *habitant* militia, 30 Christian Senecas, Mohawks and Oneidas from Caughnawaga, 25 Abenakis, 8 officers, 6 cadets, one armorer and Father Jean de Bonnecamps, professor of hydrography at the Jesuit College in Quebec.

Carefully stored among the brandy kegs, guns, and rock-hard slabs of pemmican on the floor of one canoe were a dozen engraved lead plates recently received from Paris. The engravings proclaimed:

> In the year 1749, during the reign of Louis XV, we, Céloron, commander of a detachment sent by M. the Marquis de la Galissonière, commander in chief of New France, for the restoration of tranquility in some villages of these districts, have buried this plate at _____, this _____ July, near the river Ohio, otherwise Beautiful River, as a monument of the renewal of possession which we have taken of the said river Ohio and of all those that therein fall, and of all the lands on both sides as far as the sources of the said rivers, as enjoyed or ought to be enjoyed by the preceding Kings of France and as they therein have maintained themselves by arms and by treaties, especially by those of Riswick, of Utrecht and of Aix-la-Chapelle.

The maps in Captain Céloron's strongbox showed the precise route that the expedition was to take via the Niagara and Lake Chautauqua portages to the Allegheny, thence southwest to the Beautiful River. The location details and date would be engraved on each plate by the armorer during the formal ceremony at each burial site down the seven hundred miles from Niagara to the Beautiful River's junction with the Mississippi.

Louis Joncaire's sons led a delegation of sachems to the fort to give formal greetings and wampum pledges of peace. The eight iron cannon and single mortar then usable in the House of Peace attic fired a salute.

The formal seizure of the Ohio valley by New France began on July 15, after a two-day delay to "await our Indians who were amusing themselves with drinking rum at the portage with a band of their comrades who were returning from Oswego."

A smaller flotilla that started up the St. Lawrence from the La Chine Rapids soon after Céloron's was equally important to Governor Beauharnais' master-plan. The lead canoe of this procession held a cowled 41-year-old Sulpician missionary. During his fourteen years in New France, Father François Picquet had mastered the languages and protocol of the Algonquins and the Five Nations.

Father Picquet ordered his flotilla into the natural harbor now surrounded by the city of Ogdensburg. That summer and fall he and his *habitants* built La Présentation Mission. (The British came to dread it as *Oswegatchie*.) It was to be another shanty-town for Senecas, Cayugas and Onondagas.

Niagara was the scene of one of the Indian revival meetings that Father Picquet, escorted by seven *habitants* and "five faithful savages," conducted during the summer of 1751. An "imposing figure of a gay disposition," the Father was as skilled in mob psychology as any of the Mormon, Methodist or Spiritualist divines who would fire religious passions throughout upstate New York a century later. "He sang and composed canticles, now in French and now in Iroquois, with which he amused the savages. ... His mechanical ingenuity often won admiration." At the village of the Seneca portage carriers, thirty-nine "found the Christ," abandoned their huts, and followed the missionary down lake. At Irondequoit, in typical display of revival-meeting wonders, Seneca converts staged a rattlesnake hunt and killed forty-two "without once being bitten."

Approximately four hundred Indian families moved to La Présentation during 1751 and 1752. They reduced the warrior-power of the Six Nations by a third.

Another step toward fulfillment of the master plan for the Ohio was detailed to Chabert Joncaire during conferences at Montreal in the summer of 1750. Chabert was appointed Master of the Niagara Portage. A fort would be built a mile and a half behind the falls, midway between Grass Island and the mouth of Gill Creek. It would be advisable, too, to build a carriage house, since a vehicle would shortly be shipped up the lake for the use of officers and their families crossing the portage.

The village of Fort Little Niagara—also called Fort du Portage—that Chabert developed between the fall of 1750 and 1759 included a warehouse, a stable 100 feet long, a 42-foot barn, a shed 40 feet long, log houses and, inevitably, a stockade. The portage equipment eventually totaled 36 goods carts, 12 horse sleds, four "drags with wheels and chains," and a *calèche*, or carriage.

Fourteen miles south, just beyond the beginning of the Niagara River, a shallow creek drained into Lake Erie. The soil in the creek valley was excellent. Chabert sent *habitants* and Seneca women down to develop vegetable gardens, wheat and oat fields and a fruit orchard. The stands of grass were so lush that he pastured the brood mares, stallions and colts of the portage herd here, too. Consequently, he named the creek *Rivière aux Chevaux*, The River of Horses. (Nobody knows why, or how, sometime between 1760 and 1790, the British changed the name to Buffalo Creek.) Along the river shore, near the Little Rapid, the *habitants* built a blacksmith shop; a storehouse for "harness, saddles, nails, bar iron and charcoal"; a hundred-foot "cedar barn," as well as "sleeping sheds for the Indians" and cabins for the blacksmith, herdsmen and farm overseers.

Little Niagara was still under construction when Senecas, Delawares and Shawnee began delivering English traders whom they had captured in the Ohio valley. Ralph Kilgore and Morris Turner, both from Lancaster, Pennsylvania, were captured near the Forks of the Ohio in 1750 and brought to Niagara. John Peter Salling of Williamsburg, Virginia, was "redeemed by the governor of Canada" after six years as an Indian slave and a Niagara prisoner. During 1751, Governor Clinton demanded the release from "imprisonment in irones near Oniagara of six Englishmen, subjects of the King my Master, who were peacefully pursuing a Lawful Trade with the Indians." A Seneca delegation visited Johnson to warn him that "Your castle must be guarded well this winter." Chabert Joncaire was offering £1,000 apiece for the scalps of Johnson and the most feared Pennsylvanians, George Croghan and James Lowry.

Ange, the Marquis Duquesne, a Navy veteran, became New France's Governor General during the summer of 1751. His orders from Louis XV were to "build on *La Belle Rivière* such forts as are absolutely necessary." The campaign began at Niagara during March 1753, when Captain Paul de la Malgue, Sieur de Marin, and the Chevalier le Mercier sailed in with 250 carpenters, boatmen, masons and smiths. The two schooners stationed at Frontenac began a weekly shuttle service of troops and supplies. Onondaga sent a messenger to William Johnson with the rumor that "an army of 20,000 French and hordes of Caughnawagas, Ottawas, Lakes and Miamis are invading the Ohio."

The Army of the Beautiful River never exceeded twenty-three hundred men. About seventeen hundred were *habitant* militia. Not more than two hundred were garrison troops from Frontenac and Montreal. The rest were "Christian Iroquois" and Algonquins from the Jesuit and Sulpician mission towns.

Captain Marin's orders were to build and garrison forts at Presque Isle on the Lake Erie shore, at the headwaters of the Rivière au Boeuf fourteen miles south and at Joncaire's beloved Venango on the Allegheny.

Major Michael Jean Pean, a wealthy Quebec trader, was Marin's second in command. His nomination for the post by François Bigot, the Intendant, was—rumor said—due to Madame Pean's consent to become Bigot's mistress as soon as her husband could be inveigled out of town. This David-Bathsheba echo was in keeping with Bigot's plan to juggle a fortune out of the expedition's costs.

Harvests were puny on the lower St. Lawrence farms during 1752. This gave Bigot an alibi for buying six thousand quarts of flour and corn in New England, smuggling it into Montreal and charging it to the Royal Treasury at three times its cost.

The canoes and schooners unloaded more than five hundred tons of these supplies, plus a score of brass and iron cannon, at the Niagara dock that summer. Neatly packaged among the salt pork kegs, wine casks and corn sacks were the bundles of velvet, damask, ladies' shoes, silk stockings and Paris perfumes that Bigot, Pean and their confederates had purchased as "King's stores," doublebooked, and were now prepared to peddle either to the Indians or to the traders out of Detroit, Mackinac, Vincennes and Kaskaskia.

But by July, Pean was writing reports to Quebec about "rascally thefts." Gossip about the Pean-Bigot "sideline" had been whispered uplake. The ravishing mounds of supplies warehoused at the head of the La Chine Rapids and at Frontenac invited *coureurs de bois,* porters, clerks and officers to plunder. Pean fretted:

> I have endless anxieties. At Niagara they have found barrels filled with stones instead of pork. . . . The casks of wine and brandy have nearly all been opened. They are but half full. . . . All the flour that M. Repentigny had left was entirely spoiled; the sacks being rotten have tainted it.

But the cuckolded Major earned his graft by devising, and petulantly enforcing, a Niagara portage system that assured a dependable delivery routine for the Ohio forts. He decided on a maximum weight of 80 pounds for each bundle headed uplake. Niagara's Crawl-on-all-Fours bluff and the mud and sand on the portage between Presque Isle and Rivière au Boeuf made this mandatory. Consequently, the cannon had to be taken apart and the flour, corn, pork, lead, gunpowder and tools repackaged.

Pean commandeered barrack and guardroom space at both Frontenac and Niagara as repackaging centers. The *habitant* militiamen could sew. And, as with every military expedition, hundreds of "joy girls," laundresses, and even a few wives followed the troops. "I have made thirty seamstresses as nimble as our girls of Montreal," Pean wrote the Governor during August. "I begin to have hope. . . . Gaiety reigns."

The lug of the twelve thousand bundles up Duh-jih-heh-oh was the next challenge. Pean impressed militiamen, then sent agents out to the Senecas with offers of good rations and plenty of rum. It worked. "Some of them carry as many as three pieces of 80 pounds each," Pean gloated. "Everything goes ahead, day and night. One shift works while the other sleeps and eats; there is no interruption. Some bring the *bateaux* to shore; others carry them up; one part makes the portage, another fills the sacks, still others sew them."

By fall, he had most of the twelve thousand bundles under cover at the Presque Isle and Le Boeuf centers. But Pean's work schedule and the grimness of the wilderness were too much for more than four hundred of the *habitants*. They deserted. Malaria and yellow fever killed hundreds at Presque Isle, including Captain Marin, and invalided four hundred others who had to be returned to Montreal. By snowfall, the Army of the Beautiful River was reduced to eight hundred. Inevitably, the troops invalided home gossiped about the supply thefts, the bundles of silks and perfume, and the rotten pork. This information reached even to Paris.*

Several of the supply and troop flotillas for the Army of the Beautiful River camped overnight within a few miles of Fort Oswego. But Oswego's garrison totaled less than a hundred New York militiamen and officers. No repairs had been made by the British, or cannon added, since 1727. There were no brigs or schooners to attack the French flotillas or camps.

A four-man scout was ordered up the lake to join Pean's work gangs at the portage and to estimate the strength of the Army of the Beautiful River. They did. William Johnson had their report by October. Summaries of this report, hurried south, were the final alarum that caused Virginia's Governor Dinwiddie to

---

* Intendant Bigot, Major Pean, Chabert Joncaire and others were arrested and jailed in the Bastille upon their return to France as "exchange prisoners" in 1760–61. Some were fined and banished from France for life. The memoirs that Chabert Joncaire wrote while in the Bastille, as part of his defense against the "graft and treason" charges, are the best primary source for details about the Joncaires' sixty years among the Five Nations and the 1750–59 operations at the portage, Little Niagara, and the River of Horses farms.

send Christopher Gist and the young aristocrat, George Washington, west on the protest mission so competently described in Walter O'Meara's *Guns at the Forks.*

While Major Pean was still struggling to get the 80-pound bundles up Crawl-on-all-Fours, Johnson and King Hendrick rode to Onondaga. There, in a speech to the Grand Council, Johnson mourned the "weeds growing in the path between us," and asked whether the sachems had given their consent for the French invasion of the Ohio.

The Council's reply, after two days of secret discussion, ranks with the farewell speech of Chief Joseph of the Nez Percé during 1877 in its eloquent despair over white men's greed. The Council sorrowed:

> We don't know what you Christians—English and French together—intend! ! ! We are so hemmed in by both that we have hardly a hunting place left. In a little while, if we find a bear in a tree, there will immediately appear an owner of the land to challenge the property, and hinder us from killing it, which is our livelihood. We are so perplexed between both that we hardly know what to say or think.

George II's ministers finally knew what to say. Orders came to Boston, New York, Philadelphia and Williamsburg for a formal council of all the northern colonies with the Six Nations. It began on June 19, 1754. Its most memorable speech was given by the new Postmaster General of the North, Benjamin Franklin:

> It would be a strange thing if Six Nations of ignorant savages should be capable of forming a scheme for union, and be able to execute it in such a manner as that it has subsisted ages and appears indissoluble; and yet that a like union should be impractical for ten or a dozen English colonies.

The Colonial delegates voted to appeal for an Act of Parliament establishing a central government which, like that of the Six Nations, would have a representative Assembly elected from and by each Colony, in proportion to population. This was both an acknowledgement of the superiority of the Six Nations' government

and an omen of the system of representation that would be incorporated in the United States Constitution thirty-three years later.

But many of the "Ayes" were merely a form of "Bully for you!"
to Ben Franklin for his lucidity and wit. Neither the aristocrats
controlling the Assemblies and Governors' Councils back home
nor George II's ministers would permit so radical a scheme as
the United Colonies of America.

The news of Colonel Washington's defeat at Fort Necessity
was relayed east by the Senecas a week after the Council ad-
journed. Its only effect on the New York Assembly was a grudging
vote to finance "two companies of militia" for Fort Oswego.

London, meanwhile, continued diplomatic bickers with Paris
about "your violation of treaty terms." Versailles bickered back
with generalities about "the St. Lawrence and its tributaries" as
"the heartland of New France." This gave France enough time
to land the Bearne and Guienne regiments-of-the-line at Montreal
as reinforcement for the garrisons at Frontenac and Niagara.

Criticisms from Whig benches of Parliament and the prob-
ability that George II would be forced to swallow his hate and
offer William Pitt a ministry finally bumbled Great Britain to
military resolution. At the suggestion of the Duke of Cumberland, two regiments were shipped to Virginia during the winter
of 1754. Their commander was one of the spit-and-polish officers
of the Coldstream Guards. Since he had acquired one of Queen
Caroline's ladies-in-waiting as mistress and spokeslady, Colonel
Edward Braddock was promoted to Major General for the Ohio
Expeditionary Force. His instructions, prepared by the Duke of
Cumberland's staff without recourse to geography books, directed
him to march from Virginia to the Ohio valley, capture the French
fort at the Allegheny-Monongahela junction, then parade on to
Lake Erie, occupy the Niagara portage, similarly subdue Forts
Toronto and Frontenac and then—via Oswego—parade into Al-
bany for a Victory Ball.

William Johnson was one of the delegates sent to Williamsburg
to greet General Braddock and learn the orders for intercolony
participation. Braddock called Johnson to a private conference
in his suite. The King, he reported, had signed Johnson's appoint-

ment as Royal Agent not only to the Six Nations but to all the redman tribes of the North. Moreover, Johnson's skills with "these red savages" had so favorably impressed the Duke of Cumberland that Johnson was also commissioned to command an expedition against the New France fort (St. Frederic) on Lake Champlain.

Niagara? General Braddock shook his head. It was not too important. Governor Shirley of Massachusetts would lead one force against it from Oswego. Then Braddock's troops would march in from the rear. After all, the siege of this Fort Duquesne shouldn't take more than two or three days.

∿⚬∾

NINE

WHALEBOAT ARMADAS

The spring rains of 1755 sluiced new channels down the punky stockade surrounding Fort Niagara. Fireplace kindling from Captain Pean's discarded kegs caused rancid fat odors to eddy up the stairwells of the House of Peace. A few *habitant* militiamen, slate-gray in soggy mackinaws and rawhide breeches, gossiped briefly at the Iroquois Gate, then squished away on patrol.

The Army of the Beautiful River, its plunder and waggly camp followers had gone south. Captain Duplessis-Faber and thirty homesick farm boys were the sole guardians of Thundergate. That spring and on through most of the summer, two determined companies of British regulars could have, as William Johnson begged General Braddock, "severed New France at the Throat," and let the Army of the Beautiful River starve or die on torture platforms.

An excellent spy system in London, Boston and Williamsburg assured Quebec that Captain Duplessis-Faber and his farm boys were garrison enough at Niagara until late summer. More urgent matters shaped at Quebec. Governor Duquesne had requested that his resignation be accepted at once and that he be transferred back to his former post at the Admiralty in Paris. The Quebec winter and the administrative labors of organizing the Army of the Beautiful River, the Marquis explained, had undermined his health. Versailles expressed lavish regrets—and obliged. The investigation of Intendant Bigot's books and new prosperity was underway. Obviously, the Marquis was more concerned about the draughts in the Bastille than the ones at Quebec.*

The Governor General appointed as Duquesne's successor was a "native son" for whom the Quebec-Montreal politicos had been lobbying since 1751. Pierre Vaudreuil-Cavagnal was a son of the great Governor General who had plotted with Louis Joncaire about *Magazin Royal* and the House of Peace. He was born in Quebec on November 22, 1698, received the honorary appointment of Ensign when he was 6, Lieutenant when he was 13, and Captain when he became 17. Appointed Governor of Louisiana in 1742, he served commendably for eleven years.

With him, as commander-in-chief of all the military forces of New France, came one of the most renowned soldiers of Europe. Ludwig August von Dieskau was a German baron. The motto on his coat of arms boasted, "Boldness Wins." Von Dieskau, Versailles was convinced, would outplot and outfight Major General Braddock any time and under almost any circumstances.

The inaugural ceremonies for Governor Vaudreuil were held on June 23. One of the first items for the strategy conferences with Von Dieskau concerned the reports from Frontenac and La Présentation about Oswego. More English had marched down the Oswego's gorge during early June and started building shipways.

A few young women from La Présentation were ordered to Oswego for tippling and bush play. They secured enough information to satisfy Von Dieskau that three or four warships were being built but could not be launched, rigged and manned before late fall.

As for any other attack on Niagara and Frontenac out of Oswego, all the reports from Albany and Mohawk valley spies belied it. The Major General commanding the British expedition was Willam Shirley, the bumptious, fussy Governor of Massachusetts. He was a good enough attorney and speechmaker, but an extremely bad general.

In mid-July, General Shirley was still in Albany quibbling about

* Duquesne served at the Admiralty until 1776 with a record of robust health, then retired with honors and died at his estate outside Paris on September 17, 1778.

"policy," whimpering about "inadequate troops," feuding with
William Johnson over supplies and Mohawk scouts and, all in all,
displaying many of those qualities ascribed by Shakespeare to
Sir John Falstaff.

Vaudreuil agreed to Von Dieskau's proposal that a feint be
made down Lake Champlain toward Albany. Then, if the news
about Braddock was bad, a quick march through the Adirondacks
would knock out Oswego and afford the opportunity to ambush
and reambush Braddock's army while it toiled up the Allegheny
valley.

Vaudreuil reported to Versailles on July 23:

> In regard to Niagara, 'tis certain that, should the English attack
> it, 'tis theirs. I am informed that fort is so dilapidated, that it is
> impossible to put a peg in it without causing it to crumble. Stan-
> chions have been obliged to be set up against it to support it. Its
> garrison consists of thirty men without any muskets. The Sieur de
> Villiers has been detached with about twenty men to form a camp
> of observation there.

Just the year before, Captain Villiers had avenged his brother's
death by helping to defeat George Washington's four hundred at
Great Meadows. Now, as his canoe corkscrewed past the Thousand Islands and out to Lake Ontario, his thoughts brooded back
to that Pennsylvania battlefield. Had Braddock passed it yet? Was
the Army of the Beautiful River holding its own against him?

The answer echoed out to him as he rounded the point toward
Fort Frontenac. A half dozen Indians were dancing on the beach.
They stared owlishly at his canoe for a moment, then began wav-
ing tomahawks. Villiers saw blobs of hair—some carrot-red, some
brown, some ashen blond—dangling from the tomahawk handles.
Had the French, somehow, ambushed Braddock?

By the time Villiers reached Niagara, the Joncaire brothers
were back from the Ohio with news of the victory and accompanied by a flotilla of Senecas, Caughnawagas and Hurons. All of
them sported scalp trophies. Their canoes were piled with uniforms, boots and hats stripped from Braddock's dead.

In mid-August, delegations of Oneidas and Cayugas paddled in with friendship belts that they wished to present to the new Governor at Quebec. Chabert Joncaire felt it would be expedient to accompany the Senecas who had been delegated to discuss "a great peace" with the Governor. Philippe stayed at Niagara to advise the Delawares, Shawnees and Mississaugas eager to plot winter raids against the Pennsylvania and Virginia frontiers. During October, Philippe accepted the invitation to come to Onondaga Hill for discussions with the Grand Council about "a great peace with your King."

Meanwhile, during the first part of August, General Shirley petulantly followed his three regiments toward Oswego. His quarrels with Johnson and the New York Assembly about enough Indians and allocation of supplies had strained New York-Massachusetts relations so severely that the enmity would echo on into the Revolution.

Shirley demanded a council at Onondaga Hill. The sachems were preparing for the "great peace" talk with Philippe Joncaire, but they assured Shirley of "friendship for the great King George." They also reported that "Joncuer, a Frenchman, who has resided among [the Seneca] several years past, was driven away from their country about a fortnight ago; and they promise us, they will never meet him again." Unfortunately, they added, preparations for the hunting season and the urgency of guarding their villages against the French denied them the honor of sending any warriors to attack Niagara.

A gun in one hand and an axe in the other, the Oswego militia went up the gullies to select and cut timber for twenty-five hundred palisades, a new blacksmith shop and a powder magazine, and the eighteen hundred bushels of charcoal needed by the smiths. Most of the hardwood had to be boomed eight miles down the Oswego River. This simplified the ambushes by Captain Villiers and his Niagara scouts. They peeled thirty-five to fifty scalps during August and September.

Shirley reached Oswego on August 18. The Boston ship carpenters had not only launched and rigged the 40-foot brig, *Ontario*, and the decked sloop, *Oswego*, but were finishing a fleet of 230 whaleboats that would carry the troops on the weeklong

row up the lake against Niagara. Each boat had bench space for
sixteen men.

The joy-girl spies from La Présentation still had freedom of the
fort. They circulated gory details about Braddock's defeat at
Duquesne and added that "many soldiers from France reached
Frontenac a few days ago."

Shirley ordered stores and ordnance aboard the gunboats and
had the whaleboats readied. He would take six hundred men for
the attack on Niagara. When the joy-girls' stories were reported
to him, however, he postponed the takeoff and announced that
it might be more expedient to add to the Oswego defenses first.

Word of William Johnson's victory, King Hendrick's death, and
Baron Dieskau's capture at the "Bloody Morning Scout" on Lake
George on September 8 must have reached Oswego before September 20. Certainly, word did come that the two thousand
survivors of the Braddock Expedition had reached New Jersey
and were preparing to "ascend the Hudson River to the defense
of Albany in 33 vessels."

Yet Shirley assembled his officers on September 27 and harangued them for three hours about "fall storms on the lake,"
"strong reinforcements at Niagara," and others reasons for abandoning the campaign. The officers voted "Aye." Shirley appointed
Colonel Mercer resident commandant, assigned seven hundred
infantry and artillerymen as garrison, and on September 29 fled
back toward Albany.

"What wretched complaisance is this?" asked the editors of
the *Boston Gazette* two weeks later:

> Is all this mighty parade to answer no other purpose but to
> distress, if not ruin, our country, by running us in debt, in ex-
> pending upwards of 200,000 pounds Proclamation money, and
> leaving us in a worse condition than it found us? O tell it not in
> Quebeck! nor publish it in the streets of Montreal! Let the daugh-
> ters of the Popish Nunneries rejoice, and the British name be had
> in derision by the slaves of the haughty Louis!

On October 5 two *corvettes* and a schooner put out from
Frontenac. After a leisurely tack for inspection of Oswego, they
fixed a course to Niagara. The deck passengers were five com-

panies of the Regiment of Guienne, commanded by Captain
François Pouchot. They were to repair the rotten palisades of Fort
Niagara and to build new entrenchments, gun placements and
"barracks that will house 400 men."

Captain Pouchot attended first to the construction of barracks:

> It was at once necessary to build houses for these troops in the
> Canadian manner, that is, huts made of round logs of oak notched
> into each other at the corners. In this wooded country, houses of
> this kind are quickly constructed. They have a chimney in the
> middle, some windows and a plank roof. The chimney is made by
> four poles placed in the form of a truncated pyramid, open from
> the bottom to a height of three feet on the four sides, above
> which is a basket-work, plastered with mud. They take rushes,
> marsh grass or straw, which they roll in diluted clay and drive
> in between the horizontal logs from top to bottom, and then
> plaster the whole.

Next every tree and bush within a quarter mile of Fort Niagara
was cut down. Some documents assert that a system of tunnels
was built under the cleared area, and mined with kegs of gunpowder. The palisades were rebuilt with oak timbers. A moat was
added.

"M. Pouchot has built there a great work *à corne* which occu-
pies the whole extent of it," a visiting officer wrote during the
spring of 1756:

> He has made around the old fort and on the banks of the lake
> and river several redans which put them in a state of defense,
> several cannon *à barbette* placed upon the curtain and upon the
> demi-bastion to command the woods, four cannon placed at the
> end of the branch of the demi-bastion on the river, to command
> the river, and a little foot path along which they can steal. Be-
> hind the house is one battery which commands the entrance of
> the river. This point is defended even against the attack of ves-
> sels, there being shallows here a quarter of a league wide.

Oswego's seven hundred also continued to strengthen its de-
fenses and finish the fleet that would "cut New France at the
Throat." A new stockaded blockhouse on the east bank of the
Oswego delta was named Fort Ontario. A third structure, built

at the bluff top but without either tunnel or stockade connec-
tions with the other blockhouses, would be Fort George. Its
masonry and earthwork rampart was to be 20 feet thick and 12
feet high. In the spring of 1756, this rampart was only half
finished, and cannon for the blockhouse still lay in ice-rimed
mounds of sawdust and timber shavings.

The ship carpenters launched a second sloop, another schooner
and a gawky three-master that they called a snow. Since the
snow was to become the most efficient class of sailing ship on
the Great Lakes, its birth at Oswego in 1756 is significant.

According to Bernard Ericson:

> The snow was a three-masted vessel, square-rigged on fore and
> mainmasts, lateen-rigged on the mizzen. For her special lake serv-
> ice square sails gave the snow all the propelling power of a brig,
> and a lateen mizzen, the maneuverability of a sloop or schooner,
> allowing a larger, faster, more heavily armed vessel to be handled
> with the relative ease of a smaller craft with a smaller crew.

This sire was christened *Halifax*. It measured 80 feet on the
upper deck and 60 feet on the keel, and was to carry 18 six-
pounders.

But in the area surrounding Oswego, Captain Villiers's scouts
became increasingly bold. A letter written on May 20 told of it:

> There is continually Scalping Parties about this place. There
> was, the day before I got here, Eight of them Scalped and Four
> Carryed off Prisoners. The Day after I gott here, Lieut. Blair with
> a party of 25 men that was sent to protect the bateaus coming
> down here was attacked about a mile from this place. Blair and
> two of his men killed. We killed it is imagined five or six, two of
> which we got, the others were carried off.

During June, a second letter confirmed that:

> we are yet much troubled with scalping parties, large bodies ly-
> ing within 6 or 8 miles of us, and as our garrison is not sufficient
> to dislodge them, they do us much damage. We are obliged to
> have large parties to cover the carpenters, others to clear the
> woods around the garrison. . . . For these past 10 days, we have
> quitted the fort on the hill, it not being tenable.

About the first of July, Colonel John Bradstreet brought four hundred more militiamen, sixteen large cannon and other supplies in from Schenectady. During their trip back east, two weeks later, Bradstreet's boatmen were ambushed by Villiers's scouts and Indians on the Oneida-Woods Creek portage, and thirty of them were killed. Bradstreet raced the survivors down the Mohawk, reported to William Johnson, then went on to Albany to beg the leadership of a relief expedition for Oswego.

John Campbell, the fourth Earl of Loudoun, was the new Commander-in-Chief of British forces in North America. He landed at New York City on July 23, and after a week of conferences and receptions, sailed up to the "Albany wilderness." He pondered Bradstreet's "wild story" until mid-August, then ordered Colonel Daniel Webb of the Forty-Eighth Foot to organize and lead a relief expedition to Oswego. Colonel Webb shared his commander's reputation for being, as one Massachusetts editor put it, "like St. George on a tavern sign: always on horseback but never advancing."

The noose closing around Oswego was in the dexterous hands of Baron Von Dieskau's successor, Louis Joseph, the Marquis de Montcalm. He took command of the New France forces during May. In July, a man-of-war reached Quebec with letters confirming a state of war between France and Great Britain. Montcalm went to Fort Frontenac to prepare his first campaign.

Captain Villiers already had nine hundred *habitants*, Caughnawagas and La Présentations on the prowl. The Seneca, Cayuga and Onondaga warriors became so intrigued by prospects of Oswego plunder that five hundred of them daubed on war paint. Their sachems advised Chabert Joncaire to be careful because, as he alleged in his memoirs, "they represented that if I should perish, there remained no one to keep up the good understanding between them and the French."

During the night of August 2, the Oswego squadron was corked into its river anchorage by scuttling two Frontenac schooners across the channel. Between August 3 and 8, battalions of the Guienne, Bearn and La Sarre regiments ferried across the lake from Frontenac. The brass cannon captured from Braddock had

been portaged and rafted to Niagara that spring. Six of them
came down the lake, too.

Covered by *habitant* turkey-shooters during the night of August
12, the French regulars dug earthworks 180 feet from Fort Ontario's stockade. At sunup, Colonel Mercer ordered Fort Ontario
abandoned, and retreated across the harbor to the rickety 1727
blockhouse. During the crossing or later that morning, he was
killed. After a barrage from the Braddock cannon, from the guns
in Fort Ontario that the garrison had failed to spike and from the
sharpshooters crouched behind Fort George's unfinished parapet,
Lieutenant Colonel John Littlehales ran up a white flag.

Stories differ about the surrender. New York claimed there
were 1,520 people still alive at Oswego. New France said 1,700,
"of whom 120 were women."

Boston and New York newspapers claimed that Lieutenant
Colonel Littlehales "sold out for French gold." John Newkirk, the
Indian interpreter at Oswego, later reported that:

> the Garrison behaved monstrously ill, that the Officers were de-
> jected and the men all Drunk, having knocked the heads out of
> Several Casks of Rum, and drank it till they were all Drunk as
> Beasts. Colonel Mercer, one of the Gunners and Eight men were
> all that was killed on our side & but three of the French, one of
> whom was killed by a French Indian accidentally.

Governor Vaudreuil wrote that General Montcalm "turned the
guns of his troops on the Indians to prevent a massacre of the
prisoners." But "eyewitness accounts" published in British periodi-
cals claimed that the French warriors "murthered several of our
soldiers as they stood on the parade and scalped all our sick in
the hospital." A party of twenty-five Mississaugas who went to
the Oswego siege from Niagara returned there with twelve scalps
and "three ship carpenters they led away as prisoners." Such were
the conflicting reports of the destruction of the forts at Oswego.

By August 16, the cannon and "enough supplies to provide
Niagara and Frontenac the coming winter" had been loaded on
the Oswego schooners, and the prisoners were on their way to
Montreal in the captured whaleboats. The snow *Halifax* and the
brigs had been burned and scuttled.

As a parting shot that damaged British prestige almost as much as Oswego's capture, General Montcalm instructed Chabert Joncaire to tell the Grand Council at Onondaga that "We do not invade your territory like the English. We give this back to you. Remain quiet on your mats and do not meddle with anything."

Colonel Webb's relief column was in camp at the Woods Creek portage when scouts brought a report of the Oswego siege. Webb ordered his supply train burned and fled. His men burned every blockhouse east to Canajoharie.

Five companies of the French regiments routed up the lake after the Oswego campaign. Carpenters and stone masons went with them to complete the Niagara redoubts. General Montcalm's engineers insisted that blocks for the redoubt facing come from the same quarry near Frontenac that had supplied the facing for the House of Peace. The two captured Oswego schooners became stone carriers.

The fall of Oswego, coming thirteen months and five days after the defeat of Braddock, brought scores of Indian delegations to Niagara. Ouillas from the forests of Kentucky and Indiana, Sioux with gifts of wild rice from their Minnesota lake shores, Ottawas, Hurons, Shawnee—all of them wished to present friendship belts; raise the hatchet for New France; and, of course, receive gifts of guns, cooking pots, brandy, blankets, and more brandy. "They smoked, drank one another's health and were content," Pouchot reported of one council that included Cayugas, Ottawas, Senecas, Hurons, Sioux and Ouillas.

Most of the delegations were willing to detour for plunder raids on the Pennsylvania and New York frontiers en route to meetings with Governor Vaudreuil at Quebec. Then they could bring in prisoners and scalps, and receive more gifts.

One band of forty reported that their raids extended to the mid-Hudson valley during May 1757. They brought a middle-aged Palatine woman named Muller back to Niagara on their way west. On July 27, Charles Peller, Marie Catherine Heilerin, and Marie Blanche were brought in from Pennsylvania by Seneca raiders. During August, Chabert Joncaire returned from council meetings with a blood-smeared sack slung across his pommel. He dumped the thirty-eight scalps it held on the guardroom floor for

Pouchot to count. The Senecas had charged him with delivering it to the fort, "to show this proof of the blows we have struck against the English."

General Montcalm reported that "among all the news from Niagara . . . the Delawares and Shawanese have made many prisoners, taken many scalps, destroyed houses, carried off families and cattle. They took a young English officer, whom they ate, he seeming quite fat."

A party of Mississaugas returned from a raid that took them "within sight of Albany." They expressed regrets that a Negro slave chased near Schenectady had got away, and asked, "Is the flavor of the black man's meat better than the Englishman's?" Captain Pouchot did not report his reply.

Testimony by deserters and exchange prisoners indicates that British prisoners at Niagara during 1757 and 1758 sometimes totalled 150. The officers, such as the Highlanders of Forbes's command routed near Duquesne, had given their parole so they had limited liberties. But privates and frontiersmen were confined in the cells on the ground floor of the House of Peace and used as slave labor. George Akes and David Barry, both New Englanders, claimed that they were in Niagara prison gangs for fourteen years; Edward Hoskins, also a New Englander, said he was held there for ten years.

Records about the women and children brought in by the Indians is more vague. Many were claimed by the raiders and adopted into their clans. Thus Mary Jemison of Marsh Creek, near Gettysburg, Pennsylvania, survived a family massacre. She married a Delaware named Sheninjee, was a mother at 15 and a widow at 19. She then married a Seneca named Hiokatoo when she was 20 and had six more children. Famous after 1800 as "the White Woman of the Genesee," she spent the final decade of her 91 years on the Buffalo Creek Reservation enjoying her thirty-nine grandchildren. Similarly, Marie Catherine Heilerin was adopted by the Senecas and "the old woman named Muller" was led off to the Ohio valley.

Scores of others escaped the hatchet, to be sold—for a blanket or some brandy—to the Niagara garrison as washerwomen, cooks or clerks. Isabel Stockton, carried off from Winchester, Virginia; Margaret Painter, brought in from Pennsylvania during 1757; Molly Heysham, captured in "the Blue Mountains"; and "several small children whose parents have been killed by Indianes" were among those known to have been at Fort Niagara in the late 1750's.

With the fear of attack allayed by the destruction of Oswego, wives and joy-girls were permitted in from Montreal. There were formal receptions and banquets at the House of Peace. A wife with a flair for the theater recruited and rehearsed a cast and stage-hands from the garrison. During February 1757, the Niagara Players presented *Le Viellard Dupé* (The Old Man Duped). Neither the script nor the name of the author survives. Commenting on Niagara in his journal, Montcalm noted that "The officers there make very good cheer, the region abounding with deer, bears and wild turkeys, which are superior to the ordinary kind."

The Seneca and Mississauga hunters sold wild turkeys at the fort for the equivalent of one cent and deer carcasses for fifty cents each, or, in current trade values, a pint of cognac. Rattlesnake meat was a favorite in Seneca stews, but there were only a few devotees of its musky richness at the fort!

Captain Pouchot and most of the battalions were transferred east during the fall of 1757. The command was taken over by Captain Jean Vassan. The Joncaires continued their organization of Indian raiding parties from Little Niagara.

However, Indian mutters of discontent were rising. The British Navy had established another blockade. There had been late storms and scanty crops in New France. Blankets, when obtainable, cost twenty-five beaver skins apiece. Diluted cognac brought eight pelts the jug. The Seneca porters of the portage sent a protest to Governor Vaudreuil against the increasing use of horse carts, driven by soldiers, on the route: "It robs us of the living we were promised forever here."

Then, with the speed of thunderheads growling down the Oswego gorge, Colonel Bradstreet led the British back. On August 20, 1758, a company of Rogers's Rangers reached Oswego and made a cautious examination of the fort ruins and the lake shore.

On the bluffs, Mohawk and Oneida scouts signaled, "No enemy in sight."

The next day, more than a hundred whaleboats swirled in 2,800 New York, New Jersey and Massachusetts militiamen. After them came raftloads of cannon, ammunition, journeycake, salt pork and, of course, rum. Colonel Bradstreet and Colonel Charles Clinton had kept their orders secret. This time, no Seneca or Onondaga spy was to be given the opportunity to get word to the Joncaires or Father Picquet that this blow was aimed at Fort Frontenac.

The triple purpose of the raid was, first, to destroy the winter supplies for Niagara and the Ohio forts that must be warehoused at Frontenac; second, to cripple the New France fleet on Lake Ontario and, third, to restore British prestige in the eyes of Senecas, Cayugas, Tuscaroras and Onondagas.

All afternoon and evening of August 21, Colonel Clinton recorded in his journal, the expedition raced to transfer the cannon, ammunition, and five days' rations to the whaleboats, and to cache emergency supplies near the Fort Ontario ruins.

The fleet moved out into Ontario "at 11 of the clock," rowed to an island that was probably Galloo, hid out during daylight of August 22, and island-hopped again that night. They used an island in the Frontenac harbor for the final hideout on August 25. Bradstreet and Clinton concluded that Frontenac's garrison did not total more than two hundred. A brig and schooner were taking on bales and boxes that must be for Niagara and the Ohio.

The siege began at dusk on August 26. The entrenchments outside the stockades were empty. Not a shot was fired from the fort as the militia marched into them and set up cannon. The barrage banged on into Sunday's dawn, August 27. A white flag went up.

Captain Pierre Jacques Payen de Noyan was in his sixties. He had worked with Louis Joncaire at *Magazin Royal* thirty-three years before. Montcalm had assigned him to the command of Frontenac because it was a quiet, comfortable post for a grandsire. The garrison given to him on this final assignment (before retirement to a cottage below Quebec) totaled 130 militia. Montcalm considered them too poorly trained for his Lake Champlain campaign.

Frontenac's defenders succeeded in "wounding only three or four" of the besiegers. No Indians came to the fort's defense.

Colonel Clinton reported that,

> The French took all their money, clothes and the best of every-
> thing they had in boats with them and were permitted to go to
> any of their own garrisons (under parole). They were not in-
> sulted or in any respect treated but with the greatest civility. . . .
> After we took out of the fort what we could carry of the best
> things, we broke the trunnions of their cannon, broke down the
> wall of the fort and burned all the houses, barracks, buildings,
> [plus] a vast quantity of provisions which were immediately to
> be sent to Niagara and other forts to the southward.

The raiders were back at Oswego by August 29. That night the furs, bale goods, small arms, cognac and other loot were un-loaded from the captured brig and schooner. At dawn on August 30, the ships were beached and burned. By September 8, every-one was back in the Mohawk valley, without loss of a man.

Only three weeks of supplies remained in the commissary at Niagara. A messenger from the Army of the Beautiful River came in with a demand to send every available man to Venango for the winter's campaign against the English. Captain Vassan kept only forty militiamen for Niagara. The Indians seemed strangely quiet. Few of them had visited the fort since mid-August. The Seneca porters seemed surlier than usual, too.

Word about the Frontenac disaster first came from the west, and it helped to explain the Indian furtiveness. A Colonial officer, en route to Montreal from Detroit, told Vassan that Indians far up Lake Erie had told him about "a great attack against Fronte-nac." Vassan ordered everything outside the stockades burned and the gates closed. A squad was preparing to fire the outbuildings when a sentry on the lake wall spotted a fleet of *bateaux*. Vassan's telescope identified the boats as French.

This relief force of fifteen hundred, led by Jean Testard de Montigny, had left Montreal the day after Indians from La Pré-

sentation reported Frontenac under siege. But the English had
vanished, Montigny told Vassan, as rapidly as they came. Only the
charred ruins of Frontenac and the hulks of the ships on the
Oswego beach testified that they had been there. Governor Vaudreuil said—Montigny went on with a slight shrug of his shoulders
—that a new shipyard was to be built near La Présentation. Another shipment of supplies was on the way. Matters seemed secure enough for the winter. But next year . . . He shrugged again.

Governor Vaudreuil and General Montcalm met during November to discuss Niagara and the Ohio forts. The Governor had
drawn up plans to send five thousand reinforcements west in the
spring. Meanwhile, Frontenac would be rebuilt and the shipyard
at La Présentation would launch a dozen brigs and schooners.

Montcalm scowled at the wall. Not even five hundred men
could be spared from the defenses of Lake Champlain. Judging
from the last reports out of Duquesne, it had already surrendered
or been abandoned to the British. His engineers reported that
Frontenac wasn't worth rebuilding. The shipyard at La Présentation would do well if it launched two ships by spring. The only
sane thing to do was abandon the Ohio, concentrate on defend-
ing the St. Lawrence valley, and pray that France could and
would break through the British blockade with more troops.

The conference ended in an angry stalemate. The Governor
insisted that Captain Pouchot and several hundred regulars be
returned to Niagara. An equal number must go to reinforce De
Lignery's Army of the Beautiful River, wherever it might be.

A relay of messengers snowshoed from Niagara to Montreal
during December with De Lignery's report about the burning of
Fort Duquesne, his retreat to Fort Michault at Venango, and his
determination to recapture the Ohio's headwaters area in the
spring.

The Senecas learned the news, and passed it quickly east. There
is evidence of long emergency sessions of the Grand Council at
Onondaga Hill during January and February 1759. Chabert Joncaire closed Little Niagara and made a month-long snowshoe
journey as far east as the Oneida castles.

During April, Chabert began another series of conferences

at Seneca and Cayuga castles. He took his son-in-law, Lieutenant La Milletière, with him. The Senecas chased them into a cabin, held them there for several days, and finally let Chabert join a delegation heading to Niagara with their sachems' announcement to "favor the English." But Lieutenant La Milletière was taken down the valley to the Mohawks. During July, a New York City correspondent for the *Boston Gazette* wrote that "Mons. Jonquier's son-in-law, whose father is a noted man among the French Indians, arrived here from Albany since our last."

During May 1758, the Grand Council had censured Johnson for recruiting Mohawks for the Abercromby expedition against Montcalm. They had said then that his life would be "in danger" if he attempted the journey to Onondaga Hill. The change in Grand Council logic between May 1758 and February 1759 was caused by too much British Navy blockade and not enough alcohol.

Evidence of the redman's acute alcoholism fumes throughout Colonial history, then hiccoughs on across the prairies, the high plains and the Rockies during the nineteenth century. The jug did a more effective job than the Army in "winning the West." New York State was the pilot project for the technique. The sachems fought its devilish influences. So did most of the French priests and Protestant missionaries. But the hunger for alcohol was a gaunt misery by 1759, as essential to the Six Nations' way of life as flintlock guns, itinerant blacksmiths, gaudy blankets, chunks of clamshell for wampum-making, yard goods and iron or copper cooking pots.

As Mary Jemison, "the White Woman of the Genesee," would explain,

> It was the practice of the Indians of our tribe to send to Niagara and get two or three kegs of rum—in all, six or eight gallons—and hold a frolic as long as it lasted. When the rum was brought to the town, all the Indians collected, and before a drop was drank, gave all their knives, tomahawks, guns and other instruments of war to one Indian, whose business it was to bury them in a private place, keep them concealed, and remain perfectly sober until the frolic ended. Having thus divested them-

selves, they commenced drinking, and continued their frolic till every drop was consumed. If any of them became quarrelsome, or got to fighting, those who were sober enough bound them on the ground, where they were obliged to lie till they got sober, and then were unbound. When the fumes of the spirits had left the company, the sober Indian returned to each the instruments with which they had entrusted him, and all went home satisfied.

The series of battles in the Lake Champlain and Lake George forests during the 1750's ended the smuggling between Montreal and Albany. The British blockade of the St. Lawrence, plus the reckless greed of Intendant Bigot and his accomplices, increased the cost of supplies and trade goods to Niagara by 800 percent between 1755 and 1759.

Hence there seems little doubt but that "the high cost of drinking" and the coincidental glut in the fur market was the *cause célèbre* that persuaded the Grand Council back toward English alliances during the winter of 1758–59. The Bradstreet-Clinton destruction of Fort Frontenac and Forbes's conquest of the Ohio's headwaters testified that Great Britain could bulldog on. The rum drought was becoming unbearable!

When the invitation came to attend an ox roast and council with Sir William Johnson * at Canajoharie, a delegation of sixty Senecas joined the flotillas down the Mohawk River. They took along several Shawnee dependents, plus avowals that "many nations up the Lakes are eager to raise the hatchet against New France." Rum was scarce up there, too.

Captain Pouchot left Montreal on March 27 to take over the command of Niagara. General Montcalm told him that only 150 of the French regimental veterans could be spared, plus three hundred *habitant* militia. At the close of the conference, Pouchot rose, saluted, and said, "It appears, sire, that we shall never meet again—unless it be on a British prison-ship."

---

* George II elevated Johnson to Sir William Johnson, Bart., during 1756, bestowing on him a gift of £5,000 and the Crown appointment as "Colonel, Agent and sole Superintendent of the Six Nations and other Northern tribes."

TEN

DEATH AT THE SHRINE

The April council at Canajoharie was excited, in anticipation of Sir William's war dance. It came on the night of April 20 and, he reported, "was continued till morning by the several Nations, and all the Indians throughout the whole ceremony expressed themselves, and behaved, with marks of the warmest zeal and sincerity." On April 21, after a closed meeting by the sachems, Sir William was assured that "It is the earnest and unanimous request of all the Nations present that you march as speedily as you can with an army against Niagara, which is in the country of the Senecas, and which they now give up, to be destroyed or taken by you. The sooner the thing is done the better."

General Jeffrey Amherst, the new British commander-in-chief, rode from Albany to Schenectady on May 7 for a formal inspection of the Niagara Expedition. Protocol was protocol, so Brigadier General John Prideaux had been given the command. Sir William was to command the Indians who, Amherst believed and wrote, "are a pack of lazy, rum drinking people, and little good." The force totaled thirty-three hundred, plus boatmen, and included the Forty-fourth and Forty-sixth American Regiments, the Fourth Battalion of the Sixtieth Royal Americans, and a poorly equipped detachment of Royal Artillery.

The green- and red-coated columns that marched past General Amherst and his staff that afternoon were the most ominous array America had yet seen. Sixteen years later, its survivors would be murdering one another. Several of its officers were destined for hero or villain roles in United States schoolbooks.

Lieutenant George Clinton, son of the Colonel Clinton who had led the Forty-sixth to the capture of Fort Frontenac, was there as a company commander of the Forty-sixth. He would serve as Governor of New York State for six terms and, in 1804, become Vice President of the United States. His elder brother, James, would sire DeWitt Clinton in 1769, and in 1779 would be co-commander of the expedition to raze the Six Nations.

Captain John Butler, son of "Old Walter," and now the squire of Butlersbury, commanded a detail of Rangers. Lieutenant Daniel Claus of the Royal Americans, and the scowling 17-year-old Mohawk, Joseph Brant, were in line, too. So was Sir William's bar-sinister son, John. Captain Charles Lee of the Forty-fourth, a survivor of the Braddock disaster, would become second only to Benedict Arnold as an American traitor.

Most ominous of all was the tall, mustached Colonel who stood a pace behind Brigadier General Prideaux. He was Frederick Haldimand, a professional soldier from Switzerland.

The route west was a familiar one up the Mohawk River to the "Great Portage," Woods Creek, Lake Oneida and the Oswego River. The stockades and blockhouses of Fort Stanwix at the Mohawk-Grand Portage junction were so new that the perfume of their cedar timbers still tingled noses a mile away.

The only loss en route was a plunder of three carts and the cartmen's scalps, achieved by a party of Chabert Joncaire's scouts. At Oswego, five hundred Six Nations warriors were waiting. During the next three days, bands of Shawnees, Hurons and Mingoes came to the edge of the gorge, gave the signal of peace, then filed down toward Johnson's tent to pledge their hatchets "agains' goddam Fraynch." By the time the whaleboats were launched and loaded, Sir William commanded the largest Indian army ever assembled by Great Britain, more than eight hundred braves.

Colonel Haldimand, as General Prideaux's second-in-command, was assigned, with thirteen hundred men, to guard Oswego and the supply route from Fort Stanwix. The company of axmen and carpenters stayed at Oswego, too. Their orders were to reopen the shipyard and build two schooners and a brig. The Indians assured Colonel Haldimand that no effort had been made to rebuild

Fort Frontenac; any French attack against Oswego would come from La Présentation or Caughnawaga.

The whaleboats pointed west on Sunday, July 1. The helmsmen were under orders to keep the craft in single file, and ten feet apart. The field order for the day ended with the threat that "the general is determined to put any officer under arrest who does not perform to a Tittle what his orders Express." Rations for four days had been prepared at Oswego and stored in each boat. They varied little from the fare being served Niagara's defenders: two pounds of bread, a half-pound of pork, and four ounces of dried beans or peas per day. A swig of hard cider was permitted with the evening meal. A lieutenant might, if he chose, reward the oarsmen with a midday swig from his personal jug of rum or applejack.

The holiday-picnic serenity of the whaleboats' six-day journey up Lake Ontario is a major mystery of the campaign. General Prideaux did not hold with the "travel by night and hide by day" routine that Bradstreet and Clinton had used for the assault on Fort Frontenac. The Niagara Expedition rowed during daylight, and in rigid military formation. The only possible defense was musketfire from the whaleboats.

The New France schooners, *Iroquoise* and *Outaouaise*, had been launched and rigged at La Présentation during April. They made their maiden voyages to Toronto and Niagara during May. Each vessel grossed 160 tons and was armed with one 18-pounder cannon, seven 12-pounders, two 8-pounders, and four swivel-guns. Either could have turned the Niagara Expedition into another Braddock catastrophe. And the thunderstorm that lashed down lake on July 2 offered cover for a surprise attack.

But the Six Nations kept the secret so well that Niagara did not receive any warning. When the Joncaire scouts came in with the cartmen's scalps they had peeled at the Woods Creek portage, Captain Pouchot ordered the *Outaouaise* down lake to explore as far as Oswego. The vessel returned to Niagara on July 3 or 4 with the report that it had run into a gale, had lost a mast, and had gone to La Présentation for repairs. But it had stopped at Oswego on the way back, and "There are no English."

On July 6, the *Iroquoise* also anchored in the Niagara. Her captain assured Captain Pouchot that "No English are at Oswego or anywhere along the shore."

The Niagara Expedition covered thirty miles on July 1 and made overnight camp on Great Sodus Bay. The next evening it beached at, or near, the La Salle-Denonville landing place on Irondequoit Bay, then laid over there through July 3 while more pork-and-beans were cooked. Patrols were sent into the woods "with their Arms and Tomahawks to git Bark for the Artillery Boats." On July 4 the line sloshed on to an inlet that the officers agreed should be called "Prideaux Bay." (But the inlet is now called Braddock's Bay.) The overnight camp on July 5 was at a creek later named for Johnson. The final 20-mile row to the high clay and gravel banks of Four Mile Creek occupied the morning and most of the afternoon of July 6.

South of a bar that storms had broken and then resilted across the mouth of Four Mile Creek, the channel widened to a marsh-rimmed pond. An Indian trail from the pond shore led through the swamp to a patch of woods, then crossed a meadow for half a mile to Fort Niagara.

The creek is not visible from Niagara's ramparts. But it was from the decks of the New France schooners as they sailed east that afternoon. Still they sailed without a challenge or a return to the Fort Niagara landing. By dusk, the Expedition's work crews had shoveled a channel through the bar until it was wide enough to pole the whaleboats and artillery barges up to the marshy pond.

The crews of the first twelve whaleboats that reached the pond ate supper on their benches and were given a dram of rum apiece. Before dawn, they were given their orders; the whaleboats and three cannon must be hauled five miles through the woods to the Niagara River. Two miles southwest of the fort, a ravine led down to the river's narrow beach. This was their objective. Their Seneca guides told them that the ravine was called *La Belle Famille*—the Happy Family—because of a shrine of the Holy Mother and Babe that stood beside the road there.

By sunup on July 7, the whaleboats were in the Niagara and

the cannon parts were aboard. The first artillery fire from the fort tried to sink the flotilla as it splashed through the mists to the west shore. Within an hour, the boatmen were cutting rushes and tree branches for the huge bundles, called *fascines*, that would serve as rampart protection for the cannon. It would take at least a week to reassemble the guns, prepare the battery, and start the barrage against the riverside walls of the fort.

Fort Niagara's first warning had come at dusk on July 6 when a wounded militiaman stumbled back to the Iroquois Gate shouting that "the woods are full of Indians!" He and two others were hunting passenger pigeons in a grove a half mile south. Indians in war paint fired at them; only he had been able to run.

Captain Pouchot ordered a squad out to rescue the other militiamen. It was ambushed. Six of its ten men were captured and led off to General Prideaux for questioning.

Captain Pouchot then ordered all 429 of the garrison to battle stations. A second patrol returned before dawn with the report that "a great number of English and Indians are on the shore of the Little Marsh."

An officer volunteered to carry messages to Little Niagara. Pouchot sent two. One ordered the Joncaires to abandon Little Niagara and retreat across the river to Grand Island. The second was to be relayed to Captain De Lignery, commanding the remnant of the Army of the Beautiful River, at Venango. It urged De Lignery to postpone the attack on the British at the Ohio's Forks and to raise Niagara's siege with an assault on the English camp "between *La Belle Famille* and the Little Marsh." He warned De Lignery, even though it seemed unnecessary, to "stay off the portage trail. Come down the west shore of the river. When you attack, we will sally out, too."

The herdsmen, farmers, blacksmith and boatmen at Little Niagara and the River of Horses totaled more than fifty. Another fifty to a hundred Senecas worked on the portage. That summer, Chabert Joncaire claimed, the crop fields along the River of Horses were "15 arpents of front by 20 in depth cultivated with the mattock and sown to grains." A herd of thirty cattle had arrived from Detroit only the week before. On July 5, the day before the Niagara Expedition landed, traders brought in thirty-nine range horses to be broken in for the portage carts. These brought the herd at River of Horses to ninety-six mares and stallions and thirty colts.

The Joncaires seem to have concluded that, despite the Senecas' recent fury against them, they could harangue most of the warriors away from the English and, with luck, even persuade them to massacre Johnson and enough of the other English officers to assure victory for De Lignery's column. They disobeyed Pouchot's instructions, assembled all the Little Niagara and River of Horses staff, and marched down the portage trail to Niagara. Scouts told Johnson that they were on the way; he decided to let them pass through, then to allow his warriors to plunder Little Niagara and the River of Horses.

"The Joncaires arrived at noon (July 10)," Captain Pouchot jotted in his journal. "They had 70 persons, several women and Indians, three Iroquois, among them Chief Kaendae."

On July 12, one of Prideaux's officers wrote that "Little Niagara has been burned by our Indianes. They ran off all the horses and cattle there, and are now peddling the beef through our camp."

There wasn't any haggling about the price of beef. Prideaux's two thousand had been eating baked beans and hardtack since June. And since the July 6 landing, every man had worked sixteen hours a day: one work-gang shift with pick or shovel; one four-hour stretch of guard duty; a four-to-five-hour detail collecting materials for or shaping the *fascines* for the siege trenches. The thirty beef carcasses were a mere snack. The deer, moose, bison and other wild meat animals were south in the mountains or west on the flatlands for summer grazing. It is reasonable to assume that the Englishmen's ancient mores against "eating horse-meat" were set aside on July 12, and that most of the River of Horses herd went on the campfire spits too.

Prideaux's siege plan depended on Colonel Haldimand's success in turning back any French relief expeditions from La Présentation or Montreal, as well as on the inability of the Army of the Beautiful River and the Detroit garrison to send much help to Niagara. Therefore, Prideaux ordered a network of trenches dug south of the fort and then pushed west toward the portage road. Gun batteries would be established in the trenches. The huge earth-filled baskets called *gabions* and the *fascine* twig bundles were to serve as ramparts. The trench batteries plus the three cannon being set up on the Niagara's west shore should be able to cripple the fort and force its surrender by late August.

Cannon fire wounded Captain Williams, the Expedition's chief engineer, during the survey for the first trench. The dig decided upon by his assistants offered the fort such an easy target that it was abandoned. An officer wrote on July 16:

> The garrison and fort are much stronger than we expected. Our trenches are carried within 250 yards of the fort. Our batteries were opened yesterday—two brass 12's, four 6's and five royal howits of eight inches. For three days past we have played upon them with eight pieces of cannon, and have set several of their buildings on fire. . . . The enemy have already fired near 6,000 cannon ball, besides thousands of small arms, but as yet have killed only three men and wounded about 20; among the latter Captain Williams, dangerously. We now have 900 Indians with us, and more daily coming in.

Boatmen, without so much as a challenge from the French schooners, brought in letters and dispatches from Oswego. Colonel Haldimand reported that an attack from La Présentation was fought off on July 5. The French and Christian-Indians, accompanied by Father Picquet, had totaled twelve hundred to fifteen hundred. Oswego's scouts sighted them on the afternoon of July 4. There had been time to build bags of flour and kegs of pork into barricades between the skeletons of Fort Ontario's chimneys before the French charge came over the hill on the morning of July 5. Only two of Oswego's defenders were killed and eleven wounded. The French lost more than a hundred.

Assured that Haldimand could keep the supply line open, General Prideaux sent Lieutenant Rutherford to the fort with a formal demand to "surrender." Pouchot read the note, smiled, and ordered a bottle of claret for the Lieutenant's "pleasure and health" while he wrote his reply. Pouchot's note was insolently

crisp: "Before I make any terms, I wish an opportunity to gain
your esteem."

The next day the Joncaires opened their campaign by sending
the aged Seneca, Kaendae, through the lines with a flag, to invite
"our brothers" to a council at the fort. The fort, they promised,
would not fire any guns while the council lasted, if the English
would hold their fire, too. The Six Nations war chiefs, Johnson,
and General Prideaux conferred briefly, and agreed. "Talk long
with our brothers," Johnson urged the delegates as they left with
Kaendae. General Prideaux ordered the trench crews to "dig
straight toward the fort and put your backs to it."

The Six Nations' delegates kept the parley going until late
evening, then decided they must "come back tomorrow night."
The English work crews, meanwhile, got a trench head thirty
yards closer to the fort. "I have learned a lesson," Captain Pouchot
jotted in his journal. "No more cease-fire during the Iroquois
parleys."

Johnson urged his Indians to more conferences "with your
blood brothers" and suggested that Kaendae and the Joncaires be
offered "safe mats with us so that our guns will not break their
heads." The offer was refused. On July 17, Kaendae told Pouchot
that "Johnson has promised them all your scalps and the plunder
of the fort. They will not leave the English." Pouchot refused the
Joncaires' request for "one more talk." He finally realized that
Johnson and Prideaux were using the Six Nations delegations as
spies to report on gunfire damage, the number of wounded and
the locations of his batteries.

The English battery that had been carried through *La Belle
Famille* to the Niagara's west shore began firing red-hot balls during the morning of July 17. It destroyed the fort's boat dock,
knocked holes in the palisades and in the roof of the House of
Peace and started fires in the barracks and warehouse.

By July 19, one English trench was within 40 yards of the
breastworks. General Prideaux posted a reward for "every French
cannonball in good enough condition to be fired back; sixpence,
New York currency, for each 12 and 9 lb. shot; fourpence for any

otheres." His general orders for July 20 began with the reminder
that "As the work draws nigh the fort, much depends on the
goodness of the fashenes and gabions. The Genl recommends it
therefore to the men, to make them of small wood and perfectly
Tite," and ended with the warning that "Any schulker who is
taken up is to be sent immediately to the proper guard, and pun-
ished in the most severest and publick manner." (Court martials
were held almost daily. There is no record of firing squad execu-
tions or of hangings, but 50-, 100-, and even 500-lash floggings
were common.)

After supper on July 20, General Prideaux and his aide, Colonel John Johnstone—no relative to Sir William—began an inspection tour of the trenches. They were approaching the parallel
forty yards from the fort when a French musketball killed Colonel
Johnstone. The General helped remove the body to the rear, com-
miserated briefly with the Expedition's triple-chinned chaplain,
Reverend John Ogilvie, then resumed his inspection. He stopped
again near the head of the parallel, to watch a crew load and fire
a coehorn mortar that had just been set up. The coehorn blew up.
A chunk of the barrel of the mortar ripped through the General's
skull. He died without regaining consciousness.

The deaths of Prideaux and Johnstone left Sir William Johnson as the ranking officer at the siege. However, the chain of
Army seniority passed to Colonel Haldimand. Johnson sent a boat
crew down the lake that night with a letter to Haldimand notify-
ing him of the tragedy and urging him to hurry to Niagara.

An hour or two later, the reports allege, a Seneca came to
Johnson's tent with word that their scouts had sighted "many
canoe and *bateaux* like big cloud" entering the Upper Niagara
from Lake Erie. It had to be a relief expedition from the Ohio
or Detroit. The probabilities were, thus, that a decisive battle of
the siege would be fought during the next forty-eight or seventy-
two hours. And Colonel Haldimand could not possibly reach
Niagara for six or seven days.

On the morning of July 21, Johnson sent another letter to
Haldimand reporting the impending battle and advising him to

stay at Oswego. Then he wrote the Expedition's Orders of the
Day, beginning, "The death of the late General Prideaux devolves
on me the command of the army."

Some of the officers threatened to revolt. At least one of them
proposed Johnson's assassination "devised as an accident." Captain Allan MacLean bribed a boat crew to leave at once with
his letter to Haldimand. It begged, "For God's sake, come and
save us. The command of this army is your due and belongs to
you. If you come, I believe we may take the place. If not, God
have mercy on us." But at the mid-morning conference, Johnson
related the Seneca report about the French force on the Upper
Niagara. Lieutenant-colonels passed the word along and cau-
tioned, "Stay with it."

During July 21 and 22, the Expedition set up its largest guns,
three 18-pounders. Rangers and Indians scouted behind the falls.
They reported that the force assembling there must total "a thousand French and twice as many Indians."

But the scouting wasn't necessary. The French knights' disdain
for "the English and their peasant archers" echoed in the strategy
of Captains De Lignery and Aubry. During the morning of July
23, they sent four Indians down the gorge with a truce flag, to
deliver messages to Captain Pouchot in the fort. The messages
boasted that rescue was at hand. De Lignery, with four hundred
survivors of the Army of the Beautiful River and 1,000 Indians,
had come up from Venango. Captain Charles Aubry, with Captain
Villiers as his second-in-command, had brought two hundred
French and six hundred Indians down from Detroit. They joined
forces at Presque Isle. Now they were ready to rout the English
via the portage road.

Captain Pouchot sighed and poured himself a goblet of wine.
Somewhere along the portage, of course, the messengers must
have exchanged insults with Johnson's Indians. This formality
over, they probably had settled into gossip and jug passing. So
now Johnson had an accurate report of both the manpower and
the route of the rescue effort!

Perhaps they could fight through. But just "perhaps"; no more.
There were not enough usable muskets left in the fort to send out a

sally force when the battle did start. All seven of the gunsmiths were working night and day at repairs. Still, fewer than a hundred muskets were usable. The red-hot shot being fired by the trans-river battery was as devastating as the 18-pounders that had started furying yesterday. All of the carpenters were on 24-hour fire duty, smashing out chunks of burning buildings with axes to prevent the cannonball fires from spreading. Three of the five cannon in one bastion had been knocked out. The artillery chief was dangerously wounded. Yesterday's barrage had killed or maimed ten more of the gun crews. So far: 109 dead and wounded. Gunwadding was so desperately scarce that straw from mattresses was being used; the bed linens would be next. And why not? None but the thirty-seven sick and seventy wounded had slept in a bed since July 7! Even the women and child prisoners were being used to fill and stack the bags of earth that weakly plugged the holes torn in the bastions.

Captain Pouchot limited his reply to a terse reminder to "follow my suggestions of the 10th regarding your route here." That should puzzle Sir William Johnson! There still couldn't be more than two hundred English guarding that damnable west shore battery. Let De Lignery and Aubry take it first and turn the red-hot shot on the English!

Neither Sir William Johnson's papers nor any of the letters written by his officers indicate that the messages from Aubry and De Lignery to Pouchot were intercepted and read. But, soon after the Indian messengers started back up the portage road, Johnson ordered 150 light infantry out to *La Belle Famille* to build a breastwork of *gabions* and *fascines* across the portage road. The commander of this detail was Captain James De Lancey, son of the former Chief Justice and Peter Warren's nephew. That evening, too, Johnson ordered an "all guns" bombardment of the fort to begin at 4 A.M. on July 24, and to continue until a "Cease Fire!" was received.

De Lancey's men made *fascines* and *gabions,* then filled the baskets with the dirt and forest trash they dug from the fifty-foot trench behind this barricade. They were finished by midnight.

De Lancey remembered that a 6-pounder shipped across to

the west shore battery was not being used. Installed behind their barricade and loaded with grapeshot, it could massacre twenty-five or thirty men per round—if the French did come in insolent full tilt down the portage road. He ordered a sergeant and eleven men to go upstream to the flotilla of whaleboats anchored there, cross the river to the west shore battery, and have the 6-pounder and some ammunition back before sunup.

The detail filed off. Sentries were assigned. The others were to sleep "until 4 of the clock." De Lancey was making a pillow from his jacket when war whoops shrieked down the gorge, trailed close by gunfire. De Lancey sent a courier to Johnson asking him to come to the barricade immediately. Then he called for a volunteer to scout upstream.

The volunteer returned before Johnson arrived. He slumped down at the trench edge, and retched. There had been enough light along the river edge, he told, to see that the whaleboats were scuttled. He crept closer to identify the round objects stuck on stakes along the shore. Then he saw the outline of human bodies sprawled beside them, and realized what the round objects were. The heads of the sergeant and the eleven men had been impaled on oar handles, then jammed into the mud. He retched again, and vomited.

Johnson assigned 600 men, under Lieutenant Colonel Massey, to join De Lancey's 138 at the barricade. Hundreds of Six Nations warriors jogged by, lifted their tomahawks in salute and disappeared into the woods.

Sunrise laid a pinkish gold halo on the roof of the shrine. It edged down to caress the weatherworn statues of Mary and her Babe. A soldier cursed. Captain De Lancey felt his throat tighten and a tear sting start in his eyes. He turned away. Colonel Massey blew his nose.

De Lignery's disdain for the English outweighed Pouchot's advice. The attack came straight down the portage road about 9 A.M. Shawnee, Mingo and Huron warriors slithered in first. A Seneca chief ran from a bush clump, holding his hands in a sign of peace and shouting, "Go home and save yourselves!" A Shawnee gutturaled back, "These English will die like Braddock."

The daubed figures clustered, gesticulated. Behind them came the clump of moccasins in march step . . . a shout . . . the rattle of bayonets snapping into position. The war whoops began.

Captain De Lancey recalled:

> They charged our breastwork with a very great noise and shouting. They began the attack on our right, and our men kept their ground and soon returned the fire. I ordered my men not to fire till they were sure of their mark, which they punctually obeyed.
>
> Part of the enemy then inclined to the left and gave us a very smart fire. We did not fire for some time, and then only about ten shots at some few of the enemy who came very near us. Very soon after this I found the enemy's fire slacken upon us upon which I sent to Colonel Massey to desire he would let me leave the breastwork and rush in on the enemy, which he granted, desired I would move slow, and advanced with his party to the right.
>
> We jumped over the Breastwork and rushed in on the enemy, who immediately gave way. They then endeavored to flank us on the left, but I ordered a party from the right to move to the left, which they did, and with them I pushed forwards to the enemy, who falling in with the party which was on my left, immediately ran away as fast as they could, and never offered to rally afterwards. A few of them remained behind and exchanged a few shot with us, and were either taken or killed.
>
> Our Indians as soon as they saw the enemy give way, pursued them very briskly, and took and killed great numbers of them. We pursued about five miles and then returned.

The death toll at the shrine of *La Belle Famille* on July 24, 1759, cannot be estimated. Johnson, in his journal for July 27, admitted, "I divided among the several Nations, the prisoners and scalps amounting to 246, of which 96 were prisoners. The officers I released from them by ransom and good words." De Lignery, mortally wounded, surrendered and died a few hours later in Johnson's tent. Captains Aubry, Villiers and Vassan surrendered. But hundreds of the French and more than a thousand Indians attempted to flee back to the boat beach on the Upper

Niagara, with Six Nations warriors in pursuit. Guesses about the French dead given in letters and newspapers during the next month range from two hundred to five hundred. The Expedition's casualties did not exceed fifty.

Pouchot ran up the white flag above Fort Niagara about 5 P.M., then gallantly invited Johnson and the officers of the Expedition to have dinner with him at the House of Peace.

Johnson accepted the invitation. His plans were made. His officers were to take any trophies of the victory they wished from the fort—candlesticks, china, a rosary, silverware, liquors. Then Pouchot, the Joncaires, and the other officers were to be confined under heavy guard because he had promised the Six Nations a night of plunder.

Captain John Butler followed Sir William through the Iroquois Gate that evening. Did he pause to glance across the river and thus see for the first time the hill where Butler Barracks would rise, and the adjacent knoll that would be his burial place?

SECTION FOUR

THE BIRTH OF UPPER CANADA

The Loyalists have settlements all along Lake St. Francis and up to Cataraqui. A year and a half ago there was scarcely one house and many have been built within six weeks. . . . It will make the voyage to Niagara infinitely more agreeable than it was, and it will soon become a very fine country, the soil in general is so rich. The American line is drawn here in Latitude 45. I cannot help thinking of the stupid Oswald who made such a foolish treaty with Franklin in giving up all the principal posts and carrying places.

—The Travel Diary of Robert Hunter, Jr., for June 28, 1785

ELEVEN

RACE WAR

The church bell and rocket bedlams loosed at Albany, New York, Boston, Philadelphia and Williamsburg by the bulletins about Fort Niagara's capture persuaded General Amherst to tear up the public reprimand he had written about Sir William Johnson. He did send Brigadier General Thomas Gage to Oswego so that the "Regulars" would have a "trained executive officer" at the front. But both Gage and Colonel Haldimand bowed to the public acclaim, too. They routinely approved Johnson's orders for repairs on the fort and the construction of shipyards.

The filth created at the fort by the Indians' "night of free plunder" caused as much clean up and repair as the British siege guns. Locks, hinges, door handles and every other piece of portable iron was pried off and taken back to the castles for blacksmithing into hatchet blades, arrowheads, spears and hoes. The flour barrels became urinals. Empty wine bottles and cognac jugs were smashed against the whitewashed walls. Beds and chairs were hatcheted to pieces, piled in corners and set afire. Over all hung the stench of gunpowder fumes, dried blood that had dripped from scalps, and warrior offal. The policing and repairs kept a thousand of the Niagara Expedition on labor detail throughout September.

Colonel Haldimand arrived from Oswego two days after Pouchot's surrender. He marched beside Johnson as the Expedition's officers and details of the Royal Americans formed a flying wedge escort, through the mob of "hung over" warriors, for the procession of French officers, women and garrison survivors to the boat landing. (The women and children were escorted to La Présentation. The officers and men went to Albany, via Oswego, for display in victory parades.)

That evening, formal services were held at the hundred-foot trench dug near the Iroquois Gate to hold the corpses brought in from *La Belle Famille*. A separate service, attended only by the officers, preceded the reburial of General Prideaux and Colonel Johnstone in the Jesuit Chapel. (Presumably Captain De Ligney and other French officers killed at *La Belle Famille* were buried at the chapel, too, although no mention of this is given in Johnson's reports or in surviving letters by members of the Niagara Expedition.)

Haldimand's familiarity with European fortresses seems to have been responsible for the decision to locate the fort guarding the Upper Niagara a quarter mile beyond Little Niagara, and to develop a shipyard on a small island opposite.

Captain John Joseph Schlosser, a German who had served with the Royal Americans since 1756, was Haldimand's recommendation as the officer to build and command Little Niagara's successor fort. Naturally, then, the palisaded village built midway between the site of the *Griffon's* shipyard and Little Niagara became known as "Schlosser's fort," and later as Fort Schlosser.

Possibly it was Schlosser who decided that the logical spot for a shipyard was the island that sat like a float valve between Grand Island and the Upper Niagara's west shore just above the rapids. The shipyard, the island's identification as Navy Island, and the chopping out of a cordell-path on the Upper Niagara's west shore came during the second, and final, year of Schlosser's command. Through 1759 and the first six months of 1760, Fort Schlosser stayed on the alert against possible French and western Indian raids.

Hence, until Governor Vaudreuil surrendered Montreal, shipbuilding at Niagara concentrated on a Lake Ontario fleet. The chopping out of brush and trees for a shipway near the west shore battery of the Lower Niagara began before August 1, 1759. "We are building a snow at Niagara that will carry ten 6-pounders,"

Johnson wrote on September 28. "But for want of ship carpenters sufficient, I fear she will not be finished timely to be of service this year. There is a very fine harbor for building vessels of any size at Niagara under command of the fort, and the greatest quantity of the best oak for that purpose I ever saw in any part of the world." (The American eagerness to brag was flourishing in 1759; Johnson had never been in "any part of the world" except Ireland, Boston and New York!) The snow, *Onondaga,* and two gunboats were launched during April 1760. At Oswego, Colonel Haldimand's carpenters built the snows, *Mohawk* and *Mississaga;* three gunboats, and two hundred whaleboats. Both the Niagara and Oswego vessels were used on the 1760 assault down the St. Lawrence against Montreal.

Although the garrison of five hundred militia Johnson left at Fort Niagara was intended as a repair force and a protection against French raids from either the Upper Lakes or Louisiana, its major problems evolved as the two old-dependables of the frontier: *disease* and *interrace relations.* The fevers struck first. During October and November they killed Lieutenant Colonel William Farquahar, the commandant, and a dozen men.

The race relations problem grew with fungus stealth and persistence. First came the traders out of Albany, New York and Boston with canoe loads of rum, blankets, ironware, rouge and other English trade goods denied the nations of the West ever since Montcalm's capture of Oswego. There was no competition now from the Joncaires or other New France traders. The price of rum became "Two Spanish Dollars the jug." Blankets rose to "Ten beaver pelts." There were arguments, threats and fights.

Some of the garrison courted Seneca girls—too boisterously. As a result, there were accusations of rape, and counter-accusations of "the pox." One argument snarled into a gunfight; a Seneca was murdered. Sociologically, the fault lay with the "white supremacy" doctrine preached since 1609 by newspapers, church sermons and tavern philosophers. Most of the garrison had been brought up in villages or on farms where parents edicted that "a good Indian is a dead Indian." The gossip about Six Nations' tortures, cannibalism and "sexy wenches" conditioned the recent Scotch, Irish and German immigrants to the same conviction.

Captain Robert Rogers and a company of Rangers reached Niagara, en route to accept the French surrender of Detroit, during October 1760. The Senecas confided some of their complaints about trade prices and soldier insolence to Rogers during the haul of his sixteen whaleboats over the portage. Perhaps Captain Schlosser confirmed the grumbles, because he took Rogers to Navy Island and asked his advice about the shipyard and the two schooner hulls that were to get underway as soon as shipwrights arrived from Oswego.

Rogers, thus, is reputed to have been the source of the rumor that came out of Detroit early in 1761. It alleged that two Senecas were haranguing the Wyandots, Chippewas, Hurons, Illini, and other Upper Lakes nations to join a redman confederacy that would massacre "every white west of Fort Stanwix" and establish the West as inviolate redman territory. One of the agitators, the report claimed, was "a natural son of Chabert Joncaire, named Tahaiadoris."

The report routed down the Mohawk to Sir William. But complaints from the Six Nations' sachems preceded it. The high prices ... the rapes ... the gunfights were all, the sachems feared, a prelude to an invasion of settlers and more rum-party land steals. Johnson agreed, went to Albany for conferences with General Amherst, and wheedled—despite the general's "drunken Indian" bias—an order that no white settlers or even hunters were to be permitted west of the Palatine villages.

But from Niagara, on July 30, Johnson wrote Amherst an angry letter:

> I see plainly that there appears an unusual jealousy amongst every Nation, on account of the hasty steps they look upon we are taking toward getting possession of their country, which uneasiness, I am certain, will never subside whilst we encroach within the limits which, you may recollect, have been put under the protection of the King in the year 1726, and confirmed to them by him and his successors ever since, and by orders to the governors not to allow any of his subjects settling therein.
>
> You promised [on April 22] to prevent any person, whatsoever, from settling or even hunting therein; but that it should remain their (i.e. the redmen's) absolute property. I thought it neces-

sary to remind your excellency thereof, as the other day on my riding to the place where my vessels are building (i.e. Navy Island), I found some carpenters at work, finishing a large house for one Mr. Stirling near the Falls, and have since heard others are shortly to be built hereabouts. As this must greatly add to the Indians' discontent, being on the carrying place and within the very limits which, by their own agreement, they are not so much as allowed to dispose of, I should be glad to know whether I can acquaint them that those people will be ordered to remove or not; and I hope from your Excellency's answer to be able to satisfy them on that head.

Indian complaints were, General Amherst believed, merely evidence that the French on the Upper Lakes and in Louisiana were making all sorts of promises to foment rebellion against Great Britain. Governor Vaudreuil's surrender of New France had not been recognized by Versailles. France and Great Britain were still at war. The Niagara portage, he decided, was military property and must be operated on military principles. He avoided Johnson's questions about the Niagara land grants and awarded a contract for Master of the Portage to John Stedman, empowering him to reorganize the delivery system. He saw no reason for barring the Niagara to settlement by a few traders and "competent men." During September, he approved the sale of a square mile of land on the west shore of the Lower Niagara to a Captain Servos for "farm purposes and construction of a grist mill."

The Stedman, Stirling and Servos families became Niagara's first settlers in 1762. That fall, a delegation of Ottawas reached the Seneca castles and asked for a council with the sachems. Their hatchets were red. They carried war belts.

Far west in the forests between Lake Erie and the Ohio valley, the spokesman for the Ottawas said, their sachem, Pontiac, had counseled with a Delaware medicine man. The medicine man had experienced a dream visit with the Master of Life. It was so vivid that he could recall every word the Master of Life uttered:

> This land where ye dwell I have made for you and not for others. Whence comes it that ye permit the Whites upon your lands? Can ye not live without them? I know that those whom ye call the children of your Great Father supply your needs, but if

ye were not evil, as ye are, ye could surely do without them. Ye could live as ye did live before knowing them—before those whom ye call your brothers had come upon your lands. Did ye not live by the bow and arrow? Ye had no need of gun or powder or anything else, and nevertheless ye caught animals to live upon and to dress yourselves with their skins.

But when I saw that ye were given up to evil, I led the wild animals to the depths of the forests so that ye had to depend upon your brothers to feed and shelter you.

Ye have only to become good again and do what I wish, and I will send back the animals for your food. I do not forbid you to permit among you the children of your Father; I love them. They know me and pray to me, and I supply their wants and all they give you. But as to those who come to trouble your lands—drive them out, make war upon them. I do not love them all; they know me not, and are my enemies, and the enemies of your brothers. Send them back to the lands which I have created for them and let them stay there. Here is a prayer which I give thee in writing to learn by heart and to teach to the redmen and their children!

Both the Seneca sachems and the Grand Council at Onondaga debated Pontiac's call to a race war for the redman's control of the West. They finally rejected the war belts. But many Seneca warriors did not agree with the decision. Some went north to join the uprising. Some who did not backed the Niagara porters' complaints to the council for drastic action about the Conestoga wagons and the soldier-drivers John Stedman had introduced on the portage haul between the top of Crawl-on-all-Fours and Fort Schlosser.

Captain Schlosser sailed up Erie and past Detroit during April 1763 on one of the first trips of H.M.S. *Michigan.* The vessel was a schooner, carrying ten to fifteen guns. She and her sister ship, H.M.S. *Huron* were the first products of the Navy Island yard and thus, of course, the largest sailing ships on the Upper Lakes since the *Griffon.* Schlosser was transferring to the command of British America's westernmost fort, St. Joseph, on the lower east shore of Lake Michigan.

Schlosser reached Fort St. Joseph about May 1. Pontiac began the siege of Detroit on May 9. On May 25, the Pottowatamies surprised Fort St. Joseph, plundered it, but spared Schlosser the torture stake or hatchet because the British would pay a handsome ransom for him.

Fort Pitt was under siege by May 27. Delawares, Miamis and Senecas captured Presque Isle, Le Boeuf and Venango during June. But warnings came to Fort Niagara and Fort Schlosser, either from Onondaga or Boughton Hill. Neither fort was stormed. The H.M.S. *Huron* and the H.M.S. *Michigan* survived.

During mid-June a company of fifty-five men from the Oswego garrison escorted a wagontrain of gunpowder, cannonballs, lead and foodstuffs over the portage to the H.M.S. *Michigan*. The *Michigan* fought a running battle up the Detroit River on June 30 to bring Fort Detroit its first reinforcements. (This feat caused the ship to be nicknamed "the Gladwin" after Major Henry Gladwin, the commander at Fort Detroit.)

A second relief expedition for Detroit crossed the portage during July. Its companies of Rangers were commanded by Captain Robert Rogers. Both the *Huron* and the *Michigan* were loading supplies, so the 260 made the trip up Erie in twenty-two whaleboats. With the providential aid of a ground fog, they fought their way into Fort Detroit at dawn on July 29.

The most critical trips up the lake would come during September and October. Pontiac's army was displaying amazing tenacity in the Detroit siege. Unless the *Huron* and *Michigan* could get adequate winter supplies to Detroit, Pontiac might force a surrender during the November-to-March freeze.

The provisions, clothing and ammunition load for a twelve-wagon train lugged up Crawl-on-all-Fours during the morning of September 14. Stedman, on horseback, led the train south along the gorge edge. Four miles below the falls, the trail arced through a boulder-littered forest 150 feet above a cave called Devil's hole.* The grade was so steep that the wagonmen walked. The only rider in the wagons was a drummer boy who had

---

* The route of Robert Moses Parkway along the gorge edge through Devil's Hole State Park approximates the position and height above the gorge of the 1763 portage trail.

hitched a "lift" on a lazy-board to visit friends at Fort Schlosser.
An early frost had dappled gold and scarlet on the oaks and
maples. A covey of doves whirred up. Their sobbing call echoed
down the gorge. But Stedman paid no attention.

The train was halfway through the field of glacier-pocked rocks
when war whoops screamed and a wall of flame exploded. Stedman threw himself flat against his horse's mane and kicked her
ribs. The screams of wounded horses blended with the shouts of
his wagonmen. Another volley banged. A hatchet whizzed past
him. Two forms, daubed in war paint, dove at his legs. He kicked
one in the face and heard a curse in Seneca. Then the distant
crash of wagons rolling into the gorge blended with the diminish-
ing whoops and screams.

Stedman's shouts of "Aaaambuuush! ! !" down the last mile of
the flatland gallop to Fort Schlosser brought "Officer of the
Guard" calls, a bugled "alert" and signal gun warnings to Navy
Island. The safety of the ships and the Detroit supplies took
priority. Schlosser's garrison was on the walls with cannon sighted
down the trail, and a boat was en route to Navy Island when
gunfire echoed again through the falls' thunder roar.

When a relief column did venture back to Devil's Hole, the
only sound was the squawking of the hawks and eagles feasting
on the sprawl of horses, mangled wagonmen and soldiers. The
second burst of fire had been the ambush of a relief column sent
up from the Lower Niagara landing at the foot of Crawl-on-all-
Fours.

The fear of a major attack against Fort Niagara, the Lower
Landing, Fort Schlosser and Navy Island was so great that the
bodies of the Devil's Hole victims lay in the woods for days. A
Lieutenant Rutherford crossed the portage a few days later. "We
saw about 80 dead bodies," he wrote. "They were unburied,
scalped and sadly mangled."

Seneca sachems eventually admitted to Sir William Johnson
that "It was done by some of our young men, without our knowledge." Honanyawus, who later took the name of Farmer's Brother,
bragged through his dotage years that he organized the ambush.
Some historians have dismissed the Devil's Hole Massacre as a

"grudge fight by the Seneca porters against Stedman's use of wagons." But since Chabert Joncaire had used horse carts on the portage for nine years, it is equally probable that the massacre was ordered by Pontiac and was an attempt to block delivery of winter supplies to Detroit.

But it did not block delivery. H.M.S. *Michigan* battled up to Fort Detroit on October 3. Two weeks later, Pontiac abandoned the siege and marched off toward the Ohio.

Captain John Montresor * was one of the passengers on this trip of H.M.S. *Michigan.* His father, Colonel James Montresor, had been Amherst's chief military engineer in 1759, hence was the strategist of the Niagara Expedition. The son came to America as an ensign with Braddock, received his engineer's commission from Governor Shirley, and in 1763 held the rank of "Engineer Extraordinary and Captain Lieutenant." During November, he returned down the lake with dispatches from Major Gladwin reporting the end of the Detroit siege. He delivered the dispatches to Major General Thomas Gage, Amherst's successor, in New York City on December 16.

Captain Montresor's familiarity with the Niagara portage and his realization that its lack of blockhouse protection had encouraged the Devil's Hole Massacre, initiated an elaborate program of construction. John Bradstreet, just promoted to Major General, was assigned to command the 1764 expedition that would bring fresh garrisons for Detroit and the Upper Lakes posts, and then force peace treaties with Pontiac's confederates. But first, General Gage ordered, the Niagara portage must be fortified and improved.

Montresor returned to Niagara on May 28 with a battalion of the Canadian Volunteers and set to work. He surveyed the portage and fixed the locations for five "redoubts with stockades" between the top of Crawl-on-all-Fours and Schlosser. As Bradstreet's troops arrived by bateau and schooner, he assigned them to the construction sites.

* The Captain bumptiously reported in his Journal that he "relieved the garrison of Detroit and men, whereby the siege was raised, they having then fourteen days' Indian corn and bear's grease to subsist on." He reached Detroit via schooner, he told, on October 3.

Between June 1 and 30, he designed and completed an elevator-lift system at Crawl-on-all-Fours that seems to have been the first form of railroad ever constructed in North America. Montresor's journal refers only to "the cradles on the top of the Mountains." . . . "The lower cradle broke this day by which 14 barrels of provisions were lost in the river. . . . A party employed in assisting in finishing the cradles, others in making a wharf of Log Work at the lower landing," and so on. Neither Montresor nor any officer or trader on the portage saw fit to give a coherent description of the device.

But in 1810 young DeWitt Clinton camped at Lewiston during a survey trip for the route of a "Hudson to Lake Erie canal." He jotted the following into his journal for August 2:

> On the top of the slope at Lewiston, we observed the old way in which the French [sic] drew up their goods. A crane was fixed on the hill, and an incline plane down the descent in which sleighs were fixed, and as goods were conveyed up in one sleigh, others were let down in another.

The first "rail-roads" that carried coal up from the mines of England's Midlands were built during the 1780's. But a cartway system called "the plateway" was used experimentally during the 1760's, and was the subject for speculative articles in engineering journals. A "plateway" consisted of two long troughs with iron bases and wooden sides, built on parallel lines of stone blocks. Donkeys could pull larger carloads of coal up steeper inclines via a plateway.

The Montresor portage elevator was, obviously, a double plateway automated by the gravity pull of the descending cart. It worked so effectively that Montresor could boast on June 23, "Provisions crossed as before, over this day & in all now at the Fort at little Niagara 4610 barrels. This carrying place from the Fort at Niagara is by mensuration 25620 yards or 14 miles and 98 yards."

The portage redoubts were up and garrisoned by July 1. Work gangs moved on to build a large pier and warehouse at Fort

Schlosser. There was almost daily alarms of "enemy raiders" but
Montresor reported only "one man of the Royal Artillery killed
and scalped by a small party of the Enemy . . . between the 4th
and 5th redoubt I constructed." The raiders, Montresor added,
"left their Tomahawk in his skull. It appears from the weapon
that they are Alleghany Indians."

Montresor's final project was protection for the cordell haulway
through the Upper Rapids into Lake Erie. On July 18 he took
450 Connecticut and New York militia to "the NW side of the
Rapids at the Point of Lake Erie" where "the Ground Extremely
rich, covered with Beach, Hickory, Walnut &c and the situation
answering expectation in every respect for my Fort, Provision
Store & wharf."

The commanding officer of the Connecticut work brigades was
a moon-faced veteran of Rogers' Rangers from Redding, Connecticut, Major Israel Putnam. Between July 18 and August 15,
"Old Put"—destined to be "the Rebels'" co-commander at the
Battle of Bunker Hill and George Washington's favorite Major
General during 1776 and 1777 . . . bossed the work gangs that
built Fort Erie.*

Montresor's most durable contributions at Niagara still tower
behind the Six Nations Gate and across the parade at the north
end of the ramparts. The massive South and North Redoubts,
forming a triangle with DeLery's House of Peace, were designed
as independent forts. Their stone walls are five feet thick. Each
has eating and sleeping accommodations for forty men. There
are 12-pounder cannon batteries on each top deck. Although their
construction was not undertaken until 1766 or 1767, they were
recommended and probably designed by Montresor as bastions

---

* Montresor referred to Joncaire's River of Horses as "Buffalo Creek." Thus
the mysterious transition that was to give New York's second largest city
its name occurred between 1759 and 1764. No journals mention bison
among the game animals on the Niagara during the 1760's. Grove McClellan,
the director who supervised Old Fort Niagara's restoration, believes that
"Buffalo" may have been an English spelling of the French or Indian pronunciation of "Beau Falon" or, in reference to the farms and pasture, "Good
composted land."

of defense in any future race war against the "fifth column" type of strategy that Pontiac had plotted for St. Joseph, Mackinac, LeBoeuf and Detroit.

DeLery's men required more than two years to build and fortify the House of Peace. Pouchot took another two years to improve the ramparts and outer defenses. Montresor built the plateway, the network of portage redoubts, the wharves at each end of the portage, and Fort Erie in less than four months, and designed the North and South Redoubts within Fort Niagara to boot. He sailed for Detroit with Bradstreet's 1979 soldiers and 310 Indians on August 14.

During April, messengers had gone up lake with peace belts from Sir William that invited Pontiac's allies to a "great council" at Fort Niagara during the summer and fall. Most of the sachems decided, like the Chippewas' Great Turtle prophet, that "Sir William will fill your canoes with presents; with blankets, kettles, gunpowder and shot and large barrels of rum, such as the stoutest will not be able to lift."

By August a panorama of redman individualism shrilled from the bullet-scarred trees of *La Belle Famille* across the Prideaux trenches to the shore of Four Mile Creek. The brush huts of Nipissings, the wigwam villages of Chippewas and Menominees, the bark-and-pole longhouses of the Six Nations, the sod and rawhide lodges of the Illini and Fox announced the mightiest assembly of Indians in colonial history.

Sir William, limping with gout and complaining of pain from his old thigh wound, sailed in on July 8 aboard the spanking new schooner, *Johnson*. His sons-in-law Guy Johnson and Daniel Claus, his son John, and his sullen brother-in-law—or was he really another son?—Joseph Brant were in attendance.

One of the Royal parchments in Sir William's luggage gave Pontiac and his allies a signal victory—*if* His Majesty's officers obeyed and scrupulously policed its edict. On October 7, 1763, George III had signed a Proclamation forbidding Colonial settlements "beyond the headwaters of rivers flowing into the Atlantic." Actually, of course, this was more cartographer ignorance, since every river east of the Rockies flows into the Atlantic.

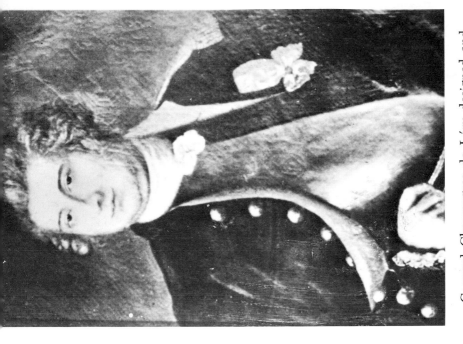

Gaspard Chaussegros de Léry designed and
built The House of Peace in 1726 and 1727.
Old Fort Niagara Association

The Iroquois Gate (until 1759) but the Six
Nations Gate thereafter. *Grove McClellan for
Old Fort Niagara Association*

The wonderful *maître* canoe shooting the St. Lawrence rapids at La Chine. *The Public Archives of Canada*

The forts and shipyard at Oswego just before its capture by Montcalm. *New York State Library*

The **SOUTH VIEW** of **OSWEGO** on **LAKE ONTARIO**

General Shirley in 1755 strengthenid & inlarged this Fort and erected two others, one Westward 170 Square with a Rampart of Earth & Stone Another on the Opposite side of the Bason, 170 Yards distant from the Old Fort. This which is called the East Fort, is built of Logs and

the Wall is surrounded by a Ditch. The Projection of the Rocks renders the Channel at the Entrance into the **Onondaga River** very Narrow, and our Vessels are generally warp'd from the Lake into the Bason.

Explanation
1. The River Onondaga
2. The Lake Ontario

A Seneca bark longhouse, as John Cornplanter recalled it in 1905. *New York State Library*

New France *voyageurs* as England's W. H. Bartlett idealized them in 1840. *Dr. Effey Riley*

GRIFFON. La Salle
ship, built on Lak[e]
Erie above the Fall[s]
1679. Drawing base[d]
on historical descri[p-]
tions. *Bernard E. Eri[c-]*
son

GUNBOAT, 176[
Shallow-draft cutt[er]
type open boats, 3[
40 feet long. Pulle[d]
by oars or driven [
simple sailing rigs.
lug-sail rig is show[
Bernard E. Ericson

HALIFAX. Oddl[y]
rigged "snow," bu[
by British at Oswe[go]
in 1756. A 200-tonn[er]
she was never arme[d]
Several variations
this type were us[
in later years. *Berna[rd]*
E. Ericson

William Johnson and King Hendrick, circa 1750. *New York State Library*

This painting is presumed
to be a life study of Robert
Cavelier, Sieur de La Salle.
Public Archives of Canada

Colonel John Butler (1790).
*The Public Archives of
Canada*

Joseph Brant, "Devil of the Mohawks" as George Catlin portrayed him. *New York State Library*

General Isaac Brock, Governor of Upper Canada, killed at the Battle of Queenston Heights. *The Public Archives of Canada*

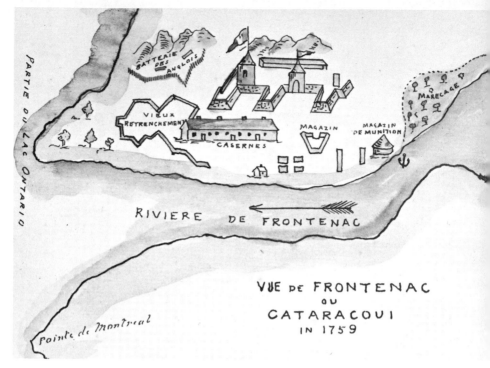

Fort Frontenac in the 1750's (NOTE—Date of "1759" has to be wrong. Bradstreet burned Frontenac in 1758.) *The Public Archives of Canada*

Indians attacking Winfield Scott at Fort George following his surrender at Queenston Heights, 1812. *New York State Library*

An 1837 drawing of Colonel Winfield Scott hauling down the Union Jack at Fort George after its 1813 surrender.

The Battle of Fort George, 1813, as depicted in American newspapers. *New York State Library*

Chapel of the Mohawks Brantford, Ontario. (Only Royal-Chapel outside the British Isles.)   *The Public Archives of Canada*

Closeup of one of the Montreal Victory medals presented to Indian chiefs by General Amherst in 1761. *The Public Archives of Canada*

Closeup of front of Montreal Victory medal above. *The Public Archives of Canada*

This stained glass window in Her Majesty's Chapel of the Mohawks, shows Queen Anne receiving King Hendrick and other Mohawk sachems. *The Public Archives of Canada*

The Cataract of Niagara, as idealized in Moll's "New and Exact Map," 1715. *New York State Library*

Captain John Montresor, builder of America's first incline-railway at the Niagara portage, 1764. *The Detroit Institute of Arts*

Major General John Sullivan, commander of the Clinton-Sullivan Expedition, 1779. *New York State Library*

Fort Erie as seen from Buffalo Creek (The River of Horses) about 1770.
The Public Archives of Canada

Fort George as seen from parapets of Fort Niagara in 1812. *Public Archives of Canada*

Colonel John Graves Simcoe, first Governor of
Upper Canada. *The Public Archives of Canada*

Fort Niagara's complex from the air. The House of Peace is at upper left.
The Iroquois (Six Nations) Gate is at right center with British Bastions
behind. *The New York State Power Authority*

This aerial view of the lower Niagara reveals the strategic checkmating by Fort Niagara (lower foreground) and Upper Canada's Fort George (upper center across the river). The "smoke" at upper right is spray from Niagara Falls. *New York State Power Authority*

But for 1764 purposes, it offered the redman evidence of His Majesty's intent. Also, it put all of the Great Lakes basin under the jurisdiction of Quebec, rather than the land-greedy Thirteen Colonies. Only His Majesty's ships were to be permitted on the Lakes.

Fort Erie was finished and Fort Schlosser's garrison had cleared the brush and trees one hundred feet back from both sides of the portage road before Sir William bade the Senecas to their peace talk. The terms he gave had already been approved by the Six Nations' Grand Council. The Seneca portage monopoly was gone—forever! John Stedman could hire and fire as Fort Niagara's commandant ordered. All of Niagara belonged to the King! Glumly, the Seneca sachems made X-marks on the agreement to transfer a land strip four miles wide from Fort Niagara to new Fort Erie to "George III and his heirs forever." The gifts of blankets and kettles Sir William gave them could be stowed in two canoes, and the rum would not allay their sorrow for more than a night.

General Bradstreet flubbed the Upper Lakes treaties so dismally that the formality of Pontiac's personal surrender was delayed until the summer of 1766. Meanwhile, Sir William and London devised a system of Indian-trade price controls that seemed trader-proof and rum-sturdy. Indian Commissaries, operated under Sir William's direction, were opened at Niagara, Detroit, Pittsburgh and other forts in the West. They administered the barter prices that Sir William and London's Board of Trade fixed. Thus, a stroud blanket two yards long cost "two good beaver or three buck pelts." A man's plain shirt, any size and the tail long, was worth "a prime doeskin." A gallon-size tin kettle cost only "two bucks," but gaudy silver arm bands were worth "four beaver or five bucks." (Rum was discreetly omitted from the price-fix. This, of course, enabled brisk individual enterprise by the commissars, with discreet kickbacks to Sir William and the fort commanders.)

Itinerant traders who operated west of Fort Stanwix were subject to fines and imprisonment. But this could usually be overlooked by means of gifts to commissars. His Majesty's Navy was tougher.

Sir William's agents escorted Pontiac down the lakes during June 1766. Perhaps "floated" was the more appropriate term! The old warrior reached Niagara in a drunken haze and sailed to Oswego so thoroughly soused that Commissar Benjamin Roberts wrote, "Pondiac said I received them very well and given them Tobacco which the Indians love . . . and rum which they loved above all things. . . . I just now offered the vessel should go to-night but he was a little drunk and did not chuse it. He kissed me. . . . The whole of them seem in good humor."

The bar menu for the peace conference with Sir William at Oswego included toddy, rum, Madeira, port, applejack. Pontiac's personal allotment of toddy—his favorite—averaged two quarts a day.

Two more years of argument passed before thirty-two hundred redmen, Governor William Franklin of New Jersey, and commissioners from Pennsylvania and Virginia met with Sir William at Fort Stanwix to fix a permanent boundary between the British and the redman. It extended south from Oswego through Stanwix, curved east of Onondaga Hill to the Delaware headwaters, then jigsawed southwest through the mountains to the headwaters of the Allegheny and beyond Pittsburgh followed the south shore of the Ohio River.

West of this line, save for "the King's Islands" at Niagara and the Upper Lakes forts, colonial settlement—as well as hunting or trapping by "whites"—was forbidden. On paper, it looked as though Pontiac had won the Race War.

But it was October 1768. Daniel Boone, the bullwhacker who first saw the Ohio as a boy wagonman with the Forbes Expedition, had already discovered the pack-pony route to Kentucky. Sir William and Benjamin Franklin were corresponding about plans for a Vandalia Company that would purchase 2,400,000 acres "west of the mountains." John Hancock sputtered against "British tyranny," possibly because customs inspectors at Boston had impounded his sloop *Liberty* with a cargo of smuggled wine. Over in Connecticut, Lieutenant Colonel Israel Putnam was drilling fellow members of the Sons of Liberty.

TWELVE

REFUGEE VENGEANCE

The French and Indian War came to Niagara by way of Oswego. So did the American Revolution. Its harbinger was Major John Butler, escorted by one hundred Mohawk warriors. He reached Fort Niagara's wharf during the afternoon of July 26, 1775.

In Boston that day Commander-in-Chief Washington's new major generals continued the discussions about the gun emplacements and infantry entrenchments that would imprison their former commander, Governor Thomas Gage, in Boston. Three of them were Niagara-Oswego veterans: Charles Lee, Philip Schuyler and Israel Putnam.

At the La Chine Rapids, Captain and Mrs. Daniel Claus and Joseph Brant walked with Guy Johnson and his two children toward the *bateaux* that would carry them to Montreal. The pine box on the ox cart following them held the body of Sir William Johnson's daughter, Mary—Mrs. Guy Johnson.

At Oswego a few Six Nations sachems still sat in the cool shadow of the traders' room, reflecting on Guy Johnson's challenge to "Join us in the feast on the flesh and blood of the Bostonians" and on the changes that had furied along the Mohawk in the twelve months since Sir William's death. Who would have dared prophesy when the death wails for Sir William keened through the castles last July that the death of the Six Nations Confederacy was also being mourned? But now? It was so!

The pattern of disaster was even more stark for John Butler as he pondered the details of transforming one of the officer rooms at the House of Peace into the new headquarters office of His Majesty's Superintendent of Indian Affairs. He knew too much about too many people! Fear and anger twitched his fingers and turned his stomach to a lead ball. Had Butlerbury been burned by the Committee of Safety rabble? Were Catherine and the children prisoners—or worse! ! !—and Walter a chained slave of the Rebels at that Connecticut copper mine?

A Revolution is a rebellion that succeeded. So the word is a semantic trap. The terror erupting throughout the Thirteen Colonies in July 1775 was still a rebellion—and by a minority. Consequently, it was also a civil war that had split the Six Nations as brutally as it was dividing the Palatines, the Hudson valley aristocrats, and the thousands of Scotch and Irish farmers who had emigrated to the Stanwix Treaty frontier since 1768.

That is why "Niagara" became both a *terror* simile and a *hope* simile between 1775 and 1796—and so remains along the shores of the Niagara, Lake Ontario and Lake Erie today.

The love children of Sir William Johnson and Catherine Weisenbergh were critically important to the development of this dual symbolism for "Niagara." So, basically, was "Old Walter" Butler's rum-treaty steal of 86,000 acres at the Mohawk-Schoharie junction.

A conference between George III's aides and the editors of *Burke's Peerage* in 1764 cleared up the sticky matter of Catherine Weisenbergh's wedding. She posthumously became Mrs. William Johnson, and, therefore, in 1765, her son became Sir John Johnson. Sometime during 1756, the 16-year-old son of one of the County Meath Johnsons landed in Boston. He slyly flaunted the phrase, "My uncle, General William Johnson . . ," and so was able to borrow money for the brig-pony-Durham-boat trip to Mount Johnson. Thus it was that Guy Johnson became a lieutenant in the Niagara Expedition. In 1762, "Uncle William" secured his appointment as Deputy Superintendent of Indian Affairs, which promoted him a rank above the competent young German refugee, Daniel Claus, and John Butler.

Inevitably, Catherine Weisenbergh's daughters fell in love with the only single white males in their father's retinue. Nancy Weisenbergh Johnson married Daniel Claus in 1762. A year later, 20-year-old Mary married "Cousin Guy."

It became obvious, even to Sir William, that his son John lacked the White Indian amorality and cunning essential to the Indian Affairs superintendency. Guy Johnson became the heir apparent for the appointment during the decade in which Cresap's War, Lord Dunmore's War, and similar frontier race wars forced the redman toward the same choice between "Tory" and "Whig" that Lexington . . . Concord . . . Bunker Hill were forcing on the whites and Negroes.

The neighborliness between the Butlers and the Johnsons was almost jovial while Sir William lived. The Butlers retained 5,000 of "Old Walter's" rum-treaty acres. The rest had been parceled out, like much of Sir William's domain, to Scotch and Irish immigrants. Their rambling, two-story home, Butlersbury, overlooked the Mohawk River near the site of Fonda. In 1775, the estate had twenty-five horses, sixty black cattle, sixty sheep and forty-five hogs. Its principal crops were wheat and hardwood lumber from the 3,000-acre forest tract. John and Catherine Butler had five children. Walter, the oldest, was a law clerk with the firm of Silvester & Van Schaack in Albany. The three girls and the other boy were being tutored by the Reverend John Stuart, the young Anglican missionary at Canajoharie. Devout churchmen, the Butlers also held a pew at St. George's Church in Schenectady. It was adjacent to Sir William's rarely used pew and to one occupied by their closest friends, the Christopher Yates family.

Because John Butler, too, was one of Sir William's deputies in Indian Affairs and respected him and understood his "Wild Irish" lusts, the Butlers held their tongues about the sequence of young Indian women who succeeded Catherine Weisenbergh as "housekeeper" at Johnson Hall. If they knew whether Joseph Brant was Molly's boy brother or just another of Sir William's bastards, they held it to frowns and headshakes. When Sir William sent the haughty, jut-jawed youngster off to Moor's Charity School in Connecticut, then sponsored him for the degree rituals at St. Patrick's Lodge of Masonry and secured his appointment

as translator and assistant to the Reverend Stuart, they hoped it
was "good riddance." But John Butler cursed out loud when he
learned that Molly Brant was gossiping up the folktale that Sir
William had beckoned Joseph Brant to his deathbed and whispered, "Control your people. I am going away." And when London did appoint Nephew Guy to be Superintendent of Indian
Affairs, the Butler-Johnson friendship began to buckle.

Guy Johnson whimpered where Sir William would have roared,
and threatened where Sir William would have coaxed. As for
Captain Claus, he was simply star-struck about being a baronet's
son-in-law.

The missionary, Samuel Kirkland, had preached among the
Oneidas and Tuscaroras since 1766. The month Sir William died,
the Oneidas asked Kirkland to come with them to a Grand Council at Onondaga. The Shawnees were warring with the Virginians
(Lord Dunmore's War) and had sent a delegation to Onondaga
with war belts, urging the Six Nations to join them in another
Pontiac-type war against the Colonials. The Grand Council lasted
a month. Reverend Kirkland's advice prevailed. The war belts
were rejected.

During May 1775, Kirkland used his peacemaker prestige to
outmaneuver Guy Johnson. Kirkland was pro-Rebel. He persuaded
the Oneidas to issue a formal declaration of neutrality "in this
grievous struggle between our white brothers." Then he went to
Onondaga, harangued the Grand Council and secured their
pledge of neutrality.

Guy Johnson was finally shrilled to action by Molly Brant. The
Mohawks would not remain neutral, she said. They would fight
for the King. But they were hemmed in on the east by the rebels'
Committees of Safety and on the west by the Kirkland-ruled
Oneidas and Tuscaroras. They must move west and live among
the Senecas. Move the Indian Superintendency to Niagara, too!
Issue the call for a great council at Oswego!

Guy Johnson decided to send his wife and children to England
"until the rebels have been put down—perhaps four, certainly not
more than six months." The Clauses settled on Montreal as a
temporary home. But Catherine Butler smiled down the invita-

tion. She and the children would be perfectly safe at Butlersbury. And she was a better farm manager than John. She had to be. He was forever riding off to Indian meetings or wars, wasn't he?

Mary Johnson developed chills during the paddle across Oneida Lake, had to be carried over the Oswego River portages, and died from pneumonia at Oswego. More than a thousand delegates had come in for the council, some from as far as Illinois. They mourned the death of the great Warrahiyageh's daughter. But a week later they rejected her husband's war belts with the plea, "We must think about this." Only the Mohawks and a few Senecas promised to take the war path. The Oneidas and Tuscaroras did not even send delegates.

The activities of John Butler between August 1775 and May 1776 are intimated in a letter written to the Crown's disbursing officers by the commanding officer at Fort Niagara, Colonel Mason Bolton, who wrote:

> I have drawn a bill of £14,760-9-5 [roughly $75,000] on account of sundries furnished Indians by Major Butler. Between us I am heartily sick of bills and accounts and if the other posts are as expensive to govern as this has been I think old England had done much better in letting the savages take possession of them than to have put herself to half the enormous sums She has been at in keeping them.

The Colonel's choler reflects the tenseness that dominated Niagara. Soon after Butler reached the fort, scouts out of Oswego reported that a force of Rebels was en route through the Adirondacks toward the St. Lawrence. Peter Brant Johnson, the first-known son of Molly Brant and Sir William, commanded the Mohawks sent down the lake to engage the invaders. They joined Ranger battalions from Oswego and Montreal and captured 140 Rebels. The Rebel commander was Ethan Allen, the bombastic Vermonter who claimed credit for the capture of Fort Ticonderoga.

Up the lake with this news came George III's August 23 Proclamation that "a state of rebellion" existed in the Thirteen Colonies and that "utmost endeavors" must be taken to suppress it. But the returning Mohawks brought the report that a second and much larger force of Rebels was advancing up the Lake Champlain route against Montreal.

During the same weeks, Butler received Governor Carleton's instructions to "keep the Indians neutral." It overruled the war-belt speech to "join us in the feast of flesh and blood on the Bostonians" that Guy Johnson had delivered at Oswego. Indian neutrality was another two-faced phrase. The Mohawks were already fighting. The Rebel army that General Richard Montgomery was leading against Montreal used Oneida and Tuscarora scouts. The Reverend Samuel Kirkland was urging the Onondagas, Cayugas and Senecas to cooperate with the Committees of Safety and the Provincial Congress by capturing every "Tory" trying to escape to Oswego or Niagara. And Sir John Johnson was still down there at Johnson Hall, playing the laird, with seven hundred soldiers and Indians guarding the stockades, cannon on the roof, all daring the Rebels to "come out and fight." Indian neutrality, thus, became for John Butler a matter of bribing the Onondagas, Cayugas and Senecas to keep the path open along the Genesee-Mohawk plow-way for anyone still loyal to His Majesty.

Montgomery's invasion kept coming. Then Indians reported that a second Rebel force, believed to be commanded by the Connecticut horse trader, Benedict Arnold, was marching through the Maine wilderness against Quebec.

Guy Johnson sent word from Montreal that he and the children were sailing to England. Governor Carleton agreed that Claus and Joseph Brant should go with them for strategy conferences in London about Indian policy. They sailed during late October. Ethan Allen was aboard, too—in chains in the brig. It was the last transport to clear Quebec before the Rebels arrived.

The Rebels—or, as they now began to call themselves, the Continentals—took Montreal on November 11. The tiny garrison at Fort Stanwix retreated to Oswego. But, Colonel Bolton and Oswego's commander agreed, Oswego could not protect Lake Ontario or Niagara from an assault up the St. Lawrence. One of the western Thousand Islands, a few miles from the rubble of Fort Frontenac, was selected as the best advance post against the

Rebels. Details out of Oswego and Niagara built a blockhouse and wharf there between November and January. The island was named Carleton, in honor of the Governor.

Sometime that fall or early winter 20-year-old Walter Butler joined his father at Niagara. A week or two later, in rode John Yost Herkimer, his brother-in-law, and several other Palatines who had decided to "stand by the King."

They confirmed John Butler's fears about Catherine and the younger children. Butlersbury had been taken "in custody" by the Provincial Congress "in lieu of John Butler's bail bond." And it had been plundered. Continental officers were riding his horses. The cattle, sheep and hogs became provisions for the Continental troops. Mrs. Butler and the children were in Canajoharie, but under house-arrest and soon to be transferred to Albany. John Yost Herkimer and his neighbors realized that the same thing would happen to their families. They wanted guns and Ranger uniforms.

It was worse than civil war. It was fratricidal war. Pro-Continental sons testified against pro-Loyalist fathers and brothers at the Committee of Safety hearings. Peter Van Schaack, the Albany attorney who had been Walter Butler's law teacher, was being held in jail as a Loyalist. The five generations of intermarriage between the Hudson valley patroon families failed to sustain the Whig versus Tory fury. The Van Rensselaers, Schuylers, Clintons, Yates, and—more hesitantly—the Livingstons had become Continentals. They were even whispering about "American independence." But the Cuylers, De Lanceys, Cartwrights held "for the King," and thousands of farmers, shopkeepers, traders and boatmen echoed them in prayers for "His Majesty's victory."

General Montgomery was killed during the Continentals' December 31 assault on Quebec. Benedict Arnold succeeded to the command, was narrowly defeated in the struggle for the Citadel, and continued to control the mid-St. Lawrence valley and Montreal through the spring of 1776.

British frigates led a fleet of transports and merchantmen through the ice floes in the St. Lawrence estuary during April 1776. Baron and Baroness Friedrich Riedesel ogled at the farmhouses that "have no pretensions to architectural beauty," "the large cloaks of scarlet cloth worn by the lower classes of Canadians," and the pretty girls "wearing large hoods which not only cover the head but almost the whole face and in the wintertime are stuffed with down." Their deck companions included Guy Johnson, Daniel Claus, Joseph Brant * and that dashing M.P. and Strand frump, Major General John Burgoyne. Stuffed below decks were 10,000 British regulars and German mercenaries.

Benedict Arnold's appeals for reinforcements did not penetrate the arguments about a Declaration of Independence at the Continental Congress or General Washington's fear of a British invasion via pro-loyalist New York City. Arnold abandoned Montreal during June and began a bulldog retreat down the Champlain trail.

Sir John Johnson and his militiamen reached Niagara about the same time. On January 13, General Philip Schuyler had written him: "If Lady Johnson is at Johnson Hall, I wish she would retire . . . and therefore enclose a passport . . . as I shall march my troops to that place without delay." Lady Johnson refused to leave. Schuyler and Sir John met on January 17. Sir John meekly gave his parole to "hold himself at the orders of the Congress, and not to abet its enemies."

But in May, after the Continentals seized Fort Stanwix, renamed it Fort Schuyler, and installed Colonel Gansevoort and two regiments, Sir John jumped parole (abandoning Lady Johnson) and fled to Niagara. He was still there when a schooner delivered the letter that Lady Johnson smuggled out of Albany. She and the baby were under house-arrest at General Schuyler's mansion. Johnson Hall had been looted. The Highlanders who had refused to flee were either killed or sent to the Connecticut copper mines that had become the Continentals' principal prison for "dangerous Tories."

The Butlers and Sir John's reunion with Guy Johnson, Claus

---

* Johnson and Claus bragged so effectively about Joseph Brant in London that he was received by George III, painted by Romney, and awarded a Captain's commission. Claus had wheedled a colonelcy. Johnson hoped for knighthood within the year, but brooded over the lack of evidence about his late wife's legitimacy at the College of Heraldry.

and Joseph Brant came during July. Guy Johnson had pledged "swarms of Six Nations warriors" to General Burgoyne and Baron Riedesel for the conquest of Albany. Brant brought along some of the scalps he and other Mohawks had peeled from disarmed prisoners after the Continentals' surrender at The Cedars a few weeks before.

Molly Brant was being just as vindictive. When Gansevoort marched his Continentals up the Mohawk, she fled to the Cayugas. Now she was riding from castle to castle along the Finger Lakes, the Genesee and the Allegheny with a red hatchet in her saddlebag.

As Loyalist refugees came to the Gate at Niagara all that summer and fall, the Butlers' lust for vengeance grew to match the Johnsons'. Many of the men and boys were scarred by the horse-whippings, thumbhangings, groin-kicks and testicle tortures that the Committee of Safety inquisitors used in order to force testimany about "Tory spies" and "plans for the Johnsons' invasion." Two of the tattered, starving creatures escorted in by Senecas were Negro slaves from Butlersbury. They brought more details about the looting and the imprisonment of Mrs. John Yost Herkimer and other Loyalist wives, eight and ten to the cell.

But the threat of Colonel Gansevoort's troops at the Mohawk headwaters kept Niagara and its Lake Ontario lifeline on the defensive during 1776. The Brants succeeded in recruiting some Senecas, Delawares and Cayugas; Joseph led them off to slash at Arnold's retreat down Lake Champlain. But Colonel Mason, backed by Governor Carleton, commandeered every refugee who could walk and every Indian willing to work to relay supplies up from Montreal and strengthen the fortifications at Carleton Island. By early winter, fifteen hundred of the Royal Highland Emigrants, Rangers and Quebec Militia were stationed there.

Arnold's suicidal attack against the Burgoyne-Riedesel fleet off Valcour Island on October 11 stopped the brag about "celebrating the New Year in the ruins of Albany." Burgoyne retreated to Montreal. There, lured on by the Johnsons and Claus, he resurrected the pincers strategy. Burgoyne and Riedesel would direct the main assault of 1777 down Lakes Champlain and George. Sir

William Howe would break through the chain of forts that Israel Putnam commanded in the Hudson Highlands. Colonel Barry St. Léger would lead the Wurttemberg Chasseurs, the regiment of Royal Greens that Sir John was recruiting, and any Indians who could be roused, against Fort Schuyler and then down the Mohawk valley. Late in November, Burgoyne sailed for London to propose the plan to the War Office. They approved it, but failed to route General Howe's orders to New York City until June 1777.

Lieutenant John Schank snowshoed into Niagara during January to discuss his new duties as Senior Naval Officer for Lakes Ontario and Erie. He inspected the Lower and Upper Niagara yards and decided on a new one at Carleton Island. During the conferences with Colonel Bolton, he described the new type of landing craft which he and Lieutenant Twiss of *Trois Rivières* had brainstormed. These *bateaux,* they decided, should have square bows that were attached to the body of the craft with bolts. These bowboards must be thick enough to stop a musket-ball and would be pierced at the upper end by loopholes. When troops stormed a beach, the bowboards could be used as portable barricades. Construction of the Schank-Twiss landing craft began at Carleton Island during March 1777.

Sir John recruited two hundred refugees for his Royal Greens; Claus was the Colonel. Between three hundred and four hundred Wurttemberg Chasseurs, all lovely targets in blue-and-yellow coats and egg-shaped brass and felt hats, came to Carleton with Colonel St. Léger in late May. Burgoyne agreed to spare two hundred British regulars, too. They went on to Oswego in the Schank-Twiss landing craft during June. The forty artillerymen reassembled the expedition's two 6-pounders, two 3-pounders, and four 5-inch howitzers. Ox teams to haul the landing craft and cannon over the Oswego portages barged down from Niagara. An Oneida scout named Silas Deane made a careful count of the troops and guns and hiked back to Fort Schuyler with the report.

Molly Brant had succeeded in recruiting three hundred Senecas. Others padded in from the La Présentation, Mississauga and Delaware villages. But fewer than five hundred Indians were at Oswego when John Butler came down from Niagara early in July.

And most of them professed that they preferred to be neutral "like our Onondaga brothers," until Butler promised "ten beaver skins for each scalp" and "all the rum you can drink after the victory." About July 15, Joseph Brant returned from a recruiting trip down the Susquehanna valley with two hundred Cayugas. In all, seven hundred hatchets joined the St. Léger Expedition.

The 65-mile haul up the Oswego and across Lake Oneida took three weeks. Somewhere along the route, a Cayuga gave Joseph Brant a message from Molly. Loyalists had sent word to her, from Canajoharie or Palatine Bridge, that the Committee of Safety had been able to recruit two regiments of militia in the valley. These were expected to march to Gansevoort's relief about the first of August. Nicholas Herkimer was their commanding officer.

Nicholas was John Yost Herkimer's brother. A brother-in-law and a nephew were also marching with Sir John's Royal Greens. Most of the men coming up valley with Nicholas Herkimer were old friends and neighbors to most of the Royal Greens. They had worked together at harvest times, on barn raisings and at husking bees. They had courted together, gone to church together, and in 1759 some of them had marched with Prideaux and Sir William.

The siege lines around Schuyler were laid out on August 4 and 5. Seneca scouts reported that Herkimer's regiments were camped less than twenty miles downstream. St. Léger ordered the Butlers and Brant to take the seven hundred Indians downriver and set up an ambush.

The sunrise of August 6 tinged lead-black and scarlet scallops on the thunderheads moving east over Lake Oneida. Nicholas Herkimer broke camp early. His militia was ten miles from Fort Schuyler. Perhaps he reasoned that the approaching storm would keep the Loyalists under cover, so there was no need to send out scouts or flankers. The wind and echoes of thunder drowned out the coded bangs of the signal guns Fort Schuyler fired as a warning to him.

John Butler had selected a wooded ravine two miles west of the Tuscaroras' village of Oriskany for the ambush. The road dipped to cross a brook and small marsh before entering the ravine. The Indians hid in bushes along the ravine's slope. They were to hold their fire until Brant blew his Ranger's whistle. Sir John, Claus and the Royal Greens waited a mile west.

Half of Herkimer's column had crossed the creek and his baggage wagons were on the bridge when Brant's whistle shrilled. More than two hundred died in the next five minutes. Herkimer's horse was killed, and he was shot through the leg. He crawled up to a tree, propped himself against it, and began shouting orders for a rally. His rear guard deployed into the woods just before the Royal Greens marched in.

Then the storm broke in such fury that Indians cowered behind rocks, muskets became too watersoaked to fire, and commands could not be heard ten feet away.

But Fort Schuyler's defenders had heard the ambush volleys and screams. Colonel Gansevoort ordered a cannon barrage against St. Léger's siege lines. Colonel Marinus Willett raced five hundred Continentals out in a sally. That decided the Battle of Oriskany. Herkimer's militia sustained more than four hundred casualties. The Senecas lost a hundred and the Royal Greens more than fifty.*

That night, Colonel Willett and a half-dozen volunteers left the fort again and, avoiding the valley towns, walked three nights and two days to General Schuyler's headquarters a few miles north of Saratoga. They found that Schuyler had just been replaced by Horatio Gates as commander of the defense against Burgoyne and Riedesel.

General Gates, for once, reached a quick decision. He assigned Benedict Arnold to take one hundred of Morgan's Riflemen and two hundred New England militia to the relief of Fort Schuyler.

On August 7 or 8, Walter Butler secured St. Léger's approval to take a patrol down valley and recruit for the Royal Greens. Sir John and St. Léger wrote a proclamation that ordered all of the "rebels in the Mohawk valley" to "lay down their arms" and invited "supporters of the King's cause" to join Sir John's Royal Greens.

Walter Butler and fifteen Royal Greens reached German Flats

---

* The next day Herkimer's leg had to be amputated. The attending doctor botched the job, and General Herkimer bled to death on the table.

on August 12, commandeered the home of a Loyalist named Shoe-maker, exchanged their green uniforms for farm clothes, then sent Shoemaker's sons out to announce a series of meetings "for the King's men." Butler made no effort to keep the meetings secret and claimed later that he was carrying "a flag of truce."

Hundreds of the valley's settlers had refused to march with the Herkimer expedition. The war, they still believed, was not of their making—or concern. But the Oriskany massacre and Walter Butler's audacity angered them to action. They surrounded Shoe-maker's, gunned down the sentries and took Walter Butler and everyone else in the house prisoner.

Benedict Arnold and Marinus Willett reached German Flats on August 20. They court-martialed Walter Butler on August 21, sentenced him to "death by hanging as a spy," and sent a flag up to St. Léger with a formal announcement of the "court's findings."

The Senecas and Cayugas were already despairing their deci-sion to follow the Butlers and Brant for an "easy plunder of the valley and reconquest of the Mohawk homelands." The news that young Butler had been captured and sentenced to death and that Arnold, "the wild man of Quebec and Valcour," was only two days' march down the valley was too much. They rioted on the morning of August 22, plundered the commissary tents, and stalked off toward their Genesee and Finger Lakes castles. Colo-nel St. Léger ordered a retreat to Oswego.

With the Burgoyne-Riedesel invasion fifty miles from Albany, Howe's frigates battering past Israel Putnam's forts in the Hud-son Highlands, and Washington retreating toward Philadelphia, Benedict Arnold ruled against a pursuit of St. Léger. He quick-marched the Morgan Riflemen and New Englanders east again, halting only long enough at Canajoharie, Butlersbury, Palatine, German Flats and Schenectady to urge the local Committees of Safety to "rally every man and boy who believes in Liberty," then pushed on to the Continentals' camps near Saratoga.

St. Léger and Sir John blamed John Butler for the departure of the Indians. In their report to Governor Carleton, they charged that "Colonel Butler withheld ammunition from Captain Brant and the Indians," thus "giving comfort to the enemy." When the report reached Montreal, Guy Johnson supplemented it with a whine to Governor Carleton that Butler's gifts to the Indians during 1775 and 1776 had been "too lavish."

This vendetta, possibly rooted in the Johnson-Claus realization that John Butler knew too much about Sir William's mistresses and their bar-sinister, conditioned Butler toward a do-or-die decision.

The St. Léger retreat, sequeled on September 19 by the Burgoyne-Riedesel failure to defeat the Continentals at the Battle of Bemis Heights, sent scores of Loyalist refugees up the valley to Oswego, Carleton Island and Niagara. From them, Butler learned that Walter was still alive and, although still under Arnold's death sentence, had been taken to Albany. Catherine and the other children were still imprisoned there. The Rebel mob might murder them, too. Life? There could be no worthwhile life without them. Die for the King? Very pretty, but the Bible was more realistic. "An eye for an eye!" Revenge! He wrote Governor Carleton for permission to organize the Loyalist refugees into a regiment of Rangers, then lead them in raids against Rebel strongholds.

The Burgoyne-Riedesel surrender at Saratoga and Howe's retreat to New York City—after burning Kingston, fifty miles south of Albany—doomed the St. Léger-Sir John dream of a triumphal return to the Mohawk valley. Many of Oswego's cannon and most of its garrison were transferred to Carleton Island. Sir John, Claus and the Royal Greens returned to Montreal.

Butler and some of the Loyalist refugees went uplake to Niagara. There, Colonel Allan MacLean, commander of the Royal Highlander Emigrants, gave Butler gruff comfort. He had detested "all of that Johnson tribe" since Sir William had usurped the Niagara Expedition's command in 1759. His old comrade and hero, General Haldimand, was—he had just learned—scheduled to replace Carleton as Governor. The "demned Johnsons" would not hoodwink Frederick Haldimand!

Carleton approved the formation of the regiment of Loyalist Rangers, gave John Butler the colonelcy, and agreed on the strat-

egy of frontier raids. Washington's army, driven out of Philadelphia, was huddled around Germantown and Valley Forge. If they
survived the winter, the wheatlands along the Schoharie and
lower Mohawk would become the most dependable source of
breadstuff supplies still available to them. Burn the wheat crops!
A matter to consider!

As for uniforms, the Butler Rangers would be outfitted like the
other Ranger regiments being formed at New York City and in
New Jersey—green jackets with yellow trim, tan breeches and a
bucket-shaped leather headgear with a horned moon of brass near
the crest.

Butler called for volunteers to go back to the Mohawk valley
and recruit. Some of them, disguised as beggars ... pedlars ...
wounded Continentals, got as far as Connecticut. By March 1778,
Butler's Rangers had three hundred men under drill; and John
Butler knew that the Christopher Yates family had not only managed to secure more comfortable quarters for Cathcrine and the
children, but had won delay after delay of Walter's hanging.

Dispatches about the treaty of alliance that Ben Franklin was
negotiating with France reached Quebec during March or early
April. Joseph Brant came up from Montreal with orders to take
war belts to the Senecas and Cayugas again. A French-Rebel
treaty would, of course, start another war between Great Britain
and France. The prospect of Rebel-French invasions should persuade the sachems toward the war path. So should Butler's orders
to "free the Wyoming valley."

Butler's Rangers marched south from Niagara during April,
weeks before Quebec learned that France and Great Britain had
declared war on March 13. Joseph and Molly Brant led in five
hundred warriors from the Allegheny and Genesee castles. At the
overnight camp near the foot of Lake Seneca, the half-breed
"Queen Esther" Montour brought in one hundred Cayugas and
announced that she would "carry a hatchet, too, to help free the
Wyoming valley."

Forty Fort, the Continentals' main defense post in the Wyoming valley, was on the site of Wilkes Barre, Pennsylvania. Across
the Susquehanna, Loyalists from Connecticut had built Fort

Wintermoot. Butler's Rangers and the Seneca-Cayuga warriors reached Wintermoot on June 30 and besieged Forty Fort on July 2. A sally failed. Forty Fort surrendered on July 4. Esther Montour and Joseph Brant screamed their warriors on to a massacre. More than three hundred were tomahawked or burned at torture stakes. The Wyoming Massacre became "the surpassing horror of the Revolution" and gave John Butler, Joseph Brant and Esther Montour reputations as "the devils of Niagara."

Yet, in his report to Colonel Bolton from Tioga, Pennsylvania, on July 12, Butler wrote, "But what gives me the sincerest satisfaction is that I can, with great truth assure you that in the destruction of the settlement not a single person was hurt except such as were in arms; to these in truth the Indians gave no quarter."

The Connecticut Loyalists abandoned Wintermoot and joined the Rangers' march north. At Tioga, Butler sent Brant with the Indians and part of the Rangers up the Susquehanna to start farm raids along the mid-Mohawk and Schoharie valleys. Other Loyalists were waiting at the Genesee castles for escort to "freedom in Canada." More than five hundred men, women and children were on the last one hundred miles of the return to Niagara.

Even Colonel Bolton managed a smile when John Butler came through the Six Nations Gate. The young Captain standing a pace behind Bolton saluted, then blurted, "Hello, Father." John Butler's arm was paralyzed in mid-salute. Then he heard Colonel MacLean boom, "Dammit, old man. Ease off! It's Walter right enough!"

On the night of April 21, Walter Butler's jailer had unlocked the cell door, handed him a cloak, muttered, "There's a horse beside the alley door," and walked off. By late May, Walter was in Montreal. During June, Governor Carleton awarded him a Captain's commission.

Colonel Bolton soon fretted back to brusqueness. There simply wasn't room for all the Rangers and their families at the Fort. But he had a plan that, he felt sure, Governor Haldimand would approve. A barracks and warehouse—with, of course, a blockhouse and boat dock—*must* be built on the west shore of the

Niagara, right about where Prideaux had set up siege guns in 1759. Rather good soil for gardens and pasture over there, too, he understood.

Governor Haldimand did approve. Construction began during September. The urgency to complete the buildings before freezing weather held John Butler at Niagara. So Colonel Bolton recommended, and Governor Haldimand approved, that Walter Butler be given command of a late fall raid against the Continentals' fort at Cherry Valley, twelve miles southwest of Canajoharie.

Thirty-five miles down the Susquehanna River from its Lake Otsego source stood the "stone houses with glass windows and brick chimneys" of the Cayugas' Unadilla castle. It had become a rest haven for Loyalists fleeing to Canada. Brant used Unadilla and Ouaquaga as bases for raids into the mid-Mohawk and Schoharie valleys. On July 18 his warriors burned Andrustown, near the head of Lake Otsego. During the night of September 17, he raided German Flats, the village where Walter Butler had been captured thirteen months before. The surprise was complete, and since even Continental reports claimed only "two whitemen, 1 Negro killed," the defense must have been slight. A report expressed to Albany the next day said, "The enemy burned 63 dwelling houses, 57 barns with grain and fodder, three grist mills, 1 saw mill, took away 235 horses, 229 horned cattle, 269 sheep, killed and destroyed hogs and burned a great many outhouses."

Colonel Ichabod Alden commanded the 250 Continentals garrisoning the Cherry Valley fort. Although raiders attempting to drive "229 horned cattle, 269 sheep" through the Otsego forests should have been easy to follow and ambush, Alden sat tight. And, survivors testified a year later, he continued to deny the Cherry Valley villagers the right to take refuge in the fort.

It had been an excellent crop year. More than 100,000 bushels of wheat were ready for the flailing floors. So, during the last days of September, three hundred of Schoharie's farmers brought their "shootin' irons" into Middle Fort to join up with two hundred Continentals sent out from Albany. The five hundred marched southwest toward Unadilla on October 2.

The column was too "Injun-wise" for Brant; he retreated to
Tioga. The Schoharians plundered and burned Unadilla on October 6. Some of them demonstrated that they could scalp as
quickly and neatly as any Seneca or Cayuga. On October 8, they
burned Brant's warehouse and stockade at Ouaquaga, thirty miles
down country. They were back at Middle Fort by October 16.
General Schuyler was confident that "these frontiers are suffi-
ciently secured from any further disturbances from the savages
at least this winter."

Walter Butler's column joined Brant's about October 20. The
story persists that Brant refused to serve under Butler's command
and sulked for a week before he called in the warriors and threw
the red hatchet against Cherry Valley.

Colonel Alden, his officers and their families found the con-
veniences at the Wells home more pleasing than the bunks and
salt pork mess available at the fort, four hundred yards away. Nor
did the Colonel seem particularly interested in his garrison's diet
or supplies. "When we were first attacked," one of his men testified during December, "we had not a pound of bread per man in
garrison. Had it not been for a barrel of powder and half a box
of cartridges belonging to the town our ammunition would have
failed us."

A sleet storm turned to mushy snow during the night of November 10. Colonel Alden, Lieutenant Colonel Stacy, Major Whiting and several other officers were still at the Wells home at 11
o'clock on the morning of the 11th when Brant's Indians bashed
in the front door.

Alden fled toward the fort and was killed. Lieutenant Colonel
Stacy surrendered. Major Whiting jumped through a window,
reached the fort, and took command of the defense.

Walter Butler commanded the attack on the fort. He claimed
later that he ordered Brant to "permit your warriors to attack
only armed men."

The siege of the fort continued for four hours—and failed. Butler ordered the retreat about 3:30 P.M. The forty homes in the
village were in flames. Brant's warriors had scalped thirty-five
women, children and unarmed men. But 173 others had fled to

safety in the woods. Captain McDonnell and the Headquarters Company of Rangers were guarding forty prisoners, including Lieutenant Colonel Stacy, Mrs. Campbell and four children, Mrs. James Moore and three children.

Word of the Cherry Valley Massacre reached Schenectady during the night of November 12, and a thousand Continentals chased the raiders past Otsego and across the Chenango hills. But the only Loyalist they caught up with was a Ranger officer waving a flag of truce. He had a letter from Walter Butler addressed to General Schuyler. It requested that "Mrs. Butler and her family" plus others named on an attached list be permitted to "go to Canada" in exchange for "an equal number of prisoners of yours taken either by the Rangers or the Indians." After passionate denial that "I wage war with Women and Children," Walter Butler had closed the missive with the threat that "If you persevere in detaining my Father's family with you, we shall no longer take the same pains to restrain the Indians from prisoners, Women or Children that we have hitherto done."

On December 18, General George Clinton wrote General Washington that "as the snow is two feet deep on the frontiers, I have ordered one hundred pair of snowshoes . . . but every acc't seems to confirm the general report that Butler and Brant with their banditti are moved to Niagara."

The Rangers and their forty prisoners reached Niagara in mid-December. Even Colonel Bolton mellowed a bit and conceded that with 111 women and 259 children at Niagara, it might be appropriate to organize "a jolly good party and gift-giving for New Year's Day."

Shortly after the New Year, General Washington ordered Major General John Sullivan to Philadelphia for a series of "important discussions." During February, General Schuyler met with General Clinton, Colonel Goose Van Schaick, and Colonel Marinus Willett. They, too, spent several days studying maps of the Six Nations homelands.

THIRTEEN

⮜～೨၆⮞

THE NIAGARA PLAN OF EDIBLE ANNEX

Gardening was an instinct, rather than a hobby, to Governor Frederick Haldimand. He had been born in Switzerland, where compost . . . animal fertilizer . . . the bank barn . . . the horse collar . . . fencing and other cornerstones of diversified agriculture evolved. So the odor of fresh loam, the military precision of vegetable rows, the crisp seasonal demands to trim, plant, weed, mulch and harvest were really hereditary instincts. Colonel Haldimand made a garden at Oswego in 1760. Brigadier General Haldimand made a garden at *Trois Rivières* in 1762. Major General Haldimand made gardens in Florida, Albany, and Boston between 1767 and 1774. Governor Haldimand hummed at his gardening in Quebec between 1779 and 1784. His hobby instinct was a critical, if subconscious, factor in the birth of Upper Canada.

Haldimand replaced Guy Carleton as Governor of Canada on July 1, 1778. His first concern about Niagara was to approve the plan for the Ranger barracks complex across the river from Fort Niagara. He suggested then that "a great advantage might be derived from the establishment of a permanent settlement at Niagara." That winter, the exodus of Loyalists and the danger of an attack by the Continentals that might cut off the Montreal-Niagara supply route caused him to order Colonel Bolton to "investigate the possibilities of farming and gardening at Niagara." On March 5, 1779, Colonel Bolton replied, "I am consulting every person here who could give me any information concerning the Plan of Agriculture."

However, the reports brought down from Detroit a week or two later caused postponement of "His Excellency's quaint hobby." Colonel Henry Hamilton, the bumptious commandant at Detroit, had gone off to Vincennes the previous summer with fifty soldiers and some Indians to "wipe out" the Virginians under George Rogers Clark. But Clark's 175 retook Vincennes, and sent "Hair-buyer" Hamilton off to the Williamsburg jail. Since Clark was receiving most of his supplies from the Spanish in New Orleans, Detroit feared an allied Spanish-Continental raid against the Upper Lakes posts.

Before April 1, Carleton Island sent another alert uplake. A large force of Continentals was en route up the Mohawk and, the spies also reported, a "huge fleet" of boats was under construction on the riverbank at Schenectady.

The pincers again? France was assembling a fleet of frigates off Newport, Rhode Island. Printed "Proclamations of Freedom" urging French-Canadians to "throw off the tyrant's yoke" were being posted on church doors from Montreal to Tadoussac. Had the United States made an agreement with France to return the New France territories to her in exchange for troops and ships in a pincers campaign against Quebec, Montreal, Carleton Island, Niagara and Detroit?

Reinforcements for Detroit, Mackinac and St. Joseph crossed the Niagara portage. Carleton Island and Niagara went on the alert and sent out scouts. John Butler took a company of Rangers south toward Tioga. Despite his fears about the young man's impetuousness and nasty temper, Colonel Bolton assigned Walter Butler to head a scout down the Allegheny for evidence of any raiders out of Pittsburgh.

On April 25, Continental troops "with a party of Onydais and a few Tuskaroras being among them," raided Oswego, took four prisoners, and almost succeeded in capturing the commanding officer. A week later, the mystery of the Schenectady *bateaux* fleet began to clear up. Colonels Goose Van Schaick and Marinus Willett led a regiment to the Onondaga homeland, burned all of the castles along Onondaga Creek, killed seventeen warriors and all the livestock, and returned to Fort Schuyler with thirty-three women and children captives "including, I fear, a child of Joseph Brant's."

On May 31, John Butler captured a Continental courier on the Genesee. After threats of Indian torture, the courier blurted that Continentals were moving up the Susquehanna. "It seems to be the intention of the Rebels," Butler wrote Colonel Bolton, "to erect a chain of forts all along their frontiers."

George Washington was gambling one third of the Continental regiments-of-the-line on a replay of the Niagara pincers. General James Clinton with five New York regiments used the fleet of new *bateaux* to row to Canajoharie. From there they cut a wagon road to Lake Otsego, then built an earth-and-brush dam across the outlet that serves as the Susquehanna's headwater. When engineers decided that the water was high enough, the dam was blown. The army boated south on the flood to Tioga. Here it joined the 2,500 Continentals, commanded by General John Sullivan, who had come up the Susquehanna from Harrisburg.

General Daniel Brodhead was to bring six hundred Continentals and Pennsylvania militia from Fort Pitt up the Allegheny-Presque Isle route to strike at Forts Erie and Schlosser. George Rogers Clark was to cut across the wilderness from the Falls of the Ohio, besiege Detroit, and wait for the Niagara breakthrough by Brodhead, Sullivan and Clinton.

Washington was planning toward the peace. The Clinton-Sullivan-Brodhead-Clark pincers was intended to be much more than a punishment for the Six Nations and eradication of the Fort Niagara "hornets' nest." It was the United States' declaration that the Fort Stanwix boundary line between white territory and red territory had been junked and that the new nation intended to settle "where it damnwell pleased," clear to the Mississippi.

Colonel Bolton dared send only one company of the Eighth Regiment to support Butler's Rangers. Haldimand ordered Guy Johnson uplake to "rouse your Indians." But only three hundred Senecas and Cayugas joined with the 250 Rangers and fifty regulars on the hills overlooking the site of Elmira.

The skirmish that took place there on August 28 would, because it was the principal engagement of the campaign, be called the Battle of Newtown. Sullivan had four thousand of the United States' best, including some of Morgan's Riflemen and several batteries of howitzers and coehorns. Butler's force totaled less than six hundred when the Continentals' cannon began firing. The Indians panicked and fled after the first salvos. Yet the Rangers managed to escape with "five men killed or taken."

The grimmest battle of the Clinton-Sullivan campaign occurred three miles southwest of the site of Geneseo on September 24 when Indians, and presumably a body of Rangers, surrounded a scouting party of twenty-six Continentals, commanded by Lieutenant Thomas Boyd and Sergeant Michael Parker.

All of the Continentals except Boyd and Parker were shot down and scalped during or after the fight. But the corpses of Boyd and Parker were found tied to trees "with wrappings of their intestines."

"It appeared," General Sullivan wrote in his official report to General Washington, "that they had whipped them in the most cruel manner, pulled out Mr. Boid's [sic] nails, cut off his nose, plucked out one of his eyes, cut out his tongue, stabbed him with spears in sundry places, and inflicted other tortures which decency will not permit me to mention; lastly, cut off his head. . . . His unfortunate companion appeared to have experienced nearly the same savage barbarity."

Spy reports from Albany and Philadelphia agreed that Sullivan would raze northwest from the Genesee to Niagara and that Brodhead had started up the Allegheny valley. Colonel Bolton prepared for an October-November siege. Governor Haldimand ordered the Ontario and Erie fleets to patrol the Niagara approaches. Sir John Johnson thundered patriotic speeches in Montreal, took his Royal Greens to Carleton Island, then decided, "We are too late to be of any help."

But General Sullivan demonstrated that he was as awed by the Niagara Legend as Governor Shirley had been in 1755. He trudged his four thousand in a mule-slow loop through the upper Genesee valley, turned east to the Finger Lakes, then returned south through "Queen Esther" Montour's village to the Susquehanna valley. His troops burned castles and corn fields, chopped down fruit trees, killed livestock, and scalped a few Indians but never got within one hundred miles of Niagara. He was fifteen miles from the Newtown skirmish site when a November blizzard whined in. He ordered all of the expedition's horses killed—thus bestowing the name of Horseheads on the subsequent village—and went home.

General Brodhead's column got as far as Venango, and then, claiming that their guides "misled us," returned to Fort Pitt. George Rogers Clark spent most of the summer building Fort Louis at the Falls of the Ohio and other posts he believed essential to protect Kentucky from the British and Indians.

But the Clinton-Sullivan campaign did cause the most terrifying winter ever experienced on the Niagara. Thus it influenced the birth of Upper Canada and the American * migration route to the West.

Between 2,500 and 3,000 Onondagas, Cayugas and Senecas fled to Fort Niagara during September and October. They built brush huts and dugouts from the Prideaux trench ruins through *La Belle Famille* and up the gorge beyond Devil's Hole. They were without food, tools, household equipment or winter clothing.

Molly Brant was escorted in during October, sent downlake to Carleton Island, and installed in a cabin. Governor Haldimand secured a Crown Pension of £100 a year for her.

Schooners brought in more sowbelly, corn meal, and bales of blankets and cloth, despite the November blizzard. Colonel Bolton established a weekly "relief line," with special allotments to the sick and the nursing mothers. The Fort physician had nightmares about outbreaks of smallpox or yellow fever.

Parade-ground snow piled into eight-foot drifts during January

* Contemporary correspondence indicates that the semantic transition from "Continentals" to "Americans" occurred during 1779–80. Loyalists then began to refer to the United States' adherents as "Americans" rather than "Rebels." The practice persists almost two centuries later. Residents south and east of the Niagara are "Americans"; residents north and west of it are not "North Americans" but "Canadians."

and February. The death toll from starvation in the caves and
dugouts is unknown, but survivors estimated it in the hundreds.
In some of the hovels, entire families froze to death. Then their
caves were buried by the snow. During April and May of 1780,
work details threw in quicklime and filled in the holes.

When salmon, sturgeon, leaf buds, tender milkweed shoots and
calamus roots replaced the ground-acorn and elm-bark stews,
more than a thousand of the redmen refugees crossed the portage
and settled on Chabert Joncaire's abandoned farmlands along
Buffalo Creek. Others went to Fort Erie, explored west, and began building longhouses in the Grand River valley.

Couriers on snowshoes took Colonel Bolton's appeal to Montreal for "vegetable and wheat seeds" on the first supply shipments
of 1780. The Butlers and Colonel MacLean waded through April
mud with him to select the locations for gardens and wheat fields
on the gentle hills behind the ranger barracks.

On July 7, Governor Haldimand wrote Bolton that London approved his plan for fort gardens and for the development of homesteads on adjacent crown lands. Rights of such tenancy, free of
rent, were to be renewed annually, at the discretion of each fort's
commander. The Crown would supply the seed, plows, and "necessary agricultural equipment." But surplus crops must be "dis-
posed of to the commanding officer for the use of troops and not
to traders or accidental travelers." For the first time, Governor
Haldimand referred to the program as "The Niagara Plan of Edible Annex to fortresses." He ordered Colonel Bolton to forward to
Detroit "the instructions for carrying it into execution."

And the war went on. Sir John satiated his glory-hunger by
directing raids into the Mohawk valley. The most devastating
were scheduled during August when the wheat was ripe. With
four hundred Butler Rangers and Royal Greens and between
three hundred and four hundred Indians, Sir John, both Butlers
and Brant followed the Southern Tier route through Tioga east to
the Schoharie valley. They besieged the Schoharians in the three
forts near Schoharie village and Middleburg. The determination
of Timothy Murphy, a veteran of Morgan's Riflemen, bullied the
Middle Fort's commander from surrender. However, thousands of

acres of wheat and hundreds of barns and homes were burned. Every domesticated animal that Brant's warriors could locate was hatcheted. During October, Canajoharie and other central Mohawk communities were plundered and burned.

Through all the worries, alarums, inspections and reports, Colonel Bolton found himself anticipating the weekly strolls behind Butler Barracks. There he observed the progress of the cabbages, sweet corn—which should be called *maize*, of course—potatoes and beans, and chatted about bug control, irrigation ditches, and similar soothing matters with the Continental prisoners who tended them. He discovered the therapeutic values of Governor Haldimand's hobby and resolved, when he went downlake on furlough that winter, to regale His Excellency with a bug-by-bug, tuber-by-tuber account of the Niagara Plan's first crop year.

Butler's Rangers returned to Niagara on October 29 or 30. Colonel Bolton called the officers into a lengthy conference. His furlough began on November 1. Everything must be in order for his successor. He would sail on October 31 aboard the new snow, *Ontario*. The ship grossed three hundred tons and carried twenty-eight guns. Her brasswork, sleek black hull, and snowy white sails sparkled at anchorage below the council room windows.

The *Ontario* sailed on schedule, with three cheers and a huzzah from the dock for Colonel Bolton. A storm was brewing to the north over the Humber. But what matter! New ship and furlough at last!

The *Ontario* was last sighted off Golden Hill, thirty miles east, just at dusk. She was running into the gale with bare poles. The gale lasted most of the night. She must have capsized and gone down with all hands near the center of the lake. No wreckage was ever discovered.

Arson, rape and torture by both Loyalists and Americans heightened the hate between Niagara and the Mohawk-Schoharie frontiersmen between 1781 and 1783. American courts declared Johnson Hall, Mount Johnson, Butlersbury and the properties of most other Tories "attainted" and their properties "real and personal" forfeit to the State.

New fears of a Detroit-Niagara assault from the west created an alert during the spring of 1781. Survivors reported that Spanish raiders, led by Don Eugenio Pourre, crossed the Mississippi and Illinois during December and in January captured Captain Schlosser's former command, Fort St. Joseph on Lake Michigan.

Catherine Butler and her four children finally reached Montreal in a prisoner exchange during June 1781. There was time for a brief reunion with Walter, probably at Carleton Island, before he took a Ranger battalion southeast on Major John Ross's arson raid.

But Colonel Marinus Willett was more alert this time. He had a thousand Continentals in chase hours after the raiders fired "near one hundred farms, three mills and a large granary for publick service" in the Warrensbush area between Schenectady and the Schoharie.

Ross ordered the retreat to Carleton Island, via Johnstown. Willett guessed the route. He managed a skirmish at Johnstown, then on October 28 quick-marched toward Canada Creek, north of Herkimer.

The raiders reached the Canada Creek fording place soon after noon on June 29. Willett's column was less than a mile behind. Walter Butler and the Rangers guarded the ford during the Loyalist crossing. Then Butler volunteered his Rangers to fight there until Major Ross had time to set up an ambush in the woods a mile west.

A mist settled in the creek valley as Willett's skirmishers crept in. The battle at the fording place lasted less than ten minutes. Three of Willett's Oneida scouts were the first Americans across the creek. They whooped and brandished their hatchets.

As Willett came up the west bank of the creek, he saw the Oneidas scalping a half dozen Rangers sprawled in the bushes. One of the bodies wore a Captain's epaulets on the bloody green and gold jacket. Willett stooped and recognized his old enemy, Walter Butler.

Willett abandoned the chase after Ross, turned the command over to a major, and galloped off toward Schenectady, carrying

Butler's scalp and wallet as evidence that "the Devil of Cherry Valley" was dead.*

Cornwallis surrendered his army of seven thousand Loyalists,‡ Hessians and British regulars ten days before Walter Butler died. Sir Henry Clinton sat tight in New York City. So did Guy Carleton, who succeeded him in February 1782.

The few skirmishes that erupted during 1782 and 1783 were products of the struggle between Governor Haldimand and George Washington for control of the West. This focused, of course, on control of the Six Nations' homelands and the Niagara gateway.

The savagery of the Butler-Johnson-Brant raids had forced the Americans to abandon Fort Schuyler. Then, when Carleton Island developed as the Loyalist bastion of the St. Lawrence headwater, Oswego had been abandoned. But when a declaration of peace became obvious, Governor Haldimand ordered the Royal Greens and Butler's Rangers to reoccupy Oswego. They did so during the summer of 1782.

* The mystery of Walter Butler's corpse has intrigued Mohawk valley history buffs and fiction writers ever since. Most historians believe the body was abandoned and "probably eaten by wolves." But the existence of a Butler family plot in the graveyard of St. George's Church at Schenectady . . . the war-proof friendship between the Butlers and the family of Colonel Christopher Yates . . . the post-Revolution marriage of Walter's brother, William Johnson Butler, to Yates' daughter, Eve, all offer circumstantial evidence for the legend that Walter Butler's corpse was secretly brought to Schenectady and buried "under the third pew from the front, in the right aisle," of St. George's. A rector who served St. George's during the 1820's is accredited as author of the following jingle:

> Beneath the pew in which you sit
> They say that Walter Butler's buried.
> In such a fix, across the Styx
> I wonder who his soul has ferried?

> And so the ages yet unborn
> Shall sing your fame in song and story,
> How ages gone you sat upon
> A Revolutionary Tory.

‡ Including the Queen's Rangers, commanded by Colonel John Graves Simcoe.

On February 8, 1783—nine weeks after the provisional peace treaty had been signed in Paris—Colonel Marinus Willett and 470 Continentals left Fort Herkimer. They were under personal orders from General Washington to "capture and hold Oswego." Willett set up a position in the woods behind Oswego on the morning of February 13. He decided to rush the fort that midnight. But five soldiers from the fort were out foraging firewood. They saw the Americans and ran. Two of them were tomahawked. The other three reached the fort and shouted the alarm. Willett abandoned the attack and ordered the march back to Herkimer.

The long wrangle over the terms of the Treaty of Paris during 1782 and 1783 involved the ownership of Gibraltar, Florida and Louisiana as well as the independence of the United States. The final terms conceded the centers of the upper St. Lawrence, Lake Ontario, the Niagara River and Lake Erie as United States-Canadian borders, very much as they are today.

But Governor Haldimand and London agreed that Carleton Island, Oswego, and the Niagara's forts and portage must not be surrendered. More than 40,000 Loyalists had fled to Canada. Their indemnity claims for property seized by the Americans would total more than £9,000,000. New settlements must be developed for them. And, if the United States did manage to survive the intrigues of France and Spain, a buffer Indian Territory for the Six Nations and the Ohio valley tribes should be set up between the United States and Canada along the Upper Lakes!

The United States sent the dignified Prussian, Baron von Steuben, to Canada during August 1783, to demand "immediate surrender" of the St. Lawrence and Great Lakes forts "in accord with the Treaty of Paris." Governor Haldimand entertained the Baron at Sorel from August 11 to August 14 and purred a lengthy "No." Congress was too involved with interstate jealousies and the incompetence of the Articles of Confederation to mount another war.

Plans for Loyalist colonization of the upper St. Lawrence and Ontario wilderness were shaping out of the Niagara Edible Annex program by the time Haldimand and Von Steuben met. John

Butler inherited supervision of the Butler Barracks gardens and farms after Colonel Bolton's death. Butler's August 25, 1783, report told that 236 acres of Niagara riverbank had been cleared and planted. The crop was expected to total 206 bushels of wheat, 46 bushels of oats, 925 bushels of corn, 632 bushels of potatoes, plus "seasonal produce." Livestock herds had increased to 49 horses, 42 cows, 30 sheep and 103 hogs.

When, that fall, Governor Haldimand wrote Butler about the Rangers' wishes for homesteads "after you are disbanded," Butler replied, "We would rather go to Japan than return among the Americans." There were 258 men in Butler's Rangers that month, and 360 wives and children were at the Barracks, too.

So the great experiment began with Butler's Rangers in the spring of 1784. Each family was awarded a grant of Crown land on the Niagara peninsula. Haldimand gave the Americans benefit of doubt and conceded that the United States just might survive long enough to pay some of its debts and occupy the Great Lakes-Niagara south shore. Hence the farm grants were made along the Butler Barracks-Fort Erie shore of the river. The first community that developed was, naturally, adjacent to the Butler Barracks. It was named Newark because, as the bookish chaplain at Fort Niagara explained, this was a good old Saxon word meaning "New Work."

That fall, Loyalists in Nova Scotia, Quebec and Montreal were offered Upper St. Lawrence and Lake Ontario land grants. The French had chosen well in selecting the sites for Toronto and Frontenac. The harbors there were excellent. Each offered hill sites for forts that could protect its community from the Americans. Since most of its pioneers were ex-New Yorkers, Toronto took the nostalgic name of York. The town that developed behind the ruins of Frontenac became Kingston. Molly Brant was one of its first home builders.

Easier access to Upper Canada, as this Ontario frontier was soon called, had been one of the first projects ordered by Haldimand after he returned to Quebec in 1780. In 1761, he had seen scores of Amherst's soldiers perish in the La Chine Rapids. The portage there cost thousands of pounds each year to operate. He ordered William Twiss, coinventor of the radical landing craft first used on the St. Léger Expedition, to design and build a series of canals wide enough to tow *bateaux* past La Chine. The La Chine Canal, only six feet wide, was completed during 1782. It was the first ship canal in North America.

As Molly and Joseph Brant haughtily insisted, and Sir John meekly echoed,* land grants must be given, too, to the Six Nations warriors who had served, and suffered for, His Majesty. Brant and a delegation of sachems which probably included Farmer's Brother and Red Jacket, explored the Niagara peninsula during the fall and winter of 1783. They decided on the Grand River valley. Haldimand secured a Royal Grant of 768,000 acres there as the refugee homeland for Mohawks, Onondagas, Senecas and Cayugas.

Governor Haldimand was 66 on August 11, 1784. He requested retirement. Sir Guy Carleton returned as Governor of Canada that November. He grasped Haldimand's dream of an Upper Canada as a haven for Loyalists who would assure guardianship of the essential lifeline up the Lakes to the fur sources in Michigan, Wisconsin and Minnesota.

More than fifteen thousand Loyalists were pioneering Upper Canada on May 21, 1791, when Great Britain's Parliament passed the act establishing the area as a Royal Province. John Graves Simcoe, son of a Navy captain and former commander of the Queen's Rangers, came out as Upper Canada's first governor. The first sessions of the Provincial Assembly were held at Newark during the fall of 1792. One of the most meaningful laws it enacted was the decision to follow the example of Rhode Island and forbid "human slavery" in the province.

Two years later, John Jay negotiated a treaty with Great Britain that gave the United States permission to "occupy forts along the Great Lakes in accord with the Treaty of Paris" during 1796. Simcoe, still certain that war with the United States would "come soon," moved Upper Canada's capital to York, ordered construction of Fort George behind the Butler Barracks to "command Fort

* Guy Johnson and Daniel Claus both went to England during the 1780's and died there.

Niagara," and hastened completion of a portage road along the Upper Canada shore of the Niagara.

Some of the "coincidences" of history are beyond scientific explanation! Molly Brant died at Kingston on April 14, 1796. Colonel John Butler died at Newark on May 13. A shabby battalion of United States Infantry occupied Fort Niagara on August 19.

SECTION FIVE

THE FIGHT FOR THE LAKES

SIR—I beg leave to inform you that, on the morning of the 21st Nov. [1812] at 6 o'clock, a heavy cannonading opened upon this garrison, from all the batteries at, and in the neighborhood of fort George, which lasted, without intermission, until after sundown. . . . The enemy threw more than 2000 red-hot balls into it, and a number of shells, amounting to 180, only one of which did injury to our men. . . .

Our garrison was not as well provided with artillery and ammunition, as I could have wished; however, the batteries opened a tremendous fire upon them, in return, with hot shot, admirably well directed. Several times, during the cannonading, the town of Newark was in flames . . . as also the centre building in fort George. Their Messhouse, and all the buildings near it, were consumed. . . .

An instance of very extraordinary bravery, in a female, (the wife of one Doyle, a private in the U. States artillery, made a prisoner at Queenstown) I cannot pass over:— during the most tremendous cannonading I have ever seen, she attended the 6 pounder, on the old messhouse, with the red hot shot, and showed fortitude equalling the Maid of Orleans.

—Lieut. Col. George McFeeley, Commanding Fort Niagara, to Brig. Gen. Smyth, commanding the Army of the Centre

FOURTEEN

DETOUR DECADES

The memorial tablet to Sir Frederick Haldimand, K.C.B.*
in Westminster Abbey merely testifies to his services to the British
Empire and Canada. But by closing Thundergate to the United
States between 1783 and 1796, he became responsible for one of
the most significant eras in United States history: the New
Englanders' covered wagon, flatboat, ark and keelboat migration down the Allegheny and Ohio valleys. Marietta, Ohio, was
founded in 1788. So was Cincinnati. But Cleveland was not platted until 1797, Chicago was not a village until 1833, and Mil-
waukee was not founded until 1835. These dates demonstrate
Governor Haldimand's influence on the American migration
routes to the West.

Rufus Putnam and Manasseh Cutler were the principal or-
ganizers of the Ohio Company. The first "Ohio or bust!" wagon-
trains crossed the Hudson River during the fall of 1787. But
Thundergate was closed to them. So they followed the route of
General Clinton's army down the Susquehanna, picked up the
Butler-Brant trail, and took it west to the Allegheny River. There
they built flatboats for the pole-and-fend-and-cordell trip to Pittsburgh and the Ohio valley. The postwar depression and the re-
sultant Shays's Rebellion sent thousands of Yankees over this trail.
Kentucky had a population of 73,677 in 1790 and 220,955 in 1800.
By 1800, Ohio boasted 45,363 settlers and Indiana, 5,641.

* Governor Haldimand was knighted during 1785, a year before his death.

151

But of the 340,120 New Yorkers listed in the first United States census in 1790, only twenty-four lived "west of the Genesee." In 1793, two families from Massachusetts settled near Captain Montresor's abandoned plate-way, at the site of Lewiston. They were still the only Americans on that shore in 1796, when the United States Infantry occupied Fort Niagara.

Moses Cleaveland's party of forty-nine men and two women from Connecticut came up-Ontario and crossed the portage to Lake Erie during June, two months before the Infantry marched in. The Upper Canadians were gracious and provided boats for their trip up-Erie. At Buffalo Creek, the party camped at the Six Nations villages for several days while "General" Cleaveland dickered with sachems for land rights. The parley finally yielded two cows, one hundred gallons of whiskey, and $500 in trade goods as a fair price for the sixty-five miles of shoreland between the Pennsylvania border and the Cuyahoga River.

Young John Morrison adventured to Niagara from Dumbarton, New Hampshire, during 1797 or 1798. He found the Upper Canadians around Newark and new Queenston as comfortable as the homefolks and began courting Mary Campbell. They were married by the Reverend Robert Addison in the log cabin that served as the only edifice of St. Mark's Anglican Church. Mary Campbell Morrison was 14, perhaps 15.

During the fall of 1803, the Morrisons decided to homestead on Eighteen Mile Creek, fourteen miles east of the Niagara Expedition's 1759 landing place. There were three children by that time. John Morrison boated downlake alone, built a cabin, cleared five acres of land for stump farming and then brought his family in during April 1804. During the next two months, after the corn, potato and bean crops were in, he and his wife built a lean-to addition to the cabin and faced it with elm bark.

In July, Morrison made an overnight trip to Batavia, the nearest trading post, for flour, salt pork and other supplies. That dusk, just after she had put the children in their trundle beds, Mrs. Morrison heard wolves yapping on the creek bank. A front door was the next project for their home; only a stroud blanket tacked to the sill kept out the bugs, snakes and squirrels.

She stood still, and prayed.

But the pack caught the scent. The yaps crescendoed to howls and whimpers that circled closer and closer to the cabin.

John Morrison had taken the family's only gun. The young wife took the ax off its wall pegs, then stationed herself just inside the doorway.

One beast came close to the sill, snarled, but slunk back. The pack settled to a death watch, broken only by occasional whines. They stayed all night. Mrs. Morrison held her post, too.

Sunrise mysteriously triggered the pack's return to the forest. When John Morrison returned that afternoon, he found his children barricaded in the lean-to and his wife drowsing on the doorsill, with the ax on her lap.*

Knife-to-claw duels with black bears, livestock raids by eagles and bobcats, horse and cattle thefts by Indians and whites, murders by highwaymen—all these, like the wolf packs and the rattlesnake dens, gave the Niagara frontier of 1800 to 1810 an atmosphere of Deadwood Dick's Wildest West.

Troy, Cooperstown, Binghamton, Elmira, Olean and Jamestown were founded between 1788 and 1800 along the Yankees' trail to the Ohio and the Northwest Territory. Yet, in 1805, settlers west of the Genesee totaled fewer than two thousand whites and Negro slaves.

The American shore of Niagara and Lake Erie became the property of a realty investment trust called The Holland Company. The community that developed at the firm's headquarters took the Dutch Colonial name of *Batavia*. Another village promotion was laid out on Joncaire's River of Horses or, as the Loyalists and Indians had renamed it, Buffalo Creek. The promoters wanted to name it *New Amsterdam*, but the settlers refused. The village of three hundred was *Buffalo Creek* in 1805, and *Buffalo*— with a population of five hundred—in 1810.

Settlement along the American shore of Lake Ontario and the

---

* Unlike many of the Americans who migrated to Upper Canada and married Canadian girls, John Morrison fought on the side of the United States during the War of 1812. He was a Major Commandant of Niagara County Militia.

lower Niagara was just as slow. Neil McMullin, one of the first American settlers at Oswego, brought the framework for his home "ready for assembly" from Kingston, New York, in 1796. The first sawmill and shipyard were opened during 1804. The United States Navy built the U.S.S. *Oneida,* its first vessel on the Great Lakes, at the Oswego yards. The vessel grossed 43 tons and was armed with sixteen guns.

James Fenimore Cooper, recently graduated from Yale College, served as a midshipman on the *Oneida* during 1807 and 1808. Hence Oswego, nearby Carleton Island, and tiny Lewiston, at the foot of Crawl-on-all-Fours, became locales in Cooper's novels, *The Pathfinder* and *The Spy.*

Mrs. Thomas Hustler, proprietress of Hustler's Tavern at Lewiston, was not only the prototype of "Betsy Flanagan" in *The Spy* but, some believe, was the inventor of the cocktail. She became popular, the folklore attests, for the summer drink she made from seasonal fruits, loaf sugar, rye whiskey and shaved ice. Each glassful was served with a stirrer made from a red or black rooster's tailfeather. So Lewiston sippers nicknamed the drink "the cocktail." *

DeWitt Clinton, son of Brigadier General James Clinton and nephew of George Clinton—then Vice President of the United States—provided the most succinct description of the Niagara shore's development in his journal for 1810:

> *August 2d, Thursday.* Messrs. Morris and Van Rensselaer arrived here from Chippeway, and after breakfast at Mr. Barton's, we all proceeded to a village near the Falls of Niagara, along the carrying road where Judge Porter resides.... (The village of Niagara Falls is) one-quarter of a mile above the Falls, and three-quarters of a-mile from Fort Schlosser. It was established by Porter, Barton & Co., and is the best place in the world for hydraulic works. Here is a carding-machine, a grist-mill, a saw-mill, a rope-walk, a bark-mill, a tannery, Post-office, tavern, and a few houses. An acre-lot sells for fifty dollars. The rope-walk is sixty

---

* H. L. Mencken failed to list this possible origin in his discussion of the etymology of "cocktail" in *The American Language.* However, he did conclude that the word was "first used about 1806."

fathoms long; is the only establishment of the kind in the western
country, and already supplies all the lake navigation. The hemp
used in this manufactory is raised on the Genesee Flats, and costs
there from $280 to $300 per ton, and when brought here, it
amounts to $380. Tar is procured from New York, there being
no pitch pine in this country, and the price there and transportation here bring it in cost to nine dollars. It constitutes in price a
twenty-fifth part of the rope. . . .

Some of the new settlers clear the lands by beginning at the
tops of trees, and cutting the limbs. The upper ones break off the
lower, and they soon strip the loftiest hemlock. . . . We got a young
Indian here to shoot at a silver piece, by blowing through a reed
of six feet long, a small arrow surmounted with hair. He hit the
mark with great exactness, ten paces, and in this way they kill
small birds.

The absence of "shipyard" from DeWitt Clinton's list of indus-
tries at Niagara Falls indicates the advantages retained by Upper
Canada. An average of thirty thousand barrels of salt was shipped
annually from the Onondaga "salt lake" via Oswego and the Niagara portage to Presque Isle and Pittsburgh. But the schooners
that carried it from Black Rock to Presque Isle used the cordell
haul on the Upper Canada shore. The guns of Forts Chippewa
and Erie dominated the tow-way.

The portage road along the Upper Canada shore of the Niagara was, like the network of military roads connecting Kingston,
York, Newark, the Detroit River and Georgian Bay, a product of
Governor Simcoe's fear of "the inevitability of war with the
Americans." During 1792, he had secured permission to reactivate
the Queen's Rangers. Between the spring planting and fall harvest
urgencies, the Queen's Rangers served as a volunteer work force
to build roads and make "other publick improvements."

The portage road they created had its northern terminal across
the river from Crawl-on-all-Fours, seven miles above Newark and
Fort George. The docks and warehouses built there became the
nucleus of Queenston, just as the American village opposite became Lewiston. The road was nine miles long, extending to the
Chippewa River, three miles above the falls. Fort Chippewa was

the loading terminal for Lake Erie transportation. It had quarters for one officer and thirty-six men.

The Upper Canada portage and the eighteen-mile sail and cordell between Chippewa and Fort Erie operated with the same spit-and-polish precision that John Stedman and Captain Montresor had developed on the La Salle-Joncaire shore. Its wagon-trains were painted each spring. The harness brass sparkled. Each train had a cavalry escort and operated on a punctual schedule. These efficiencies attracted many American traders and travelers.

Augustus Porter migrated to Niagara from Connecticut during 1803 or 1804 and became one of the owners of the American portage company. His brother, Peter O. Porter, joined him during 1806. A shrewd attorney and promoter, Peter Porter had already accumulated a fortune and built a mansion at Canandaigua, the namesake village of one of the Finger Lakes. The Porters tried to win portage trade away from the Upper Canada route—and failed.

Peter Porter was elected to Congress in 1809. By 1811 he was chairman of the important Foreign Relations Committee of the House of Representatives. He became a belligerent ally of Henry Clay and John C. Calhoun in advocating a declaration of war against Great Britain, with the "easy conquest of Canada" as the initial objective. Niagara Falls gossip during the spring of 1812 allowed that war with Canada was just another of Congressman Porter's tricks to "get hold of the Queenston-Chippewa portage."

෴

FIFTEEN

"MR. MADISON'S WAR"

The War of 1812 was, emotionally, a resurgence of the American Revolution. Its land battles centered on Niagara because Clay, Calhoun, Porter, and an aggressive minority of Southerners and Westerners believed that most Canadians would welcome political union with the United States.

But American spies were inept, American commanding officers could neither agree nor command, and the predominant state militias still believed in state autonomy.

Thus, between August and mid-October 1812, the alertness of 40-year-old Isaac Brock of Guernsey enabled fifteen hundred Canadians and not more than seven hundred Indians to defeat two American armies—totalling ten thousand regulars, militia and Indians—take thirty-five hundred prisoners, and give all Canadians a new sense of national pride.

Isaac Brock was in the tradition of John Montresor and Frederick Haldimand. A descendant of the Sir Hugh Brock who migrated to Guernsey from Brittany about 1350, he followed two brothers into the army when, soon after his fifteenth birthday, his family purchased a commission for him in the Eighth (King's) Regiment. After service in Baltic and Holland campaigns against Napoleon and in Santo Domingo, he was assigned to Upper Canada during 1802 as Lieutenant-Colonel of the Forty-Ninth. His first crisis at Niagara occurred during the fall of 1803 when the garrison at Fort George mutinied against the "extreme rigour" of the discipline imposed by the fort's commander, Lieutenant Colonel Roger Hale Sheaffe.* Four of the mutineers were hanged.

Brock assumed the command at Fort George. He retained the personal command there through his promotions to Major General and Administrator of Upper Canada. Thus, while York became the official capital of Upper Canada, Newark and Fort George continued as the military headquarters.

Loyalist resentment of "Americans" still dominated the decisions of Upper Canada's Parliament. The campaigns against Ohio and Indiana Indian tribes by American expeditions out of Pittsburgh, Louisville and Cincinnati perpetuated the argument for an autonomous Indian Territory. The Loyalist fears were confirmed by Henry Clay, who boasted: "We have the Canadas as much under our command as Great Britain has the oceans; and the way to conquer her on the ocean is to drive her from the land;" and by William Eustis, the United States Secretary of War, who believed that, "We can take the Canadas without soldiers. We have only to send officers into the province and the people, disaffected towards their own government, will rally round our standard."

There were days when Isaac Brock would have agreed. Great Britain was locked in a death struggle with Napoleon. Of the five thousand British troops stationed throughout Upper and Lower Canada and the Maritimes, only 1,450 were in Upper Canada. Possibly eleven thousand militia could be raised. But more than forty thousand of the province's seventy thousand people were "late Loyalists," who had migrated up from the United States since 1790. Many of them were Quakers, Mennonites and other religious zealots forbidden to "bear arms." Thousands of others were "frontier hoboes" who came to Canada to obtain the government supplies given homesteaders and then moved on.

During 1810, General Brock began the organization of "flank companies" of forty men and a captain in each Upper Canada community. Like the Minute Men and Sons of Liberty organizations developed in New England during the 1770's, the flank companies served without pay, drilled six times a month, and were

* Born in Boston in 1763, Sheaffe too became a British "regular" at 15.

trained to operate as scouts and raiders against American invasion. By the spring of 1812, approximately fifteen hundred Upper Canadians served in flank companies.

The lack of Federal authority over the state militia, coupled with the Congress' delusions about Canada, prevented comparable military organization in western New York. Technically, General Henry Dearborn commanded United States military operations between Maine and Lake Erie. But Dearborn was 61 in 1812 and thoroughly confused by the political struggle between the antiwar Federalists of his native New England and the War Hawks of the south and west.

Stephen Van Rensselaer, eighth patroon of the huge Manor of Rensselaer in the Hudson-Schoharie valleys and a son-in-law of General Philip Schuyler, held the sociopolitical appointment of Major General of New York's 13,500 militia. Brigadier General William Wadsworth was his subcommander on the Niagara. By mid-summer, 1812, there were fifty-two hundred New York militia in camp between Fort Niagara and Lewiston. Most of them were six-month enlistees, hence due for discharge before Christmas. Their oath of allegiance pledged them to "defend the Sovereign State of New York," thus implying that they were not committed to military service outside the state.

Upriver from the New York militia camps, Brigadier General Alexander Smyth commanded 1,640 United States Army regulars and 250 United States Navy personnel at Black Rock and Buffalo. Smyth was a 47-year-old Irishman who had migrated to Virginia after the Revolution and become a lawyer. He had used political pressures to secure his Army appointment and had even less military training than Major General Van Rensselaer.

Two companies of artillery and three companies of infantry, all from the New York militia and all serving on six-month or one-year enlistments, comprised the garrison at Fort Niagara when the war began. The Canadians had moved all of the fort's guns across river to Fort George in 1796. Until spring 1812, only seven cannon had been sent uplake to replace them.

Morale was so low at the Fort and regulations so chaotic that an average of six court-martials a month were held in Sir William

Johnson's Council Room. The majority of the charges were "striking and abusing a superior officer" or "drunk and disorderly while on duty." The sentences ranged from "six cobs on the naked posterior," or "to wear a ball and chain for ten days," to "two weeks hard labor and no whiskey ration for a month."

On June 1, 1812, President James Madison read Congress the War Message that had been ghosted by Clay and Calhoun. The House debated until June 4, then approved a Declaration of War against Great Britain by a 79 to 49 vote. The Senate worried for another thirteen days, but approved on June 17 by a vote of 19 to 13. The formal announcement by the President on June 19 evoked slurring editorials against "Mr. Madison's War" in seaboard newspapers from the Penobscot to the Chesapeake and triggered riots in Boston, New York City and Baltimore.

General Brock first received the news on the afternoon of June 26 via special courier from John Jacob Astor, the New York City fur millionaire. Neither the War Department nor Albany had notified Major General Van Rensselaer. Thus Fort George was able to ferry in several more boatloads of the corn, wheat and beef that Brock's agents had purchased from New York traders.

A courier from Fort George delivered Astor's message to Lieutenant Colonel St. George at Fort Malden, opposite Detroit, on June 27.

Since June 1, General William Hull and four militia regiments had been building the United States' first fortified wagon road between the Ohio frontier and Detroit. The War Department sent its orders and announcement of the Declaration of War to General Hull by United States Mail, care of the Cleveland post office. The dispatch reached him on July 2, while his army was camped on the River Raisin, near the site of Monroe, Michigan. Hull reached Detroit on July 6 and learned that Upper Canada whaleboats from Fort Malden had captured the schooner, *Cuyahoga*, carrying all of his personal stores, clothing, official correspondence, and campaign plans.

Again, the military roads that had been built from 1792 to 1796 permitted General Brock and his staff to examine Hull's orders and campaign plans before they left Fort George for Detroit on July 27. The expedition totalled three hundred British regulars

and flank company militia. It reached Amherstburg on the Detroit River on August 14.

The American garrison at Mackinac had already surrendered.
Tecumseh, the Shawnee war chief, had arrived with seven hun-
dred warriors "to fight the Americans." But the total Upper Can-
ada force opposing General Hull's twenty-three hundred United
States Army regulars and militia was: 250 of the Forty-First Regi-
ment, 50 of the Royal Newfoundland, 30 Royal Artillery, 300
Upper Canada militia, and the 700 Indians, plus the sloop-of-war,
H.M.S. *Queen Charlotte,* and the armed brig, H.M.S. *Hunter.*

Yet Hull surrendered Detroit and all his troops on August 17.
Brock was back at Fort George by August 25. That week, the
New York militia lolled on the Niagara's bank to watch General
Hull and his army being escorted down the Upper Canada por-
tage toward prison camps at York, Kingston and Montreal.

They were forced to loll, and curse in helpless rage, because
General Dearborn had bumbled into an agreement with Sir
George Prevost, Governor General of Canada, to declare an armi-
stice. Typically, General Dearborn proclaimed the "cessation of
hostilities" on the Maine-to-Lake Erie front before receipt of the
United States War Department's decision and despite reports that
Brock had left Fort George for the Detroit-Malden battlefront.

Before dawn on October 8, Captain Jesse D. Elliott ended the
American apathy by capturing two Upper Canada ships, the brigs
Detroit and *Caledonia,* at anchor off Fort Erie. A naval officer,
Elliott had been assigned to Black Rock to develop a shipyard and
United States Navy fleet on the Upper Lakes. His first companies
of seamen from Philadelphia had reached Black Rock at noon
on October 7. He selected fifty of them, borrowed fifty Army
regulars from General Smyth, and put off from Buffalo Creek in
whaleboats at 1 A.M. on October 8. His hundred men stormed
the brigs about 3 A.M. and, as he reported to the Secretary of the
Navy on October 9,

> in the space of about ten minutes, I had the prisoners all secured,
> the top-sails sheeted home and the vessels underway.
>
> Unfortunately, the wind was not sufficiently strong to get me
> up against a rapid current, into the lake, where I had understood
> another armed vessel lay at anchor; and I was obliged to run

down the river, by the forts, under a heavy fire of round, grape and canister.

The *Caledonia* was brought in safely and beached at Black Rock. But the *Detroit* beached on Squaw Island and was temporarily abandoned. When a boatload of forty Upper Canadians from Fort Erie attempted to recapture the *Detroit,* an American artillery battery, commanded by Lieutenant Colonel Winfield Scott, opened fire, killed most of the boarding party, and demolished the ship.

Washington had countermanded General Dearborn's armistice agreement, so the state-of-war resumed along the Niagara on September 9. By October 7, the New York militia officers were reporting to General Van Rensselaer that "the men are so bored, they are threatening to desert." Van Rensselaer finally went to General Smyth's headquarters at Buffalo to suggest plans for a trans-Niagara offensive. But General Smyth was "too busy."

After Elliott's capture of the brigs, Van Rensselaer and his officers decided to undertake the invasion without the support of Smyth or his Army regulars.

The initial objective agreed upon was the Upper Canada batteries located atop the gorge bluff behind Queenston. This, the New Yorkers reasoned, would cut off the portage road and permit flanking operations against Forts Chippewa and George. The river is 1,250 feet wide and from two hundred to three hundred feet deep between Lewiston and Queenston. The Crawl-on-all-Fours ridge behind Lewiston continues behind Queenston as a steep bluff three hundred feet high.

A spy returned from Newark on October 10 with the report that General Brock "has gone off again to Detroit." General Van Rensselaer fixed the assault for 4 A.M. on October 11. He wrote in his October 14 report to General Dearborn:

> To avoid any embarrassment in crossing the river (which is here a sheet of violent eddies), experienced boatmen were procured to take the boats from the landing below to the place of embarkation. Lieut. Sim was considered the man of greatest skill for this service. He went ahead and in the extreme darkness,

passed the intended place far up the river, and there, in the most extraordinary manner, fastened his boat to the shore, and abandoned the detachment. In this front boat, he had carried nearly every oar, which was prepared for all the boats; in this agonizing dilemma stood officers and men, whose ardour had not been cooled by exposure, through the night, to one of the most tremendous N. East storms. . . . The approach of daylight extinguished every prospect of success.

The assault was rescheduled for dawn on October 13. A battalion of regulars marched in from Black Rock. The commanding officer offered them for the attack. Lieutenant Colonel Winfield Scott also sidestepped General Smyth's indifference by bringing down two 6-pounders from his "flying artillery" battery to support the crossing. Two flotillas of whaleboats, one with three hundred militia and the second with three hundred United States Army regulars, assembled for the initial crossing.

The assault began on schedule, and was promptly sighted by the Upper Canada batteries. At midstream, the lead boat of the flotilla holding the regulars lost headway and began to drift down toward Queenston. The other boats followed it. Captain John Beverly Robinson of the Upper Canada militia recalled:

Grape and musket shot poured upon the Americans. A single discharge from a brass six-pounder destroyed fifteen in a boat. Three of the *bateaux* landed below Mr. Hamilton's garden in Queenston, and were met by a party of militia and regulars, who slaughtered almost the whole of them, taking the rest prisoners. Several other boats were so shattered and disabled that the men in them threw down their arms and came on shore, merely to deliver themselves up as prisoners of war. As we advanced with our company, we met troops of Americans on their way to Fort George under guard . . . and suffering from wounds of all description.

The second flotilla pulled through the gunfire, reached the Upper Canada shore, then fought up a path to the top of the bluff and captured the battery there.

General Van Rensselaer joined the second crossing of boats. Lieutenant Colonel Scott, a redhead 6 feet 4 inches tall, turned the command of his guns over to an aide, stalked down the bank, and asked permission to "join the excitement." The two officers and another two hundred militia reached the captured battery, and discovered that more than half of the initial three hundred were casualties, including most of the officers.

"For some time after I passed over," Van Rensselaer said in his official report, "the victory appeared complete. . . . By this time I perceived my troops were embarking very slowly. I passed immediately over to accelerate their movements."

Typically, the American spy's October 10 information about Upper Canada's forces and General Brock's whereabouts was false. Brock was still at Fort George. The gunfire awakened him. He ordered Roger Hale Sheaffe, still his second in command, to march out with half the garrison troops and the flying artillery. Brock raced on ahead with his aide, Lieutenant Colonel MacDonell.

Two companies of the Forty-Ninth Regiment and approximately one hundred militia were at Queenston when they arrived. General Brock ordered an immediate assault against the Americans atop the bluff, then recklessly led the two hundred up the portage road. He was in field uniform; the morning sun shimmering on his shoulder epaulets made him a prime target. A bullet through the chest killed him almost instantly.

The Canadians retreated, carrying General Brock's body back to Queenston. Then Lieutenant Colonel MacDonell divided the command into two columns and stormed the bluff again. MacDonell was killed, and the charge was repulsed.

But another fifty Americans had been killed or wounded, and others had fled. By noon, only three hundred Americans defended the hilltop. Brigadier General Wadsworth, the senior officer, asked Lieutenant Colonel Scott to assume the command "because, Sir, you know best professionally what should be done."

No reinforcements had appeared at the blufftop for two hours. Scott could hear drums beating in Queenston and shouts of command. He ordered a squad to scout down the path toward the landing place and try to get an appeal for more troops over to General Van Rensselaer.

The scouts stared across the Niagara at General Van Rensselaer riding slowly through masses of New York militiamen. He was waving his sword at the Canadian shore. A few men moved forward, paused, glanced at their companions, then slouched back into the silent blue mass.

"I rode in all directions—urged men, by every consideration to pass over; but in vain," General Van Rensselaer admitted in his official report. "Lieut. Col. Bloom, who had been wounded in action, returned, mounted his horse, and rode through the camp; as did also Judge Peck, who happened to be here, exhorting the companies to proceed; but all in vain."

When General Van Rensselaer sheathed his sword, lowered his head, and walked his horse off toward Lewiston, the sergeant of Scott's detail kicked blindly at a tree, growled, "You bastards are on your own!" and started back up the hill. Most of the detail followed him.

Roger Hale Sheaffe brought 380 of the Forty-First Regiment and three hundred of the York Militia to reinforce the two hundred Canadians at Queenston. In mid-afternoon, 140 Indians and Negroes * from the Grand River filed in and volunteered to fight against the Americans.

Sheaffe deployed his nine hundred around three sides of the American position and, about 4 P.M., began the attack. The Canadian fire was so effective that Scott abandoned the hill and began a slow retreat to the river bank.

Hundreds of the New York militia peered around rocks on the American shore as Scott, Wadsworth and their men slid to the water's edge. Blood-flecked and splintered by Canadian musketballs, the boats strained at their mooring lines as though murmuring, "We'd come if we could!" But the American boatmen had fled. No one moved out from the rock and hummock shelters.

Scott continued the fight for another fifteen minutes. But the Indians were moving in. Half the powder horns were empty. General Wadsworth agreed that they should surrender. Scott sent

---

* Canadian records of the battle state that approximately fifty of the 140 volunteers from the Grand River reservation were ex-slaves who had fled the United States and had been given homesteads on the Grand River reservation.

a young officer down the slope toward Queenston, waving a white kerchief knotted to a musket. A musket blazed. An Indian ran out, slashed off the young officer's scalp, waved it at the American shore, and swaggered back into the forest.

Scott tied his kerchief on the point of his sword, ordered two captains to join him, and started down the river bank toward Queenston. Two Indians fired on them as they stepped out of the brush onto the portage road. The bullets went wild. The redmen started across the road with hatchets raised. Scott waved the kerchief and shouted, "We're surrendering." A Canadian officer shouted back. The Indians turned and stalked off.

During the next two hours, Scott, Wadsworth and the cluster of officers standing under guard at Queenston gaped as column after column of Americans shuffled down the portage road toward Fort George. The polite youngsters commanding their guard provided the explanation. Another five hundred Americans had walked out of the Queenston Heights forests after the Scott-Wadsworth surrender. Some claimed that, after crossing the Niagara, they had decided, "We never wanted to fight you folks, anyhow." Others protested that their officers had deserted them. (The official figures of the Battle of Queenston Heights indicate that ninety Americans were killed on the Heights and as many more on the river, and that nine hundred surrendered. The Canadian and Indian casualties totaled fewer than a hundred.)

The battle had not ended for Colonel Scott. That evening, soon after he and the officers had been escorted to a room at Fort George, two Indians pushed past the guards and demanded that Scott "show us your wounds." Scott recognized them as the pair who had fired at him on the portage road.

"You missed," Scott jeered, and spread his arms in evidence.

"We no miss now," the eldest Indian hissed, and swung back his tomahawk.

But the Canadian sentry bellowed, "Officer of the Guard!" then whirled, straight-armed one Indian against the wall, and seized the second one by the scalplock. Thus, within a three-hour period, Upper Canadians twice saved the life of the future General-in-Chief of the United States Army and conqueror of Mexico.

General Van Rensselaer ordered Fort Niagara to fire minute-gun memorial salutes the next day during General Brock's funeral. During the salutes, the weary patroon stood at full-dress attention on the west rampart. Then he shook hands with his staff, took a final salute at the Six Nations Gate, and began the week's ride to Albany to submit his resignation.

Alexander Smyth worked his way to the command of Niagara's Army of the Centre. He spent the first week of his promotion scrawling proclamations that sent ripples of "Goodgawdamighty" giggles along both banks of the river. "Hull and Van Rensselaer," Smyth wrote in one Order of the Day, "were merely popular persons destitute alike of theory and experience in the art of war. In a few days the men under my command will plant the American standard in Canada. They will conquer or die. Will you stand with your arms folded and look at this interesting struggle?"

Both regulars and militia stood with arms folded while October scarlet sombered to November tan and the first tinkle ice feathered the shallows. Smyth fixed three dates for the "invasion," and canceled all of them. A landing near Fort Erie was attempted on the night of November 28, but was repulsed, with eighty casualties. Before dawn on December 1, Smyth ordered fifteen hundred regulars and Pennsylvania militia into boats at Black Rock. Then he asked his officers for a vote of confidence. A few muttered, "No." He called off the attack.

Peter O. Porter had returned to the Niagara. During the afternoon of December 1, he wrote the War Department and described Smyth as "a damned coward." He read the letter to some fellow officers. Smyth challenged Porter to a duel. On December 3, Porter and Smyth were rowed out to Goat Island at the brink of the falls, with seconds and a physician. They fired, missed, shook hands, then returned together to Niagara Falls for a mid-morning pick-me-up.

But the War Department had had enough. Smyth was recalled and given an extended furlough "for personal reasons." The regulars went into winter quarters. The militia, save for three companies assigned to Fort Niagara, walked off home. American destiny prepared to focus on two men named Brown.

⌒〜☙◌〜⌒

SIXTEEN

THERE WERE THESE TWO MEN NAMED BROWN...

Soldiering, like farming, was a seasonal profession. During the spring, you drilled ... listened to speeches ... drilled ... repaired wagons and roads ... listened to more speeches. Through summer and fall, you marched ... fought dysentery and fever ... fought battles ... and, if your general was smart or lucky, looted and burned enemy homes. In the winter, you repaired gear and drilled while the generals and politicians defended their failures, then plotted new ways to get you killed next summer. This routine was more complex for the militiaman since, as a homesteader, he was also obligated to spring planting and fall harvesting.

The garrison troops retained at Fort Niagara, Niagara Falls and Buffalo during the winter of 1812–13 pursued the dull routine. The activity that would prove most significant to the next summer and fall battles centered at two wilderness outposts: Sackets Harbor, New York, and Erie, Pennsylvania.

Jacob Jennings Brown was the Brigadier General of New York Militia commanding the defenses of Sackets Harbor. Noah Brown —not even a remote cousin—was the master shipbuilder ordered in from the Brooklyn Navy Yard to build a United States Navy fleet behind the ruins of the *Belle Rivière* forts at Presque Isle.

Buffalo's settlers had cut a wagon track through the forests from Batavia to Buffalo Creek.* This became the principal route for supplies and troops. But Buffalo Creek was too shallow for

* The New York Central Railroad and the Thomas E. Dewey Thruway follow this route.

schooners or brigs. The nearest harbor down the American shore of Lake Erie was the bay behind the fishhook-shaped peninsula the French called Presque Isle.

On Lake Ontario, the vigorous development of forts and a shipyard at Kingston by the Upper Canadians caused Oswego to be rejected as a principal military base by the Americans. Carleton Island became a United States possession in 1796; but United States Navy officials rejected it, too. Instead, they chose the island-encircling protection of Sackets Harbor, forty miles northeast of Oswego and opposite Kingston, as the United States' principal naval base for Lake Ontario and the upper St. Lawrence.

The choice had been made during the spring of 1812, before the declaration of war. Jacob Brown and Lieutenant Melancthon Woolsey—just assigned to Lake Ontario from the U.S.S. *Constitution*—were responsible for the speedy construction of barracks, a shipyards, warehouses and redoubts. On July 19, Woolsey's cannoneers had fought off an attack by six Upper Canada ships out of Kingston. By September, General Brown was in Ogdensburg with four hundred militiamen, raiding Upper Canada shipping as far east as the La Chine Canal.

Jacob Jennings Brown, Winfield Scott and Andrew Jackson would prove to be the three most capable American military leaders of the War of 1812. Brown's death in 1828, after seven years as General-in-Chief of the United States Army, denied him the folk-hero acclaim accorded "Old Fuss and Feathers" Scott and "Old Hickory" Jackson. Consequently, too little is known about Brown's premilitary career.

Born to a Quaker household in Bucks County, Pennsylvania, during 1775, Brown obtained enough education to become a country school teacher before he was 20. He soon abandoned this to go to Ohio as a surveyor. But by 1799, he was on the headwaters of the Black River, seventy-five miles north of Fort Schuyler.* He became a real estate promoter, opened a feed store and by 1801 had developed a community large enough to be labeled "Brownsville" by the gazetteers.

* The village adjoining Fort Schuyler, then known as Lynchville, would incorporate in 1819 as Rome.

His success was implemented by a love for books and the friendships he won by quietly sharing the book learning with his patrons and neighbors. He subscribed to the publications of the agricultural societies in Philadelphia, New York City and Boston. Thus he became the North Country authority on Merino sheep, the radically new guano fertilizer, the Shaker and Quaker convictions about cover crops and "clean seeds," as well as the latest British theories on "horse-hoeing husbandry." In effect, he became the Black River valley's "County Agent."

By 1809, Brown was convinced that there would be another war with Great Britain. He began to organize militia units and to study military journals and books as assiduously as he had studied the publications "for the advancement of agriculture." Regional tradition reports that he went to New Haven to visit Eli Whitney, questioned him about his interchangeable-parts musket and then insisted that the North Country militia use it. He was just as firm in demands for state aid to build a military road up the Black River valley that would supplement the perilous Lake Oneida-Oswego-Lake Ontario route.

When the war did come, the North Country had the best militia units in the state. Even more important, its members respected "General Jake" and his decisions. The verve of the Brown militia was a boon to Henry Eckford and Commodore Isaac Chauncey.

A 40-year-old Connecticutman, Chauncey had achieved a commendable record aboard the U.S.S. *Constitution* during the Tripoli campaign and was a Captain at 34. He was Washington's choice to command the American fleets on the Great Lakes and upper St. Lawrence. Eckford was sent up from New York City during September with one hundred shipwrights to supervise the Sackets Harbor shipyard. Brown called for volunteers from the militia to become shipyard helpers during the winter. More than two hundred signed on. After October, the yard launched a fighting ship every six weeks. By April 1813, Commodore Chauncey's fleet consisted of the 593-ton frigate, *Madison,* eleven schooners and two transports. A 700-ton frigate, almost ready for launching, would be armed with twenty-eight "long twenty-fours."

Brown's militia brought the cannon, brass and canvas in, some by sledge up the Black River, some up the lakeshore from Oswego. More than nine hundred sailors were recruited for the Ontario fleet. The majority were "deep water" youngsters from Gloucester, Marblehead and other New England fishing towns.

But the Upper Canada shipyard at Kingston kept pace, ship for ship. Captain Sir James Yeo, a veteran of the Napoleonic Wars, reached Kingston during the late fall of 1812 to develop and command the Upper Canada fleets on the Great Lakes. By spring, 1813, his Ontario fleet included the 637-ton frigate, *Wolfe*, the smaller frigate, *Royal George*, seven brigs and schooners, and scores of gunboats and barges. On the planning boards were the specifications for the *St. Lawrence*, a 2300-ton three-decker that was to carry a hundred guns and a crew of 640 men.

The Upper Canada fleet on the Upper Lakes that spring totalled twenty fighting ships, including the 490-ton flagship, H.M.S. *Detroit*, and the 400-ton H.M.S. *Queen Charlotte*.

The only Americans ships above the falls were Captain Elliott's three schooners, a sloop, and a supply ship—all trapped at the Black Rock anchorage—and a few trading schooners and fishing boats at Erie, Cleveland and Sandusky.

Noah Brown snowshoed up the Joncaire-*Belle Rivière* trail from Pittsburgh during January. A native of Long Island born in 1769, he had signed on as a 15-year-old apprentice at the United States' new Brooklyn Navy Yard. He and his brother, Adam, became the Yard's most competent shipmasters. They designed and built the U.S.S. *New York* and repaired the U.S.S. *Chesapeake* after its piratic mauling by the H.M.S. *Leopard* off Hampton Roads on June 22, 1807.

Noah Brown, thus, was the Navy Department's choice to live up to his given name by creating a fleet of warships for the Upper Lakes. Pennsylvania had won a narrow foothold on Erie's south shore during the interstate wrangle over Royal Charter grants. It included the Presque Isle waterfront and the pony-portage route to Fort Le Boeuf and Venango. Quaker practicality gave the foothold's only settlement the name of Erie.

A sandbar across the mouth of Erie's harbor would protect the shipyard from attack by the Canadian fleet—but would force every large hull launched there to slither helplessly out to the lake sans guns or rigging. However, the shore was fragrant with white pine and hemlock, and there was a wealth of chestnut, oak and other virgin hardwoods on the hills toward French Creek.

The Erie site had been selected by Daniel Dobbins, a lakes trader who had lost his schooner, *Salina,* at the Canadian seizure of Mackinac, but who had escaped and, folklore says, was the first person to reach Washington with the details of Hull's surrender. He had the shipyard barracks built by the time Brown arrived and had located a Canadian schooner frozen in the ice a few miles uplake.

Brown wrote:

> We went out and boarded her. She provided us with twenty barrels of pork, and a quantity of rigging and cables. We got oakum from them and burned the schooner and got her iron. . . . I rode all around the neighboring towns and bought of all the merchants every bar of iron I could find. The Government was to send iron, pitch and oakum but the roads were so bad that I had almost finished the fleet before any arrived at Erie.

The nearest iron foundry fumed at Steubenville, an Ohio valley settlement fifty miles west of Pittsburgh. Its Yankee owners agreed to make cannonballs. But the gunpowder, like the cannon, had to be boated and wagoned in from Philadelphia.

About April 1, Master Commandant Oliver Hazard Perry and Brigadier General Zebulon Montgomery Pike reached Sackets Harbor with General Dearborn.*

Perry, the 28-year-old son of a Rhode Island United States Navy captain, was the Navy Department's choice as Chauncey's sub-commander on the Upper Lakes.

Zebulon Pike, at 34, was as famous as Meriwether Lewis and William Clark. Born near Trenton, New Jersey, he received an Army lieutenancy at 20, and when 26 was given the command

---

* Augustus J. Fisher, His Majesty's Minister at Washington until the outbreak of the war, described Dearborn as "a heavy unwieldy-looking man who . . . has apparently accepted his appointment with great reluctance. . . . His military reputation does not stand very high."

of an expedition to determine the source of the Mississippi River. His subsequent adventures during 1805 and 1806 provided the United States with its most pertinent information about the land that was to become Minnesota, Colorado, New Mexico and Texas. The tallest bluff on the upper Mississippi shore and the mightiest mountain of eastern Colorado both went on 1810 maps as "Pike's Peak." His imprisonment by New Spain's authorities at Sante Fe resulted in the first American negotiations with New Spain and the first American trade ventures along the Santa Fe Trail. Now, just promoted to Brigadier General, Pike was to command assaults against Kingston, York, Fort George and Fort Erie.

John Armstrong, the new U. S. Secretary of War, had approved a complicated campaign for the two thousand Army regulars who followed Dearborn and Pike to Sackets Harbor. If Noah Brown completed a fleet at Erie, and if Chauncey's ships and Pike's regulars captured the Upper Canada shore of the Niagara, and if Master Commandant Perry defeated the Upper Canada fleet on the Upper Lakes, General William Henry Harrison's Army of the West would attack Detroit.

Kingston was as critical to the defense of Upper Canada as its predecessor, Fort Frontenac (that is, Cataraqui) had been to New France.* The War Department had ordered it to be the first goal of the 1813 campaign. General Pike agreed, and devoted his final weeks in Washington to studies of the maps and reports available at the War Department and the Library of Congress.

But Commodore Chauncey was as timid as General Dearborn. They agreed that Kingston was "too strongly defended" and so tabled the War Department instructions and decided to attack York. On April 25, the American fleet of fourteen brigs and schooners, led by the U.S.S. *Madison*, cleared Sackets Harbor for York. Brigadier General Brown with five hundred Army regulars,

---

* The capture of Kingston, Admiral Alfred Thayer Mahan concluded in his work, *Sea Power in Its Relation to the War of 1812*, would have solved "at a single stroke every difficulty.... No other harbor was tenable as a naval station; with its fall and the destruction of shipping and forts, would go control of the lake, even if the place itself were not permanently held."

the North Country militia, and the shipyard crews, was left to defend Sackets Harbor, a six-hour sail across the St. Lawrence headwater from Kingston.

Chauncey's fleet crossed the lake in two days. Generals Dearborn and Pike chose a beach near the ruins of Fort Toronto, two miles from York, for the landing. The Canadians were waiting with a thousand regulars and militia and five hundred Indians. Major General Roger Hale Sheaffe, the martinet victor of Queenston Heights, was in command.

Covered by cannon fire from the fleet, Pike's regulars carried the beach and by 10 A.M. on April 27 had thrown back a weak counterattack and were unloading artillery.

Sheaffe abandoned York about noon but directed the main magazine of the fort to be fired. The explosion of the five hundred barrels of gunpowder killed or wounded forty Canadians and 260 Americans.

When the magazine burst, General Pike was sitting on a tree stump a quarter mile away interrogating a prisoner. A fragment of the magazine's rock wall broke his back and punctured his lungs. He died an hour later.

No effort was made to pursue Sheaffe's troops. The Americans dallied at York for twelve days. Patrols were casual. Homes and public buildings were looted. The Upper Canada Parliament buildings were fired "by persons unknown" and burned to the ground. Finally on May 11 the expedition sailed back to Sackets Harbor, carefully avoiding Kingston.

General Pike was buried at the edge of the militia drill-ground.* Commodore Chauncey wrote the Navy Department for permission to name the new frigate, still on the ways, U.S.S. *General Pike*. Reinforcements and supplies arrived from Albany. On May 22, the fleet sailed west again. But this time it was observed by Upper Canada patrol boats out of Kingston.

Oliver Hazard Perry reached Fort Niagara on May 24 or 25 after a hurried trip to the Brown-Dobbin shipyard at Erie. Two

---

* Pike's grave is in the Old Military Cemetery, Broad Street, Sackets Harbor, eight miles west of Watertown off Interstate Highway 81.

480-ton brigs had already been launched at Erie and three schooners were on the ways.

Winfield Scott was back at Fort Niagara, too. He had reached Boston on a prisoners' exchange during January. The War Department promoted him to full Colonel and assigned him to General Dearborn's staff as Adjutant General.

"The winds being light from the westward, I did not arrive in the vicinity of Niagara before the 25th," Commodore Chauncey reported. "The other parts of the squadron had arrived . . . and landed their troops. . . . I immediately had an interview with General Dearborn for the purpose of making arrangements to attack the enemy." Thus, presumably, in the same House of Peace council room that had been used by the Joncaires, Captain Pouchot, Sir William Johnson, the Brants and the Butlers, the campaign for another conquest of the Niagara was detailed during the evening of May 25.

Chauncey's fleet crossed the mouth of the Niagara between 3 and 4 A.M. on May 26. "It being, however, nearly calm," Chauncey told, "the schooners were obliged to sweep into their positions." The transports anchored off Mississauga Point, a half mile north of Newark. Adjutant General Scott commanded the landing.

While Scott's regulars scrambled down the netting into the whaleboats, another ship climb was underway at Kingston. Governor Prevost and Sir James Yeo watched 750 Upper Canada troops come aboard for an attack on Sackets Harbor.

By sunup on May 27, the Americans had secured a beachhead at Mississauga. The Canadians, totaling fifteen hundred, established a defense line along the bluff. The first American charge was repulsed. The second assault, led by Scott, received a better supporting fire from the fleet. It broke through the ends of the Canadian line, turned it, then rushed on through Newark toward Fort George.

Fort Niagara and Fort George were bombarding each other with hot shot. As the musketfire moved toward Newark, Fort Niagara shifted its gun range south of George to the Canadian portage road, to harass Canadian reinforcements from Queenston.

The colonel commanding Fort George was killed. His staff ordered the fort abandoned, but had fuses laid to the three powder magazines.

The main magazine exploded just as the American advance reached the gate. Scott was thrown to the ground by the concussion. He limped into the fort and hauled down its flag while two of his captains stamped out the matches hissing toward the other magazines.

"The difference in our loss with that of the enemy is astonishing," General Dearborn told Washington. "We had 17 killed and 45 wounded. The enemy had 90 killed and 160 wounded. We have taken 100 prisoners, exclusive of the wounded."

Scott started a pursuit of the Canadians along the lake ridge. Dearborn's aides ordered him back. But Major General Sheaffe simplified the Niagara conquest. He had been en route from Kingston with three hundred reinforcements for Fort George. On the morning of May 28, he ordered Forts Chippewa and Erie abandoned, and their magazines exploded. The American troops marched in that evening. Thus the Upper Niagara's cordell-way opened for the American fighting ships at Black Rock.

But destruction of the Ontario fleet's home base had confronted Jacob Brown at Sackets Harbor, ever since the afternoon of May 27. Lookouts on Garden Island and Stony Point first sighted the Kingston fleet bearing in. Brown's network of warning guns barked all down the Black River valley. But it would take the militia twenty-four hours to march in.

Then the wind veered. It puffed offshore breezes so persistently all that night and throughout May 28 that the Canadian frigates could not come in close enough to deliver a barrage during a troop landing.

Brown wrote in his June 1 report:

> During the 28th and 29th ult., a considerable militia force came in and was ordered to the waterside, near Horse Island. Our strength at this point was now 500 men, all anxious for battle, as far as profession would go. The moment it was light enough to discover the approach of the enemy [on May 29], we found his ships in line, between Horse-Island and Stoney-Point and, in a

few minutes afterwards, 33 large boats, filled with troops, came off to the larger Indian or Garden-Island, under cover of the fire of his gunboats.

My orders were that the troops should lie close and reserve their fire, until the enemy had approached so that every shot might hit its object. It is however impossible to execute such orders with raw troops unaccustomed to subordination. My orders were, in this case, disobeyed. The whole line fired, and not without effect. But, in the moment while I was contemplating this, to my utter astonishment, they rose from their cover and fled. Col. Mills fell gallantly, in brave, but vain endeavors to stop his men. I was, personally, more fortunate:—gathering together about 100 militia, we threw ourselves on the rear of the enemy's left flank.

At the same moment, an American brigade of Light Dragoons launched a screaming charge against the opposite end of the Canadians' beachhead. They broke through and, leaving their colonel dead on the shore, slashed on.

Sir George Prevost had just landed. He saw the Dragoons breaking in on his left and Brown's militia charging recklessly toward his right. He concluded that a large force of Americans must still be in reserve and ordered a retreat to the boats. He led the way.

But Sackets Harbor's defenders were too busy to gloat. Having seen the militia fleeing, a young Navy lieutenant decided the battle was lost and so set fire to the warehouses and shipyard. He was a competent arsonist. Only a third of the supplies could be carried out of the warehouses before on the flames he had started collapsed them. It took two hundred men in bucket-and-broom brigades to douse the fires he set in the U.S.S. *General Pike*.

General Brown reported:

> After having re-embarked, they sent me a flag, desiring to have their killed and wounded attended to. I made them satisfied on that subject.... Americans will be distinguished for humanity and bravery.... Our loss in the above action was 154 killed, wounded and missing. The enemy's loss, according to his own account, in killed and wounded, was 150.

Commodore Chauncey and most of the American fleet returned to Sackets Harbor thirty-six hours after the battle. The Canadian fleet was safely back at Kingston. Chauncey decided the Kingston forts were too strong to attack "until the *General Pike* is finished." He resumed patrols along the American shore. By mid-June, Prevost and Yeo had decided it would be safe to send part of the Kingston troops to reinforce Sheaffe's army on Burlington Heights, twenty miles west of the Niagara.

On June 1, the day that Commodore Chauncey learned how Jacob Brown and the Light Dragoons had saved Sackets Harbor, Noah Brown supervised the Upper Niagara cordell that brought the first American fighting ships into Lake Erie. Captain Elliott had built or refitted five ships at the Black Rock yards: two schooners, *Somers* and *Tigress;* the 60-ton sloop *Trippe;* a supply ship, *Ohio,* and the *Caledonia* captured during the October dawn raid off Fort Erie. Adjutant General Scott assigned two hundred infantrymen aboard the vessels to serve as firepower against a surprise attack by the Canadians. Troops and flying artillery were stationed along the cordell-way, too. Ox teams did the hauling chore against the three-knot current. By dusk on June 1, the fleet was at anchor off Buffalo Creek.

But lookouts up Erie relayed a warning that H.M.S. *Detroit* and H.M.S. *Queen Charlotte* were cruising nearby. Master Commandant Perry ordered the decks cleared for action, then asked Scott to assign the two hundred infantrymen as marines for any fight that might develop during the run to Presque Isle.

The offshore breeze of May 27 to May 29 had given Jacob Brown enough time to assemble the North Country militia. A ground fog slithered down Erie on June 8 to offer a cloak for the escape of Perry's fleet to Presque Isle. With leadsmen chanting "the twain" in each bow, the five ships crept along the shoreline. Soon after dawn, they slithered over the sandbar to the protection of the Erie Navy Yard's batteries.

"Perry's Luck" became a byword that spread up the lake during the next two months to hearten the thirty-five hundred Kentuckians and Ohioans being assembled by General Harrison at Sandusky. On July 9, Canadian raiders crossed the Upper Niagara, captured and burned Fort Schlosser and the Black Rock Navy Yard, then fled back to the Beaver Dams Camp. On July 20 and 21, the H.M.S. *Detroit,* H.M.S. *Queen Charlotte* and several schooners veered in toward Presque Isle, anchored a mile off the sandbar, stayed for twenty-four hours, then sailed west without firing a shot.

The seven ships and squadron of whaleboats Noah Brown's workmen had created from Presque Isle and French Creek trees since February were almost ready for battle by mid-July. But the sandbar blocked the way for the U.S.S. *Lawrence* and U.S.S. *Niagara.* It was a drought summer. Only six feet of water covered the sandbar. The schooners and sloops could slip over it, but the *Lawrence* and *Niagara* were 480-ton brigs; each drew ten feet.

Noah Brown was as deft with wood and water as Jacob Brown was with farms and militia. When morning wind sniffs and bedtime taps on the barometer failed to reveal a "wet spell" growling down the lakes, he ordered the construction of two gawky scows. Each was to be 50 feet long, 10 feet wide and 8 feet deep.

When Brown explained the scows' purpose to Perry, the Master Commandant agreed to take the risk of mounting the cannon and loading stores on the *Lawrence* and the *Niagara* after the sandbar had been crossed.

The experiment began on August 5. The *Lawrence* was towed out to the edge of the bar. The scows were towed alongside. Then water was pumped in until the scows were barely afloat. Oak beams long enough to serve as supporting booms extended out of the *Lawrence's* gunports. They were attached to uprights pegged into the scows' floors. Finally, divers passed hemp cables under the *Lawrence* and lashed them on the scows' uprights.

The schooners, gunboats and whaleboats of Perry's fleet crossed the bar that night and formed into a defense line. Sloops scouted east and west. When the signal flags gave an "All Clear," Noah Brown sent bucket brigades into the scows. Heave by heave the bail-out began.

The support beams creaked and groaned. One stanchion split with a musketlike "bang" but held firm. Inch by inch, the emptying scows buoyed the *Lawrence's* hull. When the final buckets of water sloshed over the sides of the scows, more than four feet of the *Lawrence* hull sheathing was sun drying.

Whaleboats tied on and began the meticulous pull over the bar. By dusk, the *Lawrence* floated again, her guns were being rafted out, and Noah Brown's scows were headed back over the bar to repeat the trick with the *Niagara*.

If Commodore Chauncey and the American generals of the Ontario-St. Lawrence front had displayed the ingenuity and courage of Noah Brown and Oliver Hazard Perry, Upper Canada and Montreal could have been conquered before snowfall.

Perry's victory over the Canadian fleet at Put-in-Bay, off Sandusky, on September 10 caused Canada's Major General Henry A. Procter to order the forts and warehouses at Detroit and Malden to be burned and his force of twenty-five hundred to retreat up the Thames valley toward York and Kingston. Tecumseh opposed the flight, called Procter "a fat dog, with tail dropped between your legs," and demanded the "right to defend our lands." The opportunity came sixty miles up the Thames on October 5, when Harrison's brigades of mounted riflemen closed in. Tecumseh and his Shawnee warriors stood valiantly. Tecumseh was killed. Procter abandoned his troops and fled by wagon to Kingston.

By November most of Harrison's troops were home again, working from dawn to dusk to catch up with the wheat flailing, the corn husking, and the "hawg-butcherin'." Four of Perry's ships were being ogled by sightseers at Black Rock. Noah Brown and his crew of Erie stalwarts were rebuilding the Black Rock Navy Yard.

The War Department finally recommended Jacob Brown's promotion to Major General in the United States Army. General Dearborn had retired. Secretary Armstrong believed that "the Fighting Quaker" of Sackets Harbor was the best officer available to command the Ontario-Niagara front.

General Brown's appointment was approved on January 1, 1814, but by that time there were no American forts on the Niagara.

SEVENTEEN

STALEMATE

"Gen. Dearborn, from indisposition, has resigned his command, not only of the Niagara army but of the district," Major General Morgan Lewis wrote from Fort Niagara on June 14, 1813. "I have doubts whether he will ever again be fit for service. He has been repeatedly in a state of convalescence, but relapses on the least agitation of mind."

The description of the aged commander's condition was equally apt for the United States' Niagara army. It, too, was "repeatedly in a state of convalescence" and relapsed on "the least agitation of mind." Incompetent officers, inept militia, the British blockade of the United States' Atlantic seaboard and New England's threat to "secede from the Union" *—all these contributed to the apathy that enabled fewer than a thousand Canadians and Indians to devastate and reconquer all of Thundergate during the last two weeks of 1813.

General Lewis, too, was a product of the system that permitted politicians to reward exofficeholders, patroons, and status-hungry merchants with important posts in the United States Army or the state militia. He was another General Van Rensselaer. A 59-year-old attorney, married to a daughter of Robert R. Livingston,

---

* The United States symbol of "Uncle Sam" was born during 1813 as a Boston newspaper's cartoon sneer at the "bureaucratic dictatorship" of President Madison and the War Hawks. The prototype for Uncle Sam was Samuel Wilson, the Troy, New York, meat packer who provisioned beef and pork to the New York militia. His "U.S." stamp on meat barrels caused mess sergeants to nickname it "Uncle Sam's horsemeat."

Lewis had served as New York's attorney general, as chief justice of the state supreme court, and as a one-term governor. The George, James and DeWitt Clinton faction outsmarted him in 1806 and 1807 and ended his political career. He had been rewarded with the major generalship in the state militia. Thus, as the ranking officer at Niagara, he became the acting commanding general when General Dearborn's illness became senility.

Washington approval of General Dearborn's retirement did not reach Fort Niagara until July 6. By that time, General Lewis' naïveté and Commodore Chauncey's timidity were responsible for two serious American defeats. On June 2 or 3, an American column belatedly went out to hunt down the Canadians who had abandoned Fort George. But it was trapped at Stoney Creek, five miles from the site of Hamilton, Ontario, between Canadian militia and ships from the Kingston fleet. Its commanding officers, fifty men, and all of the supplies were captured.

On June 24, an attack against the Canadians entrenched at Beaver Dams was ambushed. Lieutenant Colonel Boerstler, the American commander, too promptly surrendered his 570 men and flying artillery.*

The order that approved General Dearborn's retirement on July 6 gave the Niagara command to Brigadier General John P. Boyd. A veteran of the Revolution who subsequently served as a mercenary with the British in India then became one of Harrison's aides at Tippecanoe, Boyd was as conservative as General Dearborn and as timid as Commodore Chauncey. His orders veered the Niagara troops from offense to dull defense. The Canadian

---

* The Beaver Dams victory created Canada's heroine-myth about Mrs. Laura Secord of Queenston Heights. Mrs. Secord walked twenty miles through the woods to warn the Canadians that Boerstler's raiders were on the way. Evidence indicates that other Canadian spies had preceded her, and the ambush was already planned. But there is pert significance in Mrs. Secord's act. She was a "Late Loyalist" who had moved to Upper Canada in 1793 from Massachusetts, thus was one of the "American immigrants" that Henry Clay and the War Hawks believed "would welcome release from British tyranny." Her husband was wounded at the defense of Queenston on October 13, 1812. American soldiers had looted her home during May, 1813.

raids on Fort Schlosser and Black Rock during July were undertaken because the Canadian command knew Boyd's policy and
reputation.

Commodore Chauncey ventured uplake again during late July.
He took Adjutant General Scott and two brigades aboard for
raids against the Canadians at Burlington Heights. The fleet anchored in Burlington Bay on July 29 and sent scouts ashore. They
reported that "between 600 and 800 of the enemy are posted upon
a peninsula of very high ground, strongly entrenched and defended by about eight pieces of cannon."

This was too much for Chauncey. He had only two frigates,
four schooners, a brig, 250 infantrymen, a company of artillery
and 200 marines. He scuttled off to York. Most of York's troops
were en route to Burlington Heights. He ordered the public store-
houses plundered again, and had the eleven boats in the harbor
sunk and the barracks and warehouses burned. Then, after landing Scott and the troops at Niagara, he hurried back to the protection of the North Country militia at Sackets Harbor.

During September one of the most infamous officers in the history of the United States Army arrived at Niagara to organize
another "Montreal by Christmas" expedition. James Wilkinson
had engaged in treasonable political intrigue ever since, as secretary of the Board of War, he joined the Conway Cabal against
George Washington. He had been an intimate of Aaron Burr and
narrowly escaped indictment at Burr's trial for treason. His most
recent court-martial had been ordered by President Madison during July 1811. Yet, in 1813, he was promoted to Major General,
then ordered to Niagara to organize and command an army of
eight thousand for "the conquest of Canada."

The arrival of Wilkinson and thousands of troops, followed by
news of Procter's defeat and Tecumseh's death on the Thames,
caused the Canadians to withdraw toward Kingston and prepare
for the long-expected attack there. Even Winfield Scott was taken
in by this. On October 11 he wrote:

> The enemy has treated me with neglect . . . and has abandoned
> the whole peninsula. They burnt everything in the store in this

neighborhood:—3,000 blankets, many hundred stand of arms; also the blankets in men's packs, and every article of clothing not in actual use.

General Boyd, Scott, and the Army regulars on the Niagara left to join Wilkinson's St. Lawrence valley fiasco on October 11. The Niagara command fell to Brigadier General George McClure of the New York militia.

McClure promptly ran into the States' Rights bugaboo when most of the militia at Fort Niagara refused to cross the river and "serve in a foreign land." Anyway, their pay was three-months overdue and their enlistments expired on December 10. The ration meats were maggoty. Their officers were ordering court-martials for minor rule breaking. So many supplies were stored at the two forts that most of the barracks had to be used as ware-houses and two hundred militiamen were forced to live in tents.

Wilkinson listened too well to Chauncey and by-passed King-ston. His incompetence at the Battle of Crysler's Farm on No-vember 11 hamstrung the drive against Montreal. Similar timidity and slipshod strategy had already stalled the American army General Wade Hampton commanded on Lake Champlain. A few days after the Crysler's Farm battle, the Canadian command sent one thousand regulars and militia uplake to attack McClure's command on the Niagara.

McClure blew it. After dinner time on December 10, he sent patrols to each of the eighty homes in Newark. Everybody was to be out of town within two hours! All buildings would be burned. The thermometers stood at 15 degrees that evening, and were dropping.

Some refused to believe the order until the Fort George maga-zines exploded and walls of flame crackled up at the end of the street. Most of the four hundred residents found shelter at Queenston and St. David's. Lewiston families sent boats across the Niagara with offers of shelter and hot food. Messengers galloped to Black Rock and Buffalo to bring doctors for the scores suffering from frostbite and shock. A delegation of Buffalo and Black Rock merchants and militia, led by Peter Porter, rode into Fort Niagara the next afternoon to demand an explanation and plan a defense against the retaliation certain to follow.

But McClure had fled that morning. His excuse was that he was going downlake to "raise recruits." The news of his cowardice preceded him. At Batavia and along the Genesee, women screamed, "Shoot him, damn him! Shoot him! ! !"

Civilian anger against McClure was shared by the militia. When their enlistment time ended, the paymaster admitted that he had only enough currency on hand to cover one of the three-months wages due them. He offered a bounty for reenlistments. But, the reports to the War Department say, "the militia . . . became a disaffected and ungovernable multitude. . . . A very inconsiderable number were willing to engage for a further term of service on any conditions."

Between 250 and 300 of the Niagara garrison packed their duffels and walked off toward home during December 11 and 12. There was validity, then, for McClure's ride east to "recruit." By the night of December 12, Captain Nathaniel Leonard, the acting commandant, had four hundred privates, nine lieutenants, two ensigns and a surgeon left in the garrison. Leonard was an artilleryman and was more concerned about the "two hours of practice daily" for his cannon than he was about sentry duty or patrols along the portage road.

When word of McClure's action reached Washington, Secretary of War Armstrong sent an abject apology to Sir George Prevost, alleging that Newark's burnout had been "unauthorized by the American government and abhorrent to every American feeling." But neither Prevost nor the British War Office believed Armstrong. The burning of the United States Capitol, the White House, and other government properties on August 24, 1814, was Great Britain's meticulously planned retaliation for York and Newark.

Between 1 and 2 A.M. on December 18, boats with muffled oars carried six hundred Canadians across the Niagara to the shore of Five Mile Meadow, between *La Belle Famille*'s forest and Lewiston. Upstream at Queenston, another four hundred with several detachments from the Grand River reservation, crouched

waiting for General Phineas Riall's command to take to the boats
and invade Lewiston.

Colonel John Murray had planned the attack and proposed it to
Lieutenant General Sir Gordon Drummond, the new commander-
in-chief of Upper Canada. Drummond's only change was to order
that Fort Niagara be taken "by the bayonet" and without quarter.
The thermometers had dropped to zero. A stiff wind out of the
west magnified the thunder of the falls.

Captain Leonard lived at Five Mile Meadow and was at home
and asleep. Two American gun batteries, aimed at Fort George,
were located at *La Belle Famille*. But the crews were asleep in
their log cabins, and the sentries, too, had come in "out of that
danged wind." A light still flickered at a tavern in Youngstown,
where four lieutenants from the Fort were intent on alleviating
the short-pay distress by means of a whist game.

The Canadians' massacre of the gun crews at *La Belle Famille*
was as methodical as a November pigsticking. At Youngstown,
folklore favors a grim pun as the only anecdote of the night.
After the tavern was surrounded, the anecdote alleges, Colonel
Murray and several of his aides tiptoed through the front door
and listened long enough to catch the yawning conversation at
the whist game. When one of the players muttered, "What's
trump?", Colonel Murray shouted, "Bayonets are trump!" and led
the charge into the room. (This anecdote neglects the fact that
the stabbings were delayed long enough for Murray to offer "safe
conduct" to anyone who would reveal the night's password at
Fort Niagara. One of the lieutenants blurted it, and was given
parole; so—as an officer and a gentleman—he dined at the officers' mess and played whist with the Fort George subalterns for
the rest of the winter. The other whist players were gutted in
their chairs.)

The change of guards at the Six Nations Gate was scheduled
for 4 A.M. As relief sentries marched up, Colonel Murray appeared, hiccoughed, mumbled the password, and gave the name
of one of the whist players. A sergeant growled a sarcasm about
"all night horsin' around!" then saluted and stepped back. Murray's sword split his windpipe. The Canadians raced in, stabbing.

The sentries on the walls got in a few volleys. They killed six and wounded five of the ghostlike figures charging across the parade ground. The signal that was to warn Lewiston was fired, but the wind off the falls drowned its echo over the seven miles. The signal rockets for General Riall burst above the river before 5 A.M. A dawn count totalled sixty-five American dead, fourteen wounded, and 344 prisoners. The loot count took days. More than four thousand muskets and sidearms were cached in the barracks warehouses, along with seven thousand pairs of shoes, roomsful of blankets and overcoats, rum, wine, salted and smoked meats, cheese and flour. General Drummond's quartermasters estimated its value at £200,000.

Riall's column crossed to Lewiston about dawn. He fired Lewiston, marched unopposed up the portage road to Niagara Falls, set the village afire, chased the garrison out of Fort Schlosser after a volley or two, doubled back to let the Indians burn and plunder the shack settlement on the Tuscarora reservation, and was back at Fort George for a late dinner. On December 29, his troops rowed to Black Rock, led a march on Buffalo, routed the militia there in a fifteen-minute skirmish and fired the town. Then General Riall let the troops and Indians relax in a night of drunken plunder.*

Colonel Lewis Cass led a scout downlake from Erie, Pennsylvania, about January 8 and prepared a report to the War Department that is the most coherent contemporary one about the Murray-Riall conquest. On January 12 he wrote:

> The fall of Niagara has been owing to the most criminal negligence. The force in it was fully competent to its defense. The

---

* Jonas Harrison, U.S. Collector of Customs for the District of Niagara, lived at Lewiston. He and his family fled to Batavia with other Lewiston refugees. From Batavia he wrote Samuel H. Smith, U.S. Commissioner of Customs, a letter alleging the "indiscriminate slaughter of men, women and children." In a December 31 letter to Richard Rush, U.S. Comptroller of the Treasury, Harrison claimed that Lewiston was littered with "bodies with their heads cut off, their bodies torn open and their hearts taken out—some scalped, some not." Commenting on the Harrison letters in 1885, Peter Porter's son, John, wryly observed, "There were only two people killed at Lewiston, both men. One of them a Dr. Alvord and the other was a Gillet."

conduct [of the officers] ought to be strictly investigated. The force of the enemy [at Lewiston, Black Rock and Buffalo] has been greatly magnified. From the most careful examination, I am satisfied that not more than 650 of regulars, militia and Indians landed. To oppose these, we had from 2,500 to 3,000 militia. All except a very few of them, behaved in the most cowardly manner. They fled without discharging a musket. The enemy continued on this side of the river until Saturday. All their movements betrayed symptoms of apprehension. A vast quantity of property was left in the town uninjured. Since Jan. 1, they have made no movement. They continue to possess Fort Niagara.

Buffalo's Orsamus Turner recalled, from the distortion-fraught viewpoint of the 1830's:

stirring and diversified scenes of flight and refuge. . . . During the latter part of the 30th, and forenoon of the 31st, the road from Willink to Turners Corners in Sheldon presented one continuous column of retreating soldiers, men, women and children from Buffalo, families from the settlements in all the southern portion of what is now Erie County, and the Indians en masse from the Buffalo Reservation. . . . Bread, meats and drinks soon vanished from the log taverns on the routes. . . . It was a crisis of suffering and privation; a winter of gloom and despondency. Language at this distant day is inadequate to enable the reader to fully realize the then condition of the Holland Purchase. Throughout all the back settlements, there were the half deserted neighborhoods; the solitary log house, no smoke rising from its stick chimney; cattle, sheep and swine hovering around and looking in vain for some one to deal out their accustomed food.

When Major General Jacob Brown brought forty-five hundred United States regulars and state militia back to the Niagara in March 1814, he used the Rochester-Batavia-Buffalo road and established his base camp at Buffalo. Winfield Scott returned, too, newly promoted to Brigadier General. Jacob Brown sized a man up as thoroughly as he graded horses and seed corn. He decided Scott was the best tactician on the Lakes and told him to drill the men for three months. By July 1, Scott had bunioned and blistered the forty-five hundred into the best American army since 1783.

Brown's campaign plans were as thorough as Scott's drills. General George Izard, Brown's successor at Sackets Harbor, was to seize both shores of the St. Lawrence and blockade traffic between Montreal and Lake Ontario. If Commodore Chauncey could defer his peek-a-boo game with the Kingston fleet, he was to ferry supplies uplake and bombard Forts Niagara and George. Then the forty-five hundred at Buffalo would gun down the Canadian portage toward an August recapture of Forts Niagara and George and—at long last—a shore assault against Kingston.

Scott opened the campaign on July 3 by recapturing Fort Erie. The next morning—the forty-ninth Independence Day—he led thirteen hundred gray-clad regulars against the twenty-one hundred Canadians and Indians General Riall had entrenched along the Chippewa. Scott's training and crisp control produced such a classic victory during the next five hours that the War Department ordered the gray uniform worn by "the victors of Chippewa" to become the standard uniform for cadets at the new United States Military Academy at West Point. Maneuvering like automatons, the regulars poured volleys into Riall's line at sixty paces, switched to bayonets, and took the Canadian trenches. Riall left 515 dead and wounded on the field, and retreated all the way to Fort George.

On July 5, Brown's army advanced to Queenston. Messengers hurried uplake with a letter to Commodore Chauncey. "I do not doubt my ability to meet the enemy in the field and march in any direction over his country, your fleet carrying for me the necessary supplies," General Brown pleaded. "We can threaten Forts George and Niagara and carry Burlington Heights and York and proceed direct to Kingston and carry that place. For God's sake, let me see you."

A week passed.

Two weeks passed. Scouts reported that General Drummond had reached Fort George with thousands of reinforcements. The Americans fell back to the Chippewa. Then, on July 22, a letter arrived from Chauncey. "I shall afford every assistance in my power to cooperate with the army," it wheedled, "whenever it can be done without losing sight of the great object for the attainment of which this fleet has been created—the capture or destruction of the enemy's fleet. But I shall not be diverted from my efforts to effectuate it by any sinister attempt to render us subordinate to, or an appendage of, the army."

A raid back toward Queenston, commanded by Scott, on July 25 grew into the bloodiest battle of the war. The main armies, each with about three thousand men, met at Lundy's Lane, a half mile east of the falls, forty minutes before sunset. They fought until midnight.

Both Scott and Brown were wounded and carried back to Buffalo. General Drummond was wounded. Riall was wounded and captured. Bewildered without the leadership of Brown or Scott, the Americans retired to Fort Erie. The Canadians were too battered and weary to follow. Each army had lost nearly a third of its command: 860 for the Americans, 878 for the Canadians.

The wounds received by Jacob Brown and Winfield Scott were critical. Both were out of the war. General Izard succeeded to the Niagara command. Commodore Chauncey finally consented to carry him and three thousand reinforcements up lake as far as Irondequoit Bay. But the march from Irondequoit to Buffalo gave Drummond's Canadians time for a series of attacks against Fort Erie. Their attack on the night of August 15 took one of the Erie bastions.

Lieutenant Patrick MacDonogh, wounded in the bastion's defense, crawled unnoticed across the floor to an ammunition chest, opened it, and fired his pistol into it. The explosion killed or wounded more than three hundred Canadians and gave the Americans time to rally. When the battle ended, 539 Canadians were prisoners. MacDonogh's martyrdom was never acknowledged by the War Department.

George Izard, son of the South Carolina diplomat and United States Senator, Ralph Izard, had attended military schools in England, Germany and France and was as competent as Jacob Brown.

He attempted to follow Brown's campaign plan. During September and October, his reinforcements pushed the Canadians back to Queenston. Izard, too, appealed to Commodore Chauncey to come uplake and besiege Forts George and Niagara.

But Sir George Prevost was in the upper St. Lawrence valley with eleven thousand of Wellington's veterans. So, despite Prevost's cowardly retreat after Commodore Thomas Macdonough's naval victory at Plattsburg on September 11, Chauncey again refused to sail his fleet up the lake.

But Sir James Yeo brought the Canadian fleet out of Kingston and anchored it off the Niagara's mouth in support of Drummond's defense.

Still, Chauncey held to routine patrols between Oswego and the Thousand Islands. He carefully avoided Kingston.

On November 5, Izard ordered Fort Erie blown up and withdrew all of the American troops to Black Rock and Buffalo. When word came that the Treaty of Ghent had ended the war on Christmas Eve, he resigned from the Army.

Thus, save for the Canadians' tenuous occupation of Fort Niagara and Lewiston, the War of 1812 ended in a stalemate at Thundergate. Yet the import of its battles and the achievements directed by Noah Brown, Jacob Brown, Oliver Hazard Perry and Winfield Scott were vast. American control of the Upper Lakes counteracted the success of Great Britain's blockade and the easy razing of Washington, D.C.

So the Treaty of Ghent agreed that the Great Lakes should remain a freeway for both the United States and Great Britain, and that the 1783 boundaries would be restored. The Rush-Bagot Treaty, signed two years later, ruled that naval operations on the Great Lakes were restricted to "police action."

Consequently, the battlegrounds of Thundergate tested and tempered military leadership for the United States' 1820 to 1849 "march to the Pacific." When the War of 1812 began, Fort Dearborn—puny namesake of General Dearborn—was the westernmost fort in the United States north of St. Louis. But during the 1820's, Henry Leavenworth—one of Winfield Scott's aides at Chippewa and Lundy's Lane—built Fort Leavenworth on the middle Missouri and Fort Snelling near the site of Minneapolis-St. Paul, Minnesota. William J. Worth—Scott's aide-de-camp at Chippewa and Lundy's Lane—gave his name to Fort Worth, Texas. Jacob Brown, as General-in-Chief of the United States Army between 1821 and 1828, ordered the first surveys of the Santa Fe Trail, the Upper Missouri and the Yellowstone.

George Izard became the first territorial governor of Arkansas. Winfield Scott, as General-in-Chief of the United States Army from 1841 to 1861, was responsible for every military operation in the West from the Oregon and California Trail forts through the 1860 threats of "Secesh" revolts in Utah, Nevada and California.

But Noah Brown, in doughty emulation of La Salle, led the way west from Thundergate. During the winter of 1817–18, he brought thirty ship carpenters to Black Rock and began construction of a trim two-masted ship with a schooner rig. He installed two paddlewheels amidships and hooked them up to a cast-iron steam engine. He ordered a bust of Oliver Hazard Perry for the figurehead.

On Sunday, August 23, 1818, oxen hauled the vessel up the cordell-way to Lake Erie. In mid-afternoon, the S.S. *Walk-in-the-Water*, first steamship on the Upper Lakes, chuffed off on her maiden voyage to Dunkirk, Erie, Cleveland, Sandusky and Detroit. There were twenty-nine passengers. The fare to Cleveland was $15, and to Detroit $24. The trip to Detroit took 50 hours, including stops. La Salle's *Griffon*, and every sailing ship after her, had required at least 130 hours.

SECTION SIX

ALL THE PAST WE LEAVE BEHIND

All the past we leave behind,
We debouch upon a newer, mightier world, varied
world,
Fresh and strong the world we seize, world of labor
and the march,
Pioneers! O pioneers!

—Walt Whitman (1865)

EIGHTEEN

PATRIOTS AND SLAVES

The Treaty of Ghent, like every other treaty that had attempted to soothe the rivalries between inhabitants of the St. Lawrence and Mohawk-Genesee plow-ways, merely resumed the wary truce of 1783 to 1812. The forts, like old wolves guarding the wood and stone clusters they had whelped and nursed, continued to defy one another across the St. Lawrence, the Niagara, the Detroit, the St. Clair and the Sault Ste. Marie. The terms "Canuck" and "Slick Yankee" became fashionable sneer-names for translake neighbors. Boundary disputes, business recessions, nationalist cranks and the refusal of the United States to resolve the white supremacy fetish brought the forts of Niagara to battle tenseness again in 1837 . . . 1846 . . . 1862 . . . 1866. The "unguarded boundary between the Good Neighbors" was a politicians' myth.*

General Drummond's troops abandoned Fort Niagara, Lewiston and Niagara Falls during May 1815. Buffalo incorporated as a village in 1816. President James Monroe, who had served as Secretary of War between August 1814 and March 1815, became the first United States President to visit Fort Niagara when, during the summer of 1817, he reviewed troops, dined at the House of Peace, then—en route to the falls—inspected the docks and the new road being built up Crawl-on-all-Fours by Porter, Bloom & Company.

* It still is!

The martial wariness along the Niagara's shores impressed British Captain Richard Langslow, another visitor that summer. "Passed Chippeway," he recorded for September 22. "Saw some soldiers of the 70th and an officer, a company under Cpt. Swinney posted at the small fort here." On September 23 and 24, he visited officers at Forts George and Mississauga on the Canadian shore, took the half-hour ferry journey across to Fort Niagara to inspect the new gun emplacements "going on slowly," and during the next week toured Fort Tompkins, the Sailors' Battery, the Terrace Battery and Fort Porter, all on the American shore.

But the immigrant rush up the Lakes and the harvests of furs, grain, timber and ore that began to sail and barge east in 1816 caused wharves, warehouses, factories and shipyards to be built in a solid barricade from *La Belle Famille* to Lewiston. The British suffragist, Frances Wright, reported of her 1819 visit to Niagara:

> Five years since there was but one log house between Rochester and Lewiston. A citizen who got into the stage during the morning for a dozen miles, and who united the professions of doctor and farmer, told me that he had five and thirty patients within the stretch of one mile. This may convey to you some idea at once of the rapid settling of the country, and the physical evils that the first occupiers of the soil have to encounter.

Lewiston and Queenston became terminals for steamships and freighters operating down opposite shores of Lake Ontario and the St. Lawrence. Above the falls, the Black Rock and Schlosser Landing shipyards produced hundreds of canal boats, topsail schooners, two-master brigantines, three-master barkentines and steamboats.

General Lafayette visited Fort Niagara in June 1825, during his "grand tour" of the United States as a guest of Congress. His secretary, A. Levasseur, recalled:

> On leaving the Falls of Niagara, we went to Lewiston to sleep ... and the next day at five o'clock in the morning, we rode to Fort Niagara, where General Lafayette had been invited to breakfast by Major Thomson, the commandant of the garrison.

We found the major at the head of his officers, a short distance in advance of the fort, waiting to receive the general, who was saluted by twenty four guns as soon as he entered the works. Some ladies, wives of the officers of the garrison, assisted their husbands in doing the honours of the entertainment, and contributed not a little by their politeness, in making the time we passed at Niagara appear very short.

Lafayette came in gentle June, when peach and lilac blossoms framed the fort's somber walls and Solomon's-seals and daisies nodded benediction on the forgotten graves of four wars. But the trees were a black and gray lattice against steel-blue sky in December 1837, when a cry of "War! ! !" brought an alert to the Niagara and George garrisons again.

Buffalo had outbid Black Rock fourteen years before and became the west terminal for the Erie Canal. It was a bawdy metropolis of fifty thousand. Black Rock and Lewiston struggled to retain their identities by building a railroad down the gorge to connect with the Erie Canal at new Lockport. But no shovels had clanged since fall. Overexpansion brought on the "Van Buren Depression." Banks closed; hundreds of firms declared bankruptcy. Farm values along Lake Ontario crashed from a dollar to ten cents an acre. Thousands of unemployed were going west—by wagon, canalboat, and shank's mare. New York was psychologically ripe for war!

And a war had already started in Upper Canada. Demands for political reform had agitated Upper Canada for a decade. William Lyon Mackenzie, a Scotchman who came in during 1820, became the most outspoken agitator. Through the yellow-journalism techniques of the magazine, *Colonial Advocate*, which he founded at Queenston in 1824, he fomented rebellion.

York readopted its French-Indian name of Toronto in 1834. Mackenzie was elected mayor there the same year. The bitterness between his Reform party and Governor Sir Francis Bond Head became so pronounced that Mackenzie and his followers attempted to seize Toronto and set up a revolutionary government. But Mackenzie's "Patriots" were routed in a fifteen-minute skirmish at Montgomery's Tavern on December 7, 1837.

Mackenzie fled to the Niagara, was smuggled across the river to Buffalo and welcomed by those who, like Jonas Harrison, had magnified the Canadians' 1813 raids into "another Oriskany." Thus Mackenzie was able to form a Committee of Thirteen to recruit American as well as Canadian volunteers for his Patriot Army. On December 14 or 15, while Buffalo officials figuratively turned their backs, Mackenzie and a hundred followers occupied Upper Canada's Navy Island and proclaimed a provisional government. Then the garrisons at Niagara, Porter, Tompkins, George, Chippewa and Erie prepared for war again.

On December 29, the decrepit steamboat *Caroline,* 71 feet long and 46 tons gross, butted ice floes from Buffalo down to Schlosser Landing. So many volunteers for the Patriot Army were waiting beside the crates of guns and supplies stacked there that the *Caroline* spent the rest of the day ferrying them across the three miles to Navy Island. No American official attempted to halt the trips, although more than two hundred rifles and a field gun had been stolen from the Buffalo Armory the week before.

At dusk, twenty-six volunteers and a stack of boxes were still on the dock. Gilman Appleby, captain of the *Caroline,* announced that it would be too dangerous to attempt another trip to the island before dawn. He invited the men to sleep aboard, if they would help load the cargo.

Colonel Allan McNab, a Toronto barrister, commanded the Upper Canada militia assembling at Fort Chippewa. Every detail of the *Caroline* could be studied with a spyglass from the Canadian shore. That night about ten o'clock seven boats pulled out of Chippewa. They were commanded by Captain Andrew Drew, R.N. Two of the craft failed to locate the channel around Grand Island to Schlosser Landing and almost went over the falls.

The *Caroline's* watchman shouted once. A gun cracked. The Patriot volunteers and crew stumbled up to the deck. Shadowy figures jabbed them with bayonets and ordered them ashore "on the double." The body of the watchman—a stage driver named Amos Durfee—was carried down and laid on the dock. Captain Drew went to the engine room, threw chunkwood into the furnace, then ordered the mooring lines cut. He headed the *Caro-*

line due northeast toward the Upper Rapids with a whaleboat in tow. His men set fires in the cabin and prow.

A hundred feet from the rapids, Drew lashed the steering wheel. He and his aides climbed down to the whaleboat, cut it loose and pulled upstream to the Canadian shore.

The *Caroline* flamed through the Upper Rapids, lurched against Goat Island, veered toward the Canadian falls, but grounded on a rock two hundred feet from the brink. It burned the rest of the night.

By mid-morning the road to Schlosser Landing was choked with gigs, landaus, wagons and horsemen. Thousands went to Goat Island to stare at the smoldering hulk and wonder "how many murdered men are still aboard?" There were, of course, claims of "Canadian invasion" and "This is war-r! ! !"

A report went to Washington. (It was a five-day ride.) President Martin Van Buren, a New Yorker, called an emergency meeting of the Cabinet. It was decided to send Major General Winfield Scott to the Niagara Frontier with full authority "to enforce the act of neutrality ... and to defend our territory, if necessary against invasion."

Scott routed back to his old battlegrounds through New York and Albany. In New York he ordered United States Army trainees to follow him to Buffalo. At Albany, he persuaded Governor Marcy to accompany him and determine whether the state militia should be called out.

By the time Scott and Marcy reached Buffalo on January 12, Buffalo, Montreal and Toronto newspapers were haranguing toward war, with front-page articles and belligerent editorials. Mackenzie's Patriots on Navy Island and McNab's militia at Chippewa were banging at each other with musket and cannon fire.

Scott and Marcy ordered all steamboat owners on the American shore not to lease, sell or "give" transportation services to the Patriots. But, during the night of January 14, the Patriots ferried over to Grand Island. That was American territory. McNab's militia took over Navy Island on January 15. The gun duels resumed.

Scott and Marcy sent word to McNab that they were ordering the steamer *Barcelona* out to bring the Patriots back to Black Rock, under arrest. McNab sent no formal reply, but three armed schooners began to patrol the Upper Niagara between the Chippewa and Fort Erie. Many believed that McNab had instructed the ship captains to sink the *Barcelona*.

Scott's orders to the commanders of Fort Niagara and Fort Tompkins during the afternoon of January 15 were to prepare guns for barrages of the Canadian shore and to set up flying artillery batteries along the American shore between Schlosser's Landing and Black Rock. Gunfire from Black Rock would be the signal to start the barrage.

The *Barcelona* was to begin the fateful voyage at eight on the morning of January 16. At 7:30 that morning, a closed carriage led a battery of artillery through Black Rock to the *Barcelona*'s pier. General Scott and Governor Marcy stepped from the carriage. Scott wore a dress uniform. Marcy was in top hat and frock coat with a "New York True Blue" cloak fastened across his shoulders by gold spread-eagle buttons.

The artillerymen wheeled their guns to the end of the dock. Then, as the *Barcelona* cast off and churned out toward Grand Island, they sighted on the Canadian schooners.

The *Barcelona* passed the schooners without a challenge and turned in toward the scow hulk that served as Grand Island's dock. A puff of steam rose as the ship's whistle blew. The Patriots appeared from the brush, huddled in groups, argued, then ran for the ship. The whistle puffed again. More figures emerged from the brush and scrambled aboard.

The whistle puffed three times. General Scott gave an order. The artillerymen lit their fuses and held them at the ready.

Scott and Marcy stood at ramrod attention as the steamship turned just a stone's throw from one of the schooners and headed back toward Black Rock. The schooner gun crews stood with fuses smoldering, too.

But the *Barcelona* churned placidly north, cleared the end of Grand Island, and turned in toward Black Rock. General Scott's arm rose in a salute toward Canada. He took off his tricorn hat, clamped it against his chest, and bowed his thanks, too, as he barked, "Extinguish your fuses, Lieutenant."

The Patriots were disarmed as they came off the ship, then were escorted to the Armory and registered. The out of towners received canal boat or stage fare home and orders to "Be on your way before sundown." But Mackenzie was sent to Rochester with a cavalry guard, given a quick trial for "disturbing the peace," and sentenced to serve a year in the Monroe County jail.

Colonel W. J. Worth, still Scott's aide-de-camp, took a company of regulars to Fredonia. They disarmed the three hundred Patriots who had assembled there, then went to Detroit and disarmed another five hundred.

Mackenzie supporters, however, formed secret societies called Hunter Lodges in communities along the Erie, Niagara, Ontario and St. Lawrence shore. The Van Buren Depression, plus boundary disputes, kept the Lakes under a war cloud through the "54–40 or Fight" threat and the signing of the Oregon Treaty in 1846. When Army engineers came to Fort Niagara in 1839 to repair the collapsing lake wall, it was decided that they must also build an "automatic" furnace to heat cannonballs for future hot shot bombardments of the Canadian shore. Down-lake, at Kingston, Upper Canada rushed the stone behemoth, Fort Henry, to completion to "repel the American invasion," and installed 27 of its cannon on the radically new "traversing platforms."

The invasion never quite made it. But a subtler war had been going on ever since 1793. It would cause the next artillery alert crises on the Niagara in 1861. The war between refugee Negroes and slave hunters began soon after Upper Canada's first Parliament enacted a law against slaveholding. Canada became the "Promised Land" for the 700,000 slaves in the United States.

The flights to Canada, many via Niagara, began before 1795. Canadian records assert that "at least 40" of the 140 volunteers for General Sheaffe's successful assault at the Battle of Queenston Heights were "Negroes living on the Grand River Reservation." More than three hundred Negroes volunteered to serve with the Upper Canada militia during the Patriots' War. One all-Negro company was commanded by Captain John Clench. Historians estimate that more than seventy-five thousand slaves reached the "Promised Land" across the Lakes between 1820 and 1860.

Queenston and Newark were the most accessible communities in Canada east of Detroit. They became legendary throughout the Cotton Belt of the United States as the "Cities of Refuge." King's Wharf at Newark grew into a symbol of Negro freedom, "where you kneel down and give thinks to Him for deliverance."

Slavers offered $1,000 rewards for the capture of "healthy negroes." The ferry landings became too dangerous. Hundreds succeeded in swimming the river. On August 10, 1823, the Canadian steamer *Chief Justice Robinson* picked up a Negro floating on a gate twelve miles down Lake Ontario. He had escaped from Tennessee, feared the white men at the Lewiston ferry and so stole the gate, carried it down to *La Belle Famille* at night, and tried to float across to Queenston on it. When he was told that the *Robinson* was a Canadian vessel, he, too, fell to his knees and moaned, "Thank you, Lord, for deliverin' me to Canaan."

The organization of escape routes and elaborate smuggling techniques by Quakers, Methodists, Unitarians and other Abolitionist groups after 1830 took the nickname of "The Underground Railroad." Cellar and barn hideouts at Peterboro, Skaneateles, and Rochester routed the refugees toward "the Slaves' Cave" on the St. Lawrence, not far from Sackets Harbor, or to the Niagara.

The success of "The Underground" led to the enactment of the Fugitive Slave Act by Congress in 1850. It fixed a $1,000 fine and/or six-month jail sentence for "aiding the escape of a runaway slave." Slave dealers invented the charge that "Abolitionists are cannibals. They get you darkies up there, fatten you up and then boil you."

But the human smuggling continued. One "U.G.R.R. car" frequently seen on Niagara roads looked like a farm box wagon except that the driver's seat was wider than usual and had a bulky, padded back rest. The seat and back rest were hollow. Refugee slaves were carried in it from "Underground" stations in Pennsylvania to boats hidden along the Niagara shore.

During the summer of 1850, the Reverend Josiah Henson of

Chatham on the Thames crossed John Roebling's new suspension bridge to Lewiston and boarded the steam train for Lockport. A week later, he began telling the story of his flight from slavery and the six hundred slaves he had helped escape since then. His listener was Mrs. Harriet Beecher Stowe, noticeably pregnant with her seventh child. Henson's headstone claims that he was the "original of Uncle Tom" in *Uncle Tom's Cabin or Life Among the Lowly*.

But cooperation between the North's Abolitionists and correspondents in Canada failed to check the war fears that swept up the Lakes again during 1861. Great Britain was the principal customer for the South's cotton. This fact, plus old grievances against the United States, swayed Queen Victoria's government toward an alliance with the Confederacy.

James Murray Mason, the United States Senator from Virginia who had sponsored the Fugitive Slave Act of 1850, was the Confederacy's choice as its representative in London. John Slidell of Louisiana accepted a similar appointment as Confederate lobbyist at the Court of Napoleon III. Mason and Slidell ran the United States Navy blockade during the first week of November 1861, then sailed from Havana for London on the British steamship *Trent*. On November 8, the U.S.S. *San Jacinto* halted the *Trent*, shanghaied Mason and Slidell and took them to Fort Warren in Boston harbor. Exactly sixty years before, similar acts by British naval vessels had become the War Hawks' excuse for starting the War of 1812.

Demands for "War against the U.S.A." growled through both Houses of Parliament. Ten more regiments were ordered to Canada. Mason and Slidell were delivered in London during early January 1862. Secretary of State Seward sent an abject apology to the British government for "violation of the established American principle of freedom of the seas" by the *San Jacinto*'s captain, Charles Wilkes. (The gold medal voted Wilkes by the House of Representatives was never cast.)

So the fears of siege returned to Fort Niagara. Engineers came in from New York City, examined the walls, and plotted additional bunkers and gun mounts. Brick masons worked double shifts through 1862 and 1863. The garrison was doubled. Larger siege guns were installed. Cavalry patrols paced the Lewiston road, again.

Upper Canada welcomed Confederate agents and escapees from the Union prison camps as openly as she had welcomed refugee slaves five years before. When the Union won its first major land victories at Vicksburg and Gettysburg during the summer of 1863, Canadian newspapers wrote angry editorials. Parties to raise funds and collect gifts for the Confederacy became "the mode" at Hamilton, London, Toronto and Kingston. Washington reacted with a threat to scrap the Rush-Bagot Treaty and "build a score of ironclads" to patrol the Great Lakes.

Early in July 1864, James Murray Mason reached Quebec and was hurried west, with an honorary escort of Canadian officials, to the Niagara. Clement C. Clay, Jacob Thompson, James P. Holcombe and George N. Saunders were waiting at the Clifton House, a fashionable resort hotel overlooking the Canadian falls.

Horace Greeley, editor of the *New York Tribune*, had adopted a "peace at any price" policy. On or about July 13, Greeley received an invitation to come to the Clifton House and discuss peace terms with the Confederate commissioners.

The meeting was held on July 17. Mason, as spokesman, asked for United States recognition of the Confederacy as a "sovereign nation" with boundary lines to be established along the Ohio and Potomac valleys. Greeley telegraphed the offer to President Lincoln that night. Lincoln rejected it.

The role of Canadian officials, if any, in the terror campaign loosed against the United States during the next few weeks has never been revealed.

On September 19, twelve Confederate agents hijacked the Lake Erie steamer *Philo Parsons* during its run across Put-in-Bay, the scene of Perry's 1814 victory. They ordered the captain to head for nearby Johnson Island. En route they overtook and hijacked the *Island Queen*.

Johnson Island was a Union prison camp. It held thirty-five hundred Confederate officers captured during Grant's Mississippi valley and Sherman's Tennessee-Georgia campaigns. The U.S.S.

Michigan was the prison's only guardship. She had been built at the Erie yards in 1844 and was the first all-iron steamboat on the Lakes.

Annie Davis was the madame of a sporting house at Sandusky. She sent her customers' most useful gossip to the Confederacy by means of the Copperheads' Cleveland-Cincinnati relay. During August she had received orders from Mason-Thompson-Clay at the Clifton House to take her girls out to the U.S.S. *Michigan* on September 19, provide the liquor and "spike the drinks." The "escort" she brought aboard that afternoon was John Yates Beall, a 29-year-old Virginian.

The party went to full whoop. Annie planned to introduce the knockout drops in the next round. Beall had toured the ship, counted its guns, and spotted the *Philo Parsons* and *Island Queen* anchored a half mile away.

But the captain of the *Michigan* spoiled everything by clouting Beall as he reentered the cabin. The other officers leveled pistols at Annie and her girls—except for the one who was a Pinkerton detective. Five minutes later, the *Michigan* fired a warning gun at the *Philo Parsons*. Then the captain megaphoned, "The escape plot has been discovered. Miss Davis is our prisoner."

Newspaper stories about the Johnson Island raid started rumors about invasions from Canada and other "devilish plots" fomenting at the Clifton House. Jacob Thompson, it was claimed, had hired Canadian chemists to inoculate bales of wool and fur with yellow-fever germs, then ship the bales to Cleveland, Buffalo, Detroit and Chicago. Other shipments containing time bombs were to go from Canada to Portland, Boston and New York City, to start fires that would coincide with race riots incited by Confederate agents.

Troops were ordered to every ferry landing between Buffalo and Ogdensburg. All visitors from Canada were frisked for guns or "incriminating materials." All Canadian bale goods brought to United States Customs offices were opened and tested for "malignancies."

During October, a score of "hunters" and "fishermen" crossed the Lower Canada border into Vermont. They assembled outside

St. Albans on the shore of Lake Champlain and changed into Confederate uniforms. Then they raided farms for the region's excellent Morgan horses and charged into town. They took $200,000 from the banks and merchants, and fired several buildings but fled when the county sheriff rode in with a posse of farmers, boatmen and downlake merchants.

All but six of the raiders were captured. The sheriff rode his prisoners to the border and turned them over to Canadian authorities. A Montreal magistrate threw the case out of court. The United States general commanding the Vermont military district threatened that future raiders "will be pursued into Canada and destroyed."

There were conferences at Washington and Quebec. The Vermont general's order was countermanded by President Lincoln. The Montreal magistrate was publicly reproved. Five of the St. Albans raiders were rearrested and given brief jail sentences for "disturbing the peace."

The Johnson Island and St. Albans raids, the attitude of the Vermont general, and an 1866 aftermath on the Niagara all influenced the 1867 union of Upper and Lower Canada, New Brunswick and Nova Scotia into the Dominion of Canada.

Millions of Irish had migrated to the United States between 1820 and 1850. Irish laborers won the nickname of "bog trotters" by digging the Erie Canal's trough through the malarial Montezuma swamps between Syracuse and Rochester. Stubbornly, their sons and daughters progressed from "shanty" to "lace curtain" status and became a potent sociopolitical force. The zeal of "Freedom for Ireland" drew thousands of supporters to the Irish Revolutionary Brotherhood.

During the winter of 1865–66, the strategists of the I.R.B.—or Fenians—decided that the Niagara Peninsula offered an opportunity to win independence for Ireland. A Fenian army would seize the Canadian shore and Welland Canal and hold it as a hostage until Great Britain gave Ireland independence.

Federal arsenals were auctioning off war surpluses. Hundreds of cases of rifles and cartridges were shipped to Buffalo during May 1866. Every train and canal boat brought discharged sol-

diers, most of them in faded Union blues, a few in shabbier
Confederate grays. Captain John O'Neil, a 25-year-old with an
excellent war record, was the I.R.B. choice to command the
invasion.

Again, as in 1837, no steps were taken to interfere with the
"Freedom for Ireland" meetings, or the street parades behind
shamrock banners. Nothing was done to halt the trains of men
and wagons heading through Black Rock to the docks during
the afternoon and evening of May 31.

Two tugboats and a string of canal barges had moved into
the dock at Pratt's Furnace. The wagonloads of guns and ammunition went aboard them; fifteen hundred Fenian volunteers followed. Between 1 and 3 A.M. on June 1, while United States Customs patrols stayed away, the fleet crossed the Upper Niagara to
a landing near abandoned Fort Erie.

O'Neil had been promised that commissary supplies and more
volunteers would be waiting across the river. They were not. His
1,500 needed breakfast. Farm and village families along the shore
were awakened with demands for "All the grub you got." The
morning's eating cleaned out shops and home cellars.

By afternoon, O'Neil despaired of reinforcements and headed
for the Welland Canal. But eight hundred Upper Canada militia
closed in. There were a few short battles. The Fenians split up
and began to flee. O'Neil, still with seven hundred men, fought
back to the Niagara, commandeered boats, and returned to American waters.

United States Customs agents put all of the Fenians under arrest. Apologies went to Canada. General Grant sent orders to the
Fort Niagara, Fort Tompkins and Fort Porter commanders to
guard against "further Fenian activity." But O'Neil and his seven
hundred were released without trial. Canada was never reim-
bursed for the property damage or the militiamen killed or
wounded.

O'Neil's invasion and the glowering American attitude ended
an interprovince bicker about Confederation. Pro-Confederation-
ists won that year's elections in New Brunswick and Nova Scotia.
Their delegates met with representatives of Lower Canada

and Upper Canada, reached agreement, and sailed with them to London for discussions with Parliament and Queen Victoria's ministers.

The Fenians, eager to win freedom for Ireland, had pressured Canada into a union that would assure greater freedom from the United States. The British North American Act of 1867 created the Dominion of Canada.

NINETEEN

THE MEMORY PLACES

Carbon dating at the Moundbuilders' fort on the Second Mountain behind Lewiston testified that warriors and politicians had failed to achieve either peace or neighborliness on the Niagara for at least 1,700 years. After 1871, technology loomed new hope.

By 1871, a footloose young telegraph operator from the Lake Erie shore had earned enough from his inventions to take the steam train to Boston and start tinkering with electrically powered gadgets. His name was Thomas Alva Edison.

That same year, the 24-year-old son of the Professor of Elocution at Queens College, Kingston, experimented with the same mysterious force at the family home in Brantford, the namesake city of Joseph Brant. This young tinkerer's name was Alexander Graham Bell.

A 14-year-old from nearby Baden also daydreamed about the potentials of electromagnetism as the science lectures droned on at Mr. Tassie's Grammar School in Galt. His name was Adam Beck.

In the hills behind the cellar hole of Louis Joncaire's cabin at Venango, steam engines were pumping a wealth of "Seneca oil" out of the ground. (Scientists insisted that this smelly remedy for croup, diarrhea and sore muscles should be called *petroleum!*)

The inventions that developed from the electromagnetism skills of Thomas Alva Edison and Alexander Graham Bell, of the Titusville petroleum marketers, and of the Pittsburgh and Upper Lakes steel makers fostered social relationships that promised the first peace-with-understanding in Thundergate's history.

Niagara Falls powered its first dynamo in 1882. The dozen arc lights it sustained along the Black Rock shore were such a "marvel of science" that the New York Central and Erie railroads ran "Electric Light Excursion Specials" in from Cleveland, Detroit and New York City.

The first long distance telephone line was operating over the forty miles between Boston, Massachusetts, and Providence, Rhode Island. Newspaper editorials routinely sneered at the four-cycle hydrocarbon motor just invented by Dr. A. N. Otto in Germany and the toy models of flying machines that currently absorbed Dr. Samuel P. Langley, director of Allegheny Observatory at the Western University of Pennsylvania.

Peter Porter's nephew, Grover Cleveland, was performing such an efficient job as Mayor of Buffalo that the tenement vote buyers nicknamed him "The Veto Mayor." Wilfrid Laurier, a lawyer-editor from St. Lin, delivered such cogent speeches at Canada's 16-year-old Parliament House in Ottawa that it was obvious he would succeed Edward Blake as leader of the Liberal Party.

These trends, plus the enthusiastic Canada-United States agreement that a Niagara Falls honeymoon was as essential to marital happiness as a horsehair sofa and a family buggy, began to dim memories of the Niagara's ninety years of Yankee-Loyalist hate.

Fort Erie sagged to a vine-decked ruin overlooking a favorite lakeshore picnic spot. The sites of Fort Schlosser and Little Niagara were factory foundations. Forts Chippewa, George, and Mississauga became weedy shells. The United States Army built barracks and an Officers Row up-river toward *La Belle Famille* and all but abandoned Fort Niagara.

On April 2, 1917, President Woodrow Wilson asked Congress for a declaration of war against Germany. At 1 P.M. four days later, the United States and Canada finally became allies to "make the world safe for democracy."

Lake Ontario's storms initiated a campaign to "Preserve the Old Castle." It began at Youngstown and Lewiston in 1922, and soon won Canadian contributors. A large crack appeared in the protective seawall that spring. By fall it had extended up the north end of the House of Peace.

Frank H. Severance, director of the Buffalo Historical Society, had already devoted a decade to research of the New France era at Niagara. On the eve of World War I, he was permitted to examine records and original documents at the Colonial Archives of the French War Department in Paris. The publication of his two-volume masterpiece, *An Old Frontier of France,* in 1917 restored local awareness about "that old Castle down on the river bluff." The publication of *Cardigan* and other novels by Robert W. Chambers caused more civic pride in the "oldest structure in New York west of Schenectady."

William Wallace Kincaid, a Youngstown merchant, organized the initial drive to "save the Castle from tumbling into the lake." Senator James W. Wadsworth, grandson of the militia officer who fought beside Winfield Scott at Queenston Heights, was chairman of the Senate's Subcommittee on Military Appropriations. Mr. Kincaid went to Washington and told Senator Wadsworth about the cracks. An appropriation of $22,000 was secured for the repair of the seawall and the House of Peace foundations.

Alfred E. Adams, the civilian engineer sent up by the War Department to make the repairs, was an architectural historian. Adams challenged local historians with the question: "Do you want to repair this building—or restore it?"

A meeting of twenty organizations, including the Daughters of the American Revolution, Elks, U.S. Daughters of 1812, Niagara Falls Trades & Labor Council, and the Ancient Order of Hibernians, in April 1927 at the Niagara Falls Chamber of Commerce founded the Old Fort Niagara Association, Inc. The Association's purposes were "to effect restoration and maintenance of Old Fort Niagara in cooperation with the War Department of the United States, and to promote an informed interest in the history of the occupation and colonization of the North American continent."

Frank Severance's research notes reported that Gaspard de Léry's House of Peace plans, submitted to Louis XV on January 19, 1727, were still available in Paris. Myron T. Herrick, United States Ambassador to France, responded enthusiastically to the Association's appeal and forwarded copies of pertinent Jesuit and Quebec reports along with facsimiles of the De Lery data.

Development of the Dominion Archives at Ottawa as Canada's counterpart of the British Museum and the United States Library of Congress was one of the many contributions to scholarship instituted during Sir Wilfrid Laurier's tenure as Canada's Prime Minister from 1896 to 1911. All of the Dominion Archives collections and the services of its research staff were made available to the task of determining details of garrison environment and crises between 1678 and 1815.

Appeals for restoration funds revealed eagerness along both shores of the river to have "a memory place we can see and touch and understand." Newsboys gave fistfuls of pennies and nickels. House painters and carpenters drove their families down the new macadam road to Youngstown for the formality of paying $25 "to get one of those life memberships." The Buffalo Chapter, Daughters of American Colonists, voted to restore the Military Kitchen "just the way it was when Captain Pouchot commanded there." The Knights of Columbus echoed with a resolution to finance restoration of the Jesuit Chapel. The D.A.R. pledged funds to fix up the Johnson Council Room.

A $35,000 appropriation by Congress in 1931 and approval of the restoration as a work relief project during the depression years of 1930 to 1938 restored both the House of Peace and its 1727–1863 defense systems. Ownership of the buildings and grounds was transferred from the War Department to the Niagara Frontier State Park Commission, then licensed to the Old Fort Niagara Association for maintenance and operation. The scholarly tenacity of S. Grove McClellan as executive vice president-director of Old Fort Niagara between 1951 and 1965 restored scores of "original" details to the Thundergate site.

This demonstration of governmental, group and individual cooperation encouraged fort-restoration movements from the St. Lawrence to the Allegheny portage. Forts Erie, George, Toronto, Frontenac, Ontario, Presque Isle and Le Boeuf became regional parks. Construction of the St. Lawrence Seaway during the 1950's gave Canada opportunity to assemble exciting architectural and folkway details of the Upper Canada frontier at Upper Canada Village on the St. Lawrence shore near Morrisburg, Ontario. A

National Monument and museum area at Sackets Harbor was in prospect in 1967.

Now, a weeklong serendipity from Upper Canada Village to the Allegheny headwaters guarantees new perspective on "that History stuff." The convictions, regional lore, and environmental hazards of the 1776–1800 Loyalists emerge in as crisp three-dimensional quality from the oxyards, old homes, boat basin and cheese factory of Upper Canada Village as they do from the log walls, museums and loquacious young guides at Fort George and Navy Hall. Kingston's array of forts and museums offers heritage chapters from La Salle's dream of New France through World War II. The Brock monument towering above Queenston is as much of a pride symbol for Americans as for Canadians. Lithe Six Nations youngsters will grin and wave from schoolyards beside Ontario 54's bucolic route up the Grand River valley to the Chapel of the Mohawks, Joseph Brant's grave, and Alexander Graham Bell's home at Brantford.

The high points of such wanderings are of course at Fort Niagara and Lewiston. Trees, wild asters, and blackcap brambles have returned to hedge New York's Route 18-F with the serenity that roused Walt Whitman to compose "By the Blue Ontario's Shore" as he wandered there a century ago. The basso whisper of the falls is a bit softer than the echo that quickened the midnight walk of La Salle and Tonti in 1678. The falls have gouged a quarter mile back during the three centuries.

Summer is Fort Niagara's most spectacular season. Scores of college students, most of them history majors, serve as sentries and guides. The research pioneered by Frank Severance and Grove McClellan has made possible reproduction of the uniforms worn by the Bearn, Royal American, 49th, and New York militia regiments. Honor guards of New France, Loyalists, and "those Americans" stand at the Six Nations Gate. The Fleur de Lys, the Union Jack, and the 15-starred Stars and Stripes announce "Peace at last" from the triple flagpole on the drill ground.

But even in midsummer, shadows begin to gloom the Lower Niagara by 6 P.M. Then the trip through *La Belle Famille* to Lewiston reaches a mood that can transform outboard motorboats into *bateaux,* shrill a cardinal's call into a warrior's signal, and enhance the leaf rustle of the westerly breeze to the moccasined march of *coureurs-de-bois* or the gentler step of Louis Joncaire stalking a fat doe for the Sabbath feast at *Magazin Royal.*

At Lewiston, drive straight south past the road signs warning "Dead End" to the foot of Crawl-on-all-Fours. There is a small blue-and-gold marker at the parking circle. It identifies the site of La Salle's 1678 landing place and Louis Joncaire's *Magazin Royal.* Listen to the thunder of Minnesota, Illinois, Manitoba, Michigan, Indiana, Ohio, Ontario. The saga of Thundergate— the history maker—began here.

AT THIS SPOT

A Chronology

A.D. 160—The Moundbuilders manned a fort on Second Mountain of the Niagara gorge.

1500–1550—The concept of a Five Nations Confederacy grew among refugee tribes occupying the Genesee and Mohawk troughs of the glacial drainage system.

1609, July 30—Samuel de Champlain and Algonquin-Huron allies defeated Five Nations warriors—probably Mohawks—near Crown Point on Lake Champlain.

1615, November—Champlain was wounded while leading a Huron-French attack on an Onondaga "castle." Etienne Brulé *may* have fled through Niagara that winter after his capture and torture by Senecas.

1626, November—Reverend Joseph de la Roche Dallion, a Franciscan, was first European known to have visited the Niagara.

1615–1640—The Mohawks made first trade alliances with Puritans and Hudson Valley Dutch. Mohawk warriors were Puritan allies in the Pequot War, 1637.

1641–1660—Fur trade rivalry among French, Puritans and Dutch motivated the Five Nations' wars against Hurons. Five Nations won control of the Niagara portage and Lake Erie.

1669, July—Robert Cavelier, Sieur de La Salle, crossed Lake Ontario to Irondequoit Bay, conferred with Senecas at Boughton Hill, then used Niagara portage to begin two-year exploration of Ohio valley, Indiana and Illinois.

1679, January—La Salle selected bluff on eastern shore of the Niagara's mouth for Fort Condé, and shore of Cayuga Creek, behind the Falls, for construction of the *Griffon*.

1679, May—The *Griffon* was launched.

1679, Fall—Fort Condé was abandoned, then burned by Senecas.

215

1687, August—Fort Denonville was built on Fort Condé site.

1688, September 15—Fort Denonville was abandoned after Father Millet built oak cross, 18 feet high, in memoriam to eighty soldiers and boatmen who died from scurvy and Seneca ambushes during the thirteen-month occupation.

1702, April—Madame de La Mothe-Cadillac, her infant son, and Madame Alphonse de Tonti, "the first white women on the Niagara," crossed portage en route to Detroit.

1721, May 19—Charles Le Moyne, Baron de Longueuil, then Lieutenant-governor of Montreal, and Marquis de Cavagnal, son of the Governor-General, dedicated Louis Joncaire's new trading post, *Magazin Royal*, at foot of Lewiston Bluff.

1721, Fall—Captain Peter Schuyler escorted agents of Palatine German refugees from Hudson valley to Irondequoit Bay to consider area as Palatine colony. The offer was rejected.

1724, Fall—British opened "trading establishment" at site of Oswego— first British outpost on Great Lakes.

1726, June—Chaussegros de Léry began construction of Fort Niagara on promontory site of La Salle's Fort Condé and Denonville's Fort Denonville. Baron de Longueuil appointed his son, Captain Charles Le Moyne, the first commandant.

1732, Summer—Louis Joncaire opened trading post in Allegheny valley near the site of Warren, Pennsylvania.

1738, Summer—William Johnson arrived at Fort Hunter to start development of the Mohawk valley wilderness tract owned by his uncle, Captain Peter Warren, R.N.

1746, September—Governor Clinton appointed William Johnson "Colonel of the army to be raised out of the Six Nations."

1749, Summer—Céleron de Blainville commanded an expedition from Niagara down the Chautauqua-Allegheny route to formally claim the Ohio valley for New France.

1750, Summer—Daniel (Chabert) Joncaire built Fort Little Niagara (Fort du Portage) behind the Falls, near site of the *Griffon* shipyard. He was made Master of the Niagara Portage that year. (During the next five years, he developed crop and pasture lands along the River of Horses (Buffalo Creek) and built stables and smithy there.)

1750, August—The Swedish naturalist, Peter Kalm, explored the Niagara.

1751, June 27—Reverend François Picquet landed at Niagara to win Indian converts for his two-year-old Sulpician mission-town, La Présentation, at site of Ogdensburg, New York. His sermons caused 392 Seneca, Cayuga, Onondaga and Mississauga families to move to La Présentation that fall and winter.

1753, April—The advance flotilla of the "Army of the Beautiful River" (Ohio) reached Niagara. That summer and fall the expedition, totaling twenty-three hundred regulars, militia and Indians, fortified the route to the Ohio. By October, more than fifteen hundred were dead or invalided from dysentery or yellow fever. Captain Peter Marin, commander-in-chief, died at the Presque Isle base camp on October 29.

1754, June 19—Delegates of seven northern Colonies met with Six Nations sachems at Albany to strengthen treaties and plan campaigns against New France.

1754, July 3—Colonel George Washington and Virginia militia surrendered Fort Necessity.

1754, July 10—Benjamin Franklin's plea for a Colonial Union, similar to the Six Nations' Confederacy, was approved by the delegates. That winter, colony legislatures and Great Britain rejected it.

1755, April—General Braddock's conferences with six Colony Governors at Alexandria, Virginia, evolved a plan for British "pincer attacks" on Fort Duquesne and Niagara.

1755, July 9—Braddock's Expedition was annihilated by the Army of the Beautiful River, seven miles from Fort Duquesne.

1755, July 29—After long bickering about troops and Indians, Governor William Shirley of Massachusetts started for Oswego to begin attack on Niagara. His force totaled fifteen hundred regulars and militia and seventy-five to a hundred "dependable" Indians.

1755, August–September—Shirley's troops added Fort Ontario to the Oswego defenses and built the first British fighting ships on the Great Lakes, the sloops *Oswego* and *Ontario,* each 43 feet long and displacing 100 tons.

1755, October 24—Despite reports by Indian spies that "not more than sixty French and one hundred Indians" defended Niagara, Shirley abandoned the campaign.

1756, August 11—After a three-month prelude of ambushing and fire raids, the Marquis de Montcalm began the siege of Oswego with a force totaling twenty-five hundred troops and fifteen hundred Indians. Oswego surrendered on August 14. Statistics vary, but the most creditable report indicates "1,640 prisoners, of whom 120 were women, 5 flags, 120 cannon, 6 large barques, warehouses full." The British charged, and the French denied, that "more than 100 were scalped by the Indians."

1756, November—Captain François Pouchot reached Niagara with six hundred men from the Marine, La Sarre, Guienne and Bearn regiments and orders to strengthen the defense system of the fort. Most of the artillery captured from Braddock was waiting to be incorporated into the new "works."

1758, August 23—Colonel John Bradstreet and Colonel Charles Clinton, with fifteen hundred militia and Six Nations scouts, left Oswego to attack Fort Frontenac (Kingston, Ontario). Frontenac's surrender on August 28 destroyed the principal New France supply depot between Montreal and the Ohio and most of the Lake Ontario fleet. The raiders were back in the Mohawk valley by late September.

1759, July 1—A whaleboat fleet containing two thousand British regulars and Colonial militia left Oswego to besiege the Niagara forts. Brigadier General John Prideaux commanded the expedition. Colonel Frederick Haldimand remained at Oswego with one thousand three hundred troops to defend the portage route against attacks from Montreal and La Présentation. Sir William Johnson commanded the nine hundred Indian allies.

1759, July 20—General Prideaux and Colonel John Johnstone, his second in command, were killed during an inspection tour of the siege trenches.

1759, July 21—Sir William Johnson usurped command of the expedition, although it had technically passed to Colonel Haldimand at Oswego.

1759, July 24—Captain de Lignery, six hundred survivors of the Army of the Beautiful River and fifteen hundred Indians were ambushed at *La Belle Famille*, two miles from Fort Niagara.

1759, July 25—Captain Pouchot surrendered Fort Niagara to Johnson.

1760—Shipyards were opened behind the Falls and across Lower Niagara from the fort. Captain John J. Schlosser, given the command of Upper Niagara, built namesake fort near site of Little Niagara.

1761—John Stedman (Steadman) became Master of Niagara Portage. He built his home on site of Little Niagara.

1763, September 14—Senecas ambushed Stedman's wagontrain and rescue troops at Devil's Hole, leaving eighty-eight scalped dead.

1764, July to September—Captain John Montresor, Chief Engineer of British forces in North America, designed and supervised construction of "plate-way" carrier up Lewiston bluff as well as series of blockhouses along the portage route. Fort Erie was westernmost blockhouse. Lieutenant-Colonel Israel Putnam of Connecticut Militia commanded the construction battalions. Meanwhile, at Fort Niagara, Sir William Johnson negotiated peace treaties with Indian allies of the Pontiac War.

1775, July 25—Captain John Butler and a hundred Mohawks reached Niagara after flight from "Continental rebels" in Mohawk valley.

1776, June—Sir John Johnson fled to Niagara.

1777, July—Butlers, Johnsons and Brants persuaded five hundred Senecas and Cayugas to join the St. Léger Expedition.

1778, Spring—John Butler recruited regiment of Royal Rangers.

1778, July 4—More than three hundred were massacred after Butler's Rangers and Indians captured Wyoming Valley forts, at site of Wilkes Barre, Pennsylvania.

1778, August and September—Rangers and Joseph Brant's warriors burned German Flats and other "Continental" communities in Mohawk valley.

1778, October 6 to 8—Continentals out of Albany and Schoharie Valley plundered and burned Loyalist strongholds at Unadilla and Ouaquaga in Susquehanna valley.

1778, November 11—John Butler and Rangers captured fort at Cherry Valley; Joseph Brant's warriors fired village and murdered thirty women, children and aged.

1779, May—Colonel Goose Van Schaick and Colonel Marinus Willett led Continental raid through Onondaga homeland, burned castles and killed livestock.

1779, August—Butler Rangers and Indians were defeated by Clinton-Sullivan Expedition at Newtown, near site of Elmira.

1779, September to November—Clinton-Sullivan troops destroyed Cayuga and Seneca castles, livestock and orchards between Genesee valley and Finger Lakes. More than three thousand Indians fled to Niagara.

1780, Spring—After hundreds died in the winter "Starving Time" at Niagara, the first cropfields were plowed and sown on west bank of Lower Niagara.

1780, October 31—Butler Rangers and Johnson Greens returned from Mohawk-Schoharie raid.

1780, November 1—Colonel William Bolton, commander of Fort Niagara, was among those lost when the new snow, *Ontario*, foundered "with all hands" en route to Kingston.

1781, January—Ranger volunteers started east to recruit new companies in Hudson valley and New Jersey.

1781, Spring—Haldimand plan of "Edible Annex" was expanded to offer of farmland and "necessary equipment" along Lower Niagara to Loyalist refugees "until the rebellion is put down and you can return home."

1781, October 29—Captain Walter Butler was killed during skirmish at Canada Creek ford as he covered the retreat of Major John Ross's raiders.

1783, February 8—Americans failed to "capture and hold" Oswego.

1783, August—Governor Haldimand met at Sorel with Baron Von Steuben and announced refusal to obey Treaty of Paris regarding surrender of Great Lakes forts to the United States.

1784—Loyalist refugees, shipped from New York to Nova Scotia during 1783, started migration up the St. Lawrence to join Loyalists at Niagara in founding Upper Canada. Haldimand signed treaty granting "the Mohawk Nation and such other of the Six Nations Indians as wish to settle in that quarter" a tract 12 miles wide centering on the Grand River from Lake Erie to "the head of said river."

1788, June—The Reverend John Stuart, former Anglican missionary in Mohawk valley, dedicated Her Majesty's Chapel of the Mohawks near headwaters of the Grand River.

1791—Upper Canada was created by Constitutional Act of British Parliament.

1792, September 17—Lieutenant-Governor John Graves Simcoe convened first session of Upper Canada's Parliament at Navy Hall, Newark. (Denmark had abolished human slavery by royal decree that May. The Upper Canada Parliament's October decision to "prevent the introduction of Negro slaves" became the second such national law on Earth, and the first in North America.)

1795—The Jay Treaty, signed by the United States and Great Britain on November 19, hastened Upper Canada's construction of a military-roads network through Detroit-Niagara-York-Kingston and a portage road up the west shore of the Niagara. Fort George was built on the west shore of Lower Niagara "to dominate" Fort Niagara.

1795—First refugee slaves from the United States were welcomed to Indian settlements in Grand River Valley.

1796, August 11—United States Infantry occupied Fort Niagara. Two families then lived on the Niagara's American shore. That summer, Moses Cleaveland with forty-seven men and two women from Connecticut crossed the portage to locate homes on the Lake Erie shore.

1807—James Fenimore Cooper served his apprenticeship as a midshipman on the U.S.S. *Oneida*, the 43-ton brig constituting the United States Navy fleet on Lake Ontario. The "cocktail" may have originated at the Hustler Tavern in Lewiston about that time. Settlers along Buffalo Creek rejected the Holland Land Company's name of "New Amsterdam" for their village, and adopted "Buffalo."

1810, August 2 to 5—DeWitt Clinton explored Niagara as a member of New York State Commission "to study the possibility of constructing a canal to connect the Hudson River with Lakes Ontario and Erie."

1812, June 4—United States House of Representatives approved Declaration of War against Great Britain by a 79–49 vote. United States Senate approved by a 19–13 vote on June 17.

1812, October 13—Lieutenant-Governor Isaac Brock was killed; Lieu-
    tenant Colonel Winfield Scott, Brigadier General William Wads-
    worth and nine hundred Americans were captured at Battle of
    Queenston Heights.
1813, February—Noah Brown and Daniel Dobbins began boatyard at
    Erie, Pennsylvania, to build United States Navy fleet for Upper
    Lakes.
    April 27—Brigadier General Zebulon Pike was killed after leading
    successful American assault on York.
    May 27—Americans captured Forts George and Erie and released
    United States Navy Ships at Black Rock.
    May 29—Brigadier General Jacob Brown and fifteen hundred militia
    repulsed Canadian attack on Sacket's Harbor.
    July 9—Canadians raided Black Rock and burned shipyard.
    June 24—The Laura Secord legend originated when six hundred
    Americans, in "surprise attack" on Canadian stronghold at Beaver
    Dams, were ambushed and captured.
    December 10—Brigadier General George McClure ordered his
    American troops to abandon and burn Fort George and Newark.
    December 18—Canadians, under Colonel John Murray, took Fort
    Niagara "by the bayonet." General Phineas Riall's command, with
    Indians, burned Lewiston and Black Rock.
    December 29—Riall's Canadians burned Buffalo.
1814, July 3 and 4—Americans recaptured Fort Erie, then defeated
    Riall's twenty-one hundred men at Chippewa Creek.
1814, July 25—The Battle of Lundy's Lane, fought from sunset to mid-
    night less than a mile west of the Falls, was deadliest of the War
    of 1812. Americans lost 860; Canadians, 878. Generals Winfield
    Scott and Jacob Brown were wounded. General Riall was wounded
    and captured.
1814, August 15—Canadian attack on Fort Erie was repulsed after am-
    munition chest in the captured bastion exploded. Legend credits
    American Lieutenant Patrick MacDonogh with setting off the ex-
    plosion that killed him and twenty-five others and wounded more
    than three hundred.
1814, November—Americans evacuated Fort Erie, a month before the
    Treaty of Ghent ended the war.
1837, December 29—Canadian militia seized Patriots' supply ship Caro-
    line at Schlosser Landing, set it afire, then ran it down Upper
    Rapids to burn at edge of Falls.
1838, January 12 to 20—General Winfield Scott averted United States
    involvement in the Patriot War and a probable third war with
    Great Britain.

1850—The Reverend Josiah Henson of Chatham, Upper Canada, re-crossed the Niagara en route to Boston. The anecdotes he told Mrs. Calvin Stowe that summer about his flight from slavery to Upper Canada's "Promised Land" are reputed to have given Mrs. Stowe the plot outline for *Uncle Tom's Cabin* (first published in 1852).

1861—Fears that Great Britain would recognize the Confederate States of America and initiate an invasion of "the Union" via Niagara caused new installations and larger garrisons at the Niagara forts.

1864, July 17—Horace Greeley and Confederate commissioners discussed Civil War peace terms at Clifton House, Niagara Falls, Upper Canada.

1864, Fall—Raids by Confederate agents out of Canada against Johnson Island, Ohio, and St. Albans, Vermont, brought martial law to Niagara's American shore.

1866, June 1 to 3—The trans-Niagara invasion of Canada by Captain John O'Neil and fifteen hundred Fenians failed but swung legislative support to the movement for Confederation of Canadian provinces.

1867, July 1—Queen Victoria's signature on the British North American Act created the Dominion of Canada.

1927, April—Old Fort Niagara Association, Inc., was founded.

1928–40—Fort Niagara was completely renovated and its ownership transferred from the United States War Department to Niagara Frontier State Park Commission, with the Old Fort Niagara Association licensed to maintain and operate it.

1963, July—United States Department of Defense closed the Niagara army post, 286 years after La Salle built Fort Condé.

BIBLIOGRAPHY

CHAPTER 1

Hough, Jack L., *Geology of the Great Lakes*. Urbana, University of Illinois Press, 1958.

McKee, Russell, *Great Lakes Country*. New York, Thomas Y. Crowell, 1966.

Ritchie, William A., *The Archaeology of New York State*. New York, Natural History Press, 1965.

Roseberry, C. R., *Before Cayuga*. Ithaca, New York, Board of Education, 1950.

Severance, Frank H., *An Old Frontier of France*, Vol. I. New York, Dodd, Mead, 1917.

CHAPTER 2

Colden, Cadwallader, *The History of the Five Indian Nations*. Ithaca, New York, Great Seal Books, Cornell University Press, 1958.

Hassler, William II., "The Real Hiawatha," *American History Illustrated*, Vol. 1, No. 2 (May 1966), pp. 18–23.

Hunt, George T., *The Wars of the Iroquois*. Madison, University of Wisconsin Press, 1940.

Hyde, George E., *Indians of the Woodlands*. Norman, University of Oklahoma Press, 1962.

Knowles, Nathaniel, "The Torture of Captives by the Indians of Eastern North America," *Proceedings* of the American Philosophical Society, Vol. 82, No. 2 (March, 1940), pp. 151–225.

Lahontan, Baron de, *Voyages to North America*, Vols. I and II. Chicago, A. C. McClurg, 1905.

McKee, Russell, *Great Lakes Country*. New York, Thomas Y. Crowell, 1966.

Merriam, G. C., Company, Springfield, Massachusetts. Correspondence with editors of Merriam-Webster Dictionaries about the etymology of Iroquoian words.

Parker, Arthur C., *History of the State of New York*, Vol. I. A. C. Flick, New York, Columbia University Press, 1933.

————, *Seneca Myths and Folk Tales*. Buffalo, Buffalo Historical Society, 1923.

CHAPTER 3

Collection Clairambault, Vol. 1016. Ottawa, Public Archives of Canada.

Crouse, Nellis M., "The White Man's Discoveries," *History of the State of New York*, Vol. I, A. C. Flick, ed. New York, Columbia University Press, 1933.

Ericson, Bernard E., *The Evolution of Ships on the Great Lakes*. A speech delivered before the Niagara, Ontario, meeting of the Society of Naval Architects and Marine Engineers, October 12, 1962.

Hatcher, Harlan, *Lake Erie*, The American Lakes Series. Indianapolis, Bobbs-Merrill, 1945.

Hunt, George T., *The Wars of the Iroquois*. Madison, University of Wisconsin Press, 1960.

Lahontan, Baron de, *Voyages to North America*. Chicago, A. C. McClurg, 1905.

Mathews, Mitford, *A Dictionary of Americanisms*. Chicago, University of Chicago Press, 1951.

Parkman, Francis, *La Salle and the Discovery of the Great West*. New York, New American Library, 1963.

Pound, Arthur, *Lake Ontario*, The American Lakes Series. Indianapolis, Bobbs-Merrill, 1945.

Severance, Frank H., *An Old Frontier of France*. New York, Dodd, Mead, 1917.

Thwaites, R. G., ed., *The Jesuit Relations and Allied Documents*. Cleveland, A. C. McClurg, 1896–1901.

CHAPTER 4

Barber, John W. and Henry Howe, *Historical Collections of the State of New York*. New York, S. Tuttle, 1841.

Hatcher, Harlan, *Lake Erie*, The American Lakes Series. Indianapolis, Bobbs-Merrill, 1945.

Hunt, George T., *The Wars of the Iroquois*. Madison, University of Wisconsin Press, 1960.

Lahontan, Baron de, *Voyages to North America*. Chicago, A. C. McClurg, 1905.

Mathews, Mitford, *A Dictionary of Americanisms.* Chicago, University of Chicago Press, 1951.

O'Callaghan, E. C., ed., *The Documentary History of the State of New York*, Vols. I–IV. Albany, Weed, Parsons, 1849.

Parkman, Francis, *LaSalle and the Discovery of the Great West.* New York, New American Library, 1963.

Pound, Arthur. *Lake Ontario,* The American Lakes Series. Indianapolis, Bobbs-Merrill, 1945.

Severance, Frank H., *An Old Frontier of France.* New York, Dodd, Mead, 1917.

Yates, Raymond F., *Under Three Flags,* Buffalo, Henry Stewart, 1958.

CHAPTER 5

Edwards, Jonathan, *Life of the Reverend David Brainerd.* Glasgow, William Collins, 1829.

Ericson, Bernard E., *The Evolution of Ships on the Great Lakes,* a paper delivered before the Society of Naval Architects and Marine Engineers at Niagara, Ontario (October 12, 1962).

Flick, Alexander, ed., *History of the State of New York.* New York, Columbia University Press, 1933.

Graham, Lloyd, *The Niagara Country.* New York, Duell, Sloan & Pearce, 1949.

Mau, Clayton, *The Development of Central and Western New York.* Dansville, New York, F. A. Owen Publishing Company, 1958.

O'Callaghan, E. C., ed., *The Documentary History of the State of New York*, Vols. I–IV. Albany, Weed, Parsons, 1849.

Severance, Frank H., *An Old Frontier of France.* New York, Dodd, Mead, 1917.

CHAPTER 6

Flick, Alexander, ed., *History of the State of New York.* New York, Columbia University Press, 1933.

Hunter, William A., *Forts on the Pennsylvania Frontier.* Harrisburg, The Pennsylvania Historial and Museum Commission, 1960.

O'Callaghan, E. C., ed., *The Documentary History of the State of New York*, Vols. I–IV. Albany, Weed, Parsons, 1849.

Severance, Frank H., *An Old Frontier of France.* New York, Dodd, Mead, 1917.

CHAPTER 7

Barber, John W. and Henry Howe, *Historical Collections of the State of New York.* New York, S. Tuttle, 1841.

Colden, Cadwallader, *The History of the Five Indian Nations.* Ithaca, New York, Great Seal Books, Cornell University Press, 1958.

Flexner, James T., *Mohawk Baronet*. New York, Harper, 1959.
Flick, Alexander, ed., *History of the State of New York*. New York, Columbia University Press, 1933.
Hunter, William A., *Forts on the Pennsylvania Frontier*. Harrisburg, The Pennsylvania Historical and Museum Commission, 1960.
Mau, Clayton, *The Development of Central and Western New York*. Dansville, New York, F. A. Owen Publishing Company, 1958.
O'Callaghan, E. C., ed., *The Documentary History of the State of New York*, Vols. I–IV. Albany, Weed, Parsons, 1849.
Pound, Arthur, *Johnson of the Mohawks*. New York, Macmillan, 1930.
————, *Lake Ontario*, The American Lakes Series. Indianapolis: Bobbs-Merrill, 1945.
Sanford, Ezekiel, *A History of the United States Before the Revolution with Some Account of the Aborigines*. Philadelphia, Anthony Finley, 1819.
Severance, Frank H., *An Old Frontier of France*. New York, Dodd, Mead, 1917.

CHAPTER 8

Dunlap, William, *History of the New Netherlands, Province of New York and State of New York*. New York: Carter & Thorp, 1839.
Flexner, James T., *Mohawk Baronet*. New York: Harper, 1959.
Flick, Alexander, ed., *History of the State of New York*. New York, Columbia University Press, 1933.
Fregault, Guy, "The Epoch of Belle Riviere," *Pennsylvania History*, Vol. 18, No. 3 (July 1951).
Hunter, William A., *Forts on the Pennsylvania Frontier*. Harrisburg, The Pennsylvania Historical and Museum Commission, 1960.
Mau, Clayton, *The Development of Central and Western New York*. Dansville, New York, F. A. Owen Publishing Company, 1958.
Morison, Samuel E., *The Oxford History of the American People*. New York, Oxford University Press, 1965.
Pound, Arthur, *Johnson of the Mohawks*. New York, Macmillan, 1930.
Severance, Frank H., *An Old Frontier of France*. New York, Dodd, Mead, 1917.

CHAPTER 9

Dunlap, William, *History of the New Netherlands, Province of New York and State of New York*. New York, Carter & Thorp, 1839.
Ericson, Bernard E., *The Evolution of Ships on the Great Lakes*. A speech delivered before the Niagara, Ontario, meeting of the Society of Naval Architects and Marine Engineers, October 12, 1962.
Flexner, James T., *Mohawk Baronet*. New York: Harper, 1959.

Flick, Alexander, ed., *History of the State of New York*. New York, Columbia University Press, 1933.

Fregault, Guy, "The Epoch of Belle Riviere," *Pennsylvania History*, Vol. 18, No. 3 (July 1951).

Hunter, William A., *Forts on the Pennsylvania Frontier*. Harrisburg, The Pennsylvania Historical and Museum Commission, 1960.

Mau, Clayton, *The Development of Central and Western New York*. Dansville, New York, F. A. Owen Publishing Company, 1958.

Morison, Samuel E., *The Oxford History of the American People*. New York, Oxford University Press, 1965.

Pound, Arthur, *Johnson of the Mohawks*. New York, Macmillan, 1930.

Severance, Frank H., *An Old Frontier of France*. New York, Dodd, Mead, 1917.

Wainger, Bertrand M., supervisor, *New York: A Guide to the Empire State*, WPA American Guide Series. New York, Oxford University Press, 1940.

CHAPTER 10

Dunlap, William, *History of the New Netherlands, Province of New York and State of New York*. New York, Carter & Thorp, 1839.

Flexner, James T., *Mohawk Baronet*. New York, Harper, 1959.

Flick, Alexander, ed, *History of the State of New York*. New York, Columbia University Press, 1933.

O'Callaghan, E. D., ed., *The Documentary History of the State of New York*, Vols. I–IV. Albany, Weed, Parsons, 1849.

Pound, Arthur, *Johnson of the Mohawks*. New York, Macmillan, 1930.

Severance, Frank H., *An Old Frontier of France*. New York, Dodd, Mead, 1917.

CHAPTER 11

Creighton, Donald, *A History of Canada*. Boston: Houghton Mifflin Company, 1958.

Dunlap, William, *History of the New Netherlands, Province of New York and State of New York*. New York, Carter & Thorp, 1839.

Ericson, Bernard E., *The Evolution of Ships on the Great Lakes*, a speech delivered before the Niagara, Ontario, meeting of the Society of Naval Architects and Marine Engineers (October 12, 1962).

Flexner, James T., *Mohawk Baronet*. New York, Harper, 1959.

Flick, Alexander, ed., *History of the State of New York*. New York, Columbia University Press, 1933.

Graham, Lloyd, *Niagara Country*. New York, Duell, Sloan & Pearce, 1949.

Hatcher, Harlan, *Lake Erie*, The American Lakes Series. Indianapolis, Bobbs-Merrill Company, 1945.

Klinck, Carl F., ed., *Tecumseh: Fact and Fiction in Early Records*. Englewood Cliffs, N.J., Prentice-Hall, 1961.

Livingston, William F., *Israel Putnam*. New York, G. P. Putnam's Sons, 1901.

Mau, Clayton, *The Development of Central and Western New York*. Dansville, New York, F. A. Owen Publishing Company, 1958.

Morison, Samuel E., *The Oxford History of the American People*. New York, Oxford University Press, 1965.

O'Meara, Walter, *Guns at the Forks*. Englewood Cliffs, N.J., Prentice-Hall, 1965.

Peckham, Howard H., *Life in Detroit Under Pontiac's Siege*. Detroit, Detroit Historical Society, 1964.

Pound, Arthur, *Johnson of the Mohawks*. New York, Macmillan, 1930.
————, *Lake Ontario*, The American Lakes Series. Indianapolis, Bobbs-Merrill, 1945.

Severance, Frank H., *An Old Frontier of France*. New York, Dodd, Mead, 1917.

CHAPTER 12

Bradley, A. G., "Lord Dorchester," in *The Makers of Canada*, Vol. III. New York, Oxford University Press, 1926.

Bradley, A. G., *The United Empire Loyalists*. London, Thornton Butterworth, 1932.

Ericson, Bernard E., *The Evolution of Ships on the Great Lakes*, speech delivered before the Niagara, Ontario, meeting of the Society of Naval Architects and Marine Engineers (October 12, 1962).

Flexner, James T., *Mohawk Baronet*. New York: Harper, 1959.

Flick, Alexander, ed., *History of the State of New York*. New York, Columbia University Press, 1933.

Graham, Lloyd, *Niagara Country*. New York, Duell, Sloan & Pearce, 1949.

Jefferys, C. W., *The Picture Gallery of Canadian History*. Toronto, The Ryerson Press, 1945.

Mau, Clayton, *The Development of Central and Western New York*. Dansville, New York, F. A. Owen Publishing Company, 1958.

McIlwraith, Jean N. "Sir Frederick Haldimand," in *The Makers of Canada*, Vol. III. New York, Oxford University Press, 1926.

Pound, Arthur, *Lake Ontario*, The American Lakes Series. Indianapolis, Bobbs-Merrill, 1945.

Swiggett, Howard, *War Out of Niagara*. New York, Columbia University Press, 1933.

CHAPTER 13

Barber, John W. and Henry Howe, *Historical Recollections of the State of New York*. New York, S. Tuttle, 1841.

Bradley, A. G., *The United Empire Loyalists*. London, Thornton Butterworth, 1932.

Ericson, Bernard E., *The Evolution of Ships on the Great Lakes*, a speech delivered before the Niagara, Ontario, meeting of the Society of Naval Architects and Marine Engineers (October 12, 1962).

Flexner, James T., *Mohawk Baronet*. New York, Harper, 1959.

Flick, Alexander, ed., *History of the State of New York*. New York, Columbia University Press, 1933.

Jefferys, C. W., *The Picture Gallery of Canadian History*. Toronto, The Ryerson Press, 1945.

Mau, Clayton, *The Development of Central and Western New York*. Dansville, New York, F. A. Owen Publishing Company, 1958.

McIlwraith, Jean N., "Sir Frederick Haldimand," in *The Makers of Canada*, Vol. III. New York, Oxford University Press, 1926.

Pound, Arthur, *Lake Ontario*, The American Lakes Series. Indianapolis, Bobbs-Merrill, 1945.

Scott, Duncan Campbell, "John Graves Simcoe," in *The Makers of Canada*, Vol. IV. New York, Oxford University Press, 1926.

Swiggett, Howard, *War Out of Niagara*. New York, Columbia University Press, 1933.

CHAPTER 14

Edgar, Lady, "General Brock," in *The Makers of Canada*, Vol. IV. New York, Oxford University Press, 1926.

Ericson, Bernard E., *The Evolution of Ships on the Great Lakes*, a speech delivered before the Niagara, Ontario, meeting of the Society of Naval Architects and Marine Engineers (October 12, 1962).

Fay, (Captain) H. A., *Collection of the Official Accounts, in Detail, of all the Battles Fought by Sea and Land, Between the Navy and Army of the United States, and the Navy and Army of Great Britain, During the Years 1812, 13, 14, & 15*. New York, E. Conrad, 1817.

Graham, Lloyd, *Niagara Country*. New York, Duell, Sloan & Pearce, 1949.

Havighurst, Walter, *Wilderness for Sale*. New York, Hastings House, 1956.

LeDoux, Florence B., *Sketches of Niagara*. St. Catharines, Ontario, Peninsula Press Limited, 1955.

Mau, Clayton, *The Development of Central and Western New York*. Dansville, New York, F. A. Owen Publishing Company, 1958.

McNeil, Donald. Unpublished memoirs of the John Morrison family.

Pound, Arthur, *Lake Ontario*, The American Lakes Series. Indianapolis, Bobbs-Merrill, 1945.

CHAPTER 15

Edgar, Lady. "General Brock," in *The Makers of Canada*, Vol. IV. New York, Oxford University Press, 1926.

Fay, (Captain) H. A., *Collection of the Official Accounts, in Detail, of all the Battles Fought by Sea and Land, Between the Navy and Army of the United States, and the Navy and Army of Great Britain, During the Years 1812, 13, 14, & 15*. New York, E. Conrad, 1817.

Graham, Lloyd, *Niagara Country*. New York, Duell, Sloan & Pearce, 1949.

Hamil, Fred C., *Michigan in the War of 1812*, a John M. Munson Michigan History Fund Publication. Lansing, Michigan Historical Commission, 1960.

Hatcher, Harlan, *Lake Erie*, The American Lakes Series. Indianapolis, Bobbs-Merrill, 1945.

Kyte, E. C., "Fort Niagara in the War of 1812—Side-lights from an Unpublished Order-book," *The Canadian Historical Review*, Vol. 17, No. 4 (December 1936).

Mau, Clayton, *The Development of Central and Western New York*. Dansville, New York, F. A. Owen Publishing Company, 1958.

Pound, Arthur, *Lake Ontario*, The American Lakes Series. Indianapolis, Bobbs-Merrill, 1945.

CHAPTER 16

Bradley, A. G., *The United Empire Loyalists*. London, Thornton Butterworth, 1932.

Cochran, Thomas A. and William Miller, *The Age of Enterprise*. New York, Macmillan, 1942.

Ericson, Bernard E., *The Evolution of Ships on the Great Lakes*, a speech delivered before the Niagara, Ontario, meeting of the Society of Naval Architects and Marine Engineers (October 12, 1962).

Fay, (Captain) H. A., *Collection of the Official Accounts, in Detail, of all the Battles Fought by Sea and Land, Between the Navy and Army of the United States, and the Navy and Army of Great Brit-*

ain, *During the Years 1812, 13, 14, & 15.* New York, E. Conrad, 1817.

Graham, Lloyd, *Niagara Country.* New York, Duell, Sloan & Pearce, 1949.

Hatcher, Harlan, *Lake Erie,* The American Lakes Series. Indianapolis, Bobbs-Merrill Company, 1945.

Hitsman, J. Mackay, "The War of 1812 in Canada," *History Today,* Vol. 12, No. 9 (September 1962).

Mansfield, Edward M., *A Life of General Winfield Scott.* New York, A. S. Barnes, 1846.

Mau, Clayton, *The Development of Central and Western New York.* Dansville, New York, F. A. Owen Publishing Company, 1958.

Morton, W. L., *The Kingdom of Canada.* Toronto, McClelland & Stewart, 1963.

Niles, John M., *The Life of Oliver Hazard Perry.* Hartford, Oliver D. Cooke, 1821.

Pound, Arthur, *Lake Ontario,* The American Lakes Series. Indianapolis, Bobbs-Merrill, 1945.

Wood, William, *The War With the United States.* Toronto, Glasgow, Brook, 1920.

CHAPTER 17

Barber, John W. and Henry Howe, *Historical Collections of the State of New York.* New York, S. Tuttle, 1841.

Cochran, Thomas and William Miller, *The Age of Enterprise.* New York, Macmillan, 1942.

Ericson, Bernard E., *The Evolution of Ships on the Great Lakes,* a speech delivered before the Niagara, Ontario, meeting of the Society of Naval Architects and Marine Engineers (October 12, 1962).

Fay, (Captain) H. A., *Collection of the Official Accounts, in Detail, of all the Battles Fought by Sea and Land, Between the Navy and Army of the United States, and the Navy and Army of Great Britain, During the Years 1812, 13, 14, & 15.* New York, E. Conrad, 1817.

Graham, Lloyd, *Niagara Country.* New York, Duell, Sloan & Pearce, 1949.

Hamil, Fred C., *Michigan in the War of 1812.* A John M. Munson Michigan History Fund Publication. Lansing, Michigan Historical Commission, 1960.

Harrison, Jonas, "A War-Time Letter-Book," in *Publications of the Buffalo Historical Society,* Vol. V. Buffalo, Buffalo Historical Society, 1881.

Hatcher, Harlan, *Lake Erie*, The American Lakes Series. Indianapolis, Bobbs-Merrill, 1945.

Hitsman, J. Mackay, "The War of 1812 in Canada," *History Today*, Vol. 12, No. 9 (September 1962).

Kyte, E. C., "Fort Niagara in the War of 1812—Side-lights from an Unpublished Order-book," *The Canadian Historical Review*, Vol. 18, No. 4 (December 1936).

Mansfield, Edward M., *A Life of General Winfield Scott*. New York, A. S. Barnes, 1846.

Mau, Clayton, *The Development of Central and Western New York*. Dansville, New York, F. A. Owen Publishing Company, 1958.

Morton, W. L., *The Kingdom of Canada*. Toronto. McClelland & Stewart, 1963.

O'Reilly, Isabel M., "A Hero of Fort Erie," in *Publications of the Buffalo Historical Society*, Vol. V. Buffalo, Buffalo Historical Society, 1881.

Pound, Arthur, *Lake Ontario*, The American Lakes Series. Indianapolis, Bobbs-Merrill, 1945.

Wood, William, *The War With the United States*. Toronto, Glasgow, Brook, 1920.

CHAPTER 18

Cochran, Thomas and William Miller, *The Age of Enterprise*. New York, Macmillan, 1942.

Graham, Lloyd, *Niagara Country*. New York, Duell, Sloan & Pearce, 1949.

Hatcher, Harlan, *Lake Erie*, The American Lakes Series. Indianapolis, Bobbs-Merrill, 1945.

Kurtz, Henry I., "The Undeclared War between Britain and America," *History Today*, Vol. 12, No. 11 (November 1962).

LeDoux, Florence B., *Sketches of Niagara*. St. Catharines, Ontario, Peninsula Press Limited, 1955.

Mansfield, Edward M., *A Life of General Winfield Scott*. New York, A. S. Barnes, 1846.

Mau, Clayton, *The Development of Central and Western New York*. Dansville, New York, F. A. Owen Publishing Company, 1958.

Morison, Samuel E., *The Oxford History of the American People*. New York, Oxford University Press, 1965.

Pound, Arthur, *Lake Ontario*, The American Lakes Series. Indianapolis, Bobbs-Merrill, 1945.

Shaw, Ronald E., *Erie Water West*. Lexington, University of Kentucky Press, 1966.

Wallace, W. Stewart, *The Family Compact*. Toronto, Glasgow, Brook, 1920.

Yates, Raymond F., *Under Three Flags*. Buffalo, Henry Stewart, 1958.

CHAPTER 19

Graham, Lloyd, *Niagara Country*. New York, Duell, Sloan & Pearce, 1949.

Hultzen, Claud H., Sr., *Restoration of Old Fort Niagara*, a paper presented at the annual meeting of the Old Fort Niagara Association at Old Fort Niagara (September 15, 1936).

McClellan, S. Grove, "Old Fort Niagara," *American Heritage*, Vol. 4, No. 4.

"The Niagara Frontier Landmarks Association," *Publications of the Buffalo Historical Society*, Vol. V. Buffalo, Buffalo Historical Society, 1881.

Scovell, J. Boardman, *A Short History of the Niagara Portage*. Lewiston, New York–Queenston, Ontario, Lewiston–Queenston Rotary Club, 1949.

INDEX

ABOUT THE AUTHOR

Robert West Howard was born in upstate New York and spent most of his childhood and youth in that region. He left home at age 17 to seek a career as a newspaperman in New York City. Upon mastering a two-finger method of typing under the guidance of a YMCA counselor, he got a job with the old *New York Telegram* as a copyboy and earned $10 a week. Two years later, cub reporting chores came, and eventually the radio reviewer's chair. In the '30s following a variety of journalistic jobs, Howard was named an assistant district director of the Federal Writers Project for the Syracuse area; a few months later, he was transferred to Albany as assistant state director.

Since then his occupations have ranged from free-lance writing to stints as magazine editor, publications coordinator for the Adult Education Association of U.S.A., and vice-president in charge of public relations at Antioch College (Ohio).

Currently Bob Howard devotes his full time to writing at his home in Rochester, New York.

His wife Elizabeth is a member of the faculty in the University of Rochester's School of Education.

For recreation Mr. Howard turns to rock hounding, gardening, cooking, and furniture restoration projects.

Typography and Binding Design

by

CARL A. KOENIG